BY ONE VOTE

American Presidential Elections

MICHAEL NELSON

JOHN M. MCCARDELL, JR.

BY ONE VOTE

THE DISPUTED PRESIDENTIAL ELECTION OF 1876

MICHAEL F. HOLT

UNIVERSITY PRESS OF KANSAS

Published
by the
University
Press of Kansas
(Lawrence,
Kansas 66045),
which was
organized by the
Kansas Board of
Regents and is
operated and
funded by
Emporia State
University,
Fort Hays State
University,
Kansas State
University,
Pittsburg State
University,
the University
of Kansas, and
Wichita State
University

© 2008 by the University Press of Kansas

Library of Congress Cataloging-in-Publication Data

Holt, Michael F.

The disputed presidential election of 1876 / Michael F. Holt.

p.   cm. — (American presidential elections)

Includes bibliographical references and index.

ISBN 978-0-7006-1608-4 (cloth : alk. paper)

1. Presidents—United States—Election—1876. 2. Contested
elections—United States—History—19th century. 3. Hayes,
Rutherford Birchard, 1822–1893. 4. Tilden, Samuel J.
(Samuel Jones), 1814–1886. 5. United States—Politics and
government—1869–1877. 6. Political corruption—United
States—History—19th century. I. Title.

E680.H75 2008

973.8′3—dc22   2008027408

British Library Cataloguing-in-Publication Data is available.

Printed in the United States of America

10 9 8 7 6 5 4 3 2 1

The paper used in this publication is recycled and contains 30
percent postconsumer waste. It is acid free and meets the mini-
mum requirements of the American National Standard for Per-
manence of Paper for Printed Library Materials Z39.48–1992.

For my granddaughters,

Lila Gentry Holt and Sarah Palmer Holt

CONTENTS

For a very long time, most standard accounts of Reconstruction have identified the election of 1876 as the occasion that brought this era to an end. In the resolution of the disputed contest between Democrat Samuel J. Tilden of New York and Republican Rutherford B. Hayes of Ohio, historians have generally agreed that the nation at last turned its eyes away from the aims of the Civil War and toward the less divisive political issues, and more seductive economic opportunities, of the Gilded Age.

Moreover, virtually all textbooks view this election as the end of the first "half" of American history. It is where volume one ends and volume two begins. This delineation is only somewhat based on commercial publishing requirements. A legitimate intellectual case can be made that modern American history truly begins in the years following the Civil War, including not only the rapid expansion of the economy and the search for order among its agents and its victims but also the marginalization of fundamental racial issues for another century.

Those who seek lessons for our own time find 1876 appealing for an additional reason: it is one of only four presidential elections in American history when the winner of the popular vote did not receive a majority in the electoral college. Thus, not surprisingly, two new studies of 1876 appeared almost immediately after the disputed election of 2000. The 1876 election drew the highest voter turnout, 81.8 percent, of any contest in American history before or since. The loser, Tilden, won a majority of the popular vote, 51 percent, and received 250,000 more votes than the winner, Hayes. Nineteen disputed electoral votes—all in the South, including Florida—were awarded to Hayes, who, upon assuming office, withdrew the remaining federal troops from the former Confederacy.

What could possibly be left to say? Michael F. Holt, a distinguished historian of nineteenth-century politics, rises to this challenge in the pages that follow. Bringing to bear a career of careful and thoughtful voting analysis, Holt focuses on two significant but long overlooked aspects of the 1876 election. The first is the admission of Colorado to statehood, which tipped the balance in favor of the Republicans. The second is the acquiescence of the Democrats in this critical decision.

And it is in addressing this second aspect that Holt makes a truly original contribution to our understanding of the 1876 election. The Democrats had won large majorities in the 1874 congressional contests. Falling in the sixth year of the presidency of Ulysses S. Grant, this outcome seemed to indicate a Democratic triumph two years hence. Yet once the votes were tabulated in 1876, the Republicans had regained a majority in the Senate and reduced the Democratic majority in the House from seventy-nine to nineteen.

That the Republicans were able to stage such a remarkable comeback in the midst of a protracted economic depression that, a mere two years earlier, they had been blamed for shapes and directs Holt's narrative. It is a complicated story clearly told and will remind readers that the mundane task of assembling an electoral majority often reveals as much about an election's outcome as does a focus on great issues or core principles. Such a reminder may or may not have application to the 2008 election, which was in progress as this volume went to press. It will surely serve as an object lesson to those who think the last word about this, or any, election has ever been or can ever be said.

Most historically informed Americans today probably view the presidential election of 1876 primarily as a precursor of the disputed presidential election of 2000. After that latter election—and with its outcome very much in mind—two new books on the 1876 contest rapidly appeared. One was by an author with obvious Democratic proclivities, who detailed how Republicans had stolen the 1876 election just as they had that of 2000. The second was by former Chief Justice William Rehnquist, implicitly defending the Supreme Court's actions in 2000 by focusing on the role of Supreme Court justices in the resolution of the 1876 contest.

Parallels between the two elections certainly exist. In 1876, just as in 2000, the Democratic candidate clearly won a majority of the nationwide popular vote. Then, as in 2000, electoral votes, including those of Florida, were in dispute. And in 1876, just as in 2000, Republican Supreme Court justices helped declare the Republican candidate the winner, in part by overruling decisions by state courts in Florida. In other ways, however, the presidential election of 1876 is unique. It attracted a higher rate of voter participation than any other presidential election in American history. A single electoral vote determined its outcome—the narrowest margin of any presidential contest. For the only time in our history, moreover, a Federal Electoral Commission created by an act of Congress determined who would be the next president.

None of these things, however, explains why I opted to write about the 1876 election when approached by the editors of this new series by the University Press of Kansas. Rather, two other questions aroused my curiosity. The first may strike some readers as relatively small potatoes. When writing chapters on Reconstruction for a textbook some years back, I concluded that a crucial, if little noted, event in determining the outcome of the 1876 presidential election was Colorado's admission in August as the Centennial State. Statehood for Colorado was pivotal because it changed the number of electoral votes cast in the election and thus the size of the majority necessary to win. Absent Colorado's admission, and if all else had remained the same, Democrat Samuel J. Tilden would have won the election. Democrats had a huge majority in the

House of Representatives in 1876. How, I asked myself, could they have been so stupid as to allow Colorado's admission in time to participate in the presidential election? This book provides an answer to that question that differs from any offered by the few previous historians who have even bothered to ask it.

What primarily attracted me to this election, however, was something else—a curious anomaly concerning the relationship between economic conditions and political results. The presidential election of 1876 was the only time in American political history that the "out" party won the preceding off-year congressional elections in the midst of a severe economic depression (and the depression of the 1870s was particularly severe) yet failed to win the subsequent presidential election. After the panic of 1837, Whigs won the majority of congressional seats up for grabs in 1837–1838 and the presidency in 1840. After the panic of 1893, when Democrats held power, Republicans won the congressional elections of 1894 and the presidency in 1896. After the monumental crash of 1929, Democrats, railing against the hapless incumbent Republican administration, won the congressional elections of 1930 and put Franklin D. Roosevelt in the White House in 1932.

The political aftermath of the depression launched by the banking panic in September 1873 was strikingly different. As might be predicted, Democrats, who had languished out of power since 1860, won the congressional—and state—elections of 1874, and they won so overwhelmingly as to mark a revolution in the history of congressional elections. Yet Democrats lost the presidential election of 1876. The primary purpose of this book is to explain why.

Democrats at the time and most subsequent historians of the election, almost all of whom tilt toward the Democratic Party in their current political affiliation, would contend that this question is based on false premises. There is no anomaly to be explained, because the Democratic Party did in fact win the election of 1876. It got a clear majority of the popular vote, and only Republican fraud stole a rightful majority of the electoral vote from their candidate. Unspeakably corrupt Republican canvassing boards in the states whose electoral votes were in dispute dishonestly awarded their electoral votes to the Republican candidate, and then Republicans in Washington, including Republican members of the Supreme Court, counted him in, refusing to allow a recount of the popular votes actually cast that clearly showed those electoral votes belonged to the Democratic candidate. The election of 1876, therefore, was no anomaly; it was "The Fraud of the Century!"[1]

Although this charge is understandable, at least when shouted by bitter Democrats in 1876, it is questionable on at least four grounds. First, Republican returning boards in Florida, Louisiana, and South Carolina had explicit legal authority and ample reason for counting the votes as they did. Second, Democrats also tried to steal an electoral vote to which they had no right—in Oregon. Third, corruption did abound in the disputes over the electoral votes, but Democrats were just as guilty of it as Republicans. Fourth, and most important, regardless of what happened in the South, there *was* a truly astonishing comeback by the Republican Party in the northern states between 1874 and 1876, even though the hard times that had fueled Democratic victories in 1874 showed no signs of abating. Outside of the fifteen former slave states and West Virginia, which had been carved from one of them, Republicans, who had been drubbed in the congressional contests of 1874–1875, won eighteen of twenty-two states, a majority of House seats, and a majority in the popular vote of more than a quarter of a million votes cast. It is that Republican comeback in the North in the midst of a continuing depression that I seek to explain in this book.

In looking for answers, I came to realize that some of the explanations I had offered in the textbook chapters mentioned earlier required revision, if not complete abandonment. Deeper research, after all, should force historians to revise their earlier thinking. For example, I no longer believe that the Specie Resumption Act of 1875 was as powerful a weapon in the Republican arsenal as I once did. Now, moreover, I am convinced that competition between Democrats and Republicans for the votes of the Liberal Republican bolters of 1872 explains the strategies that both parties pursued in 1876. It is largely for that reason that I begin my story with the election of 1872.

Let me close this preface with a caveat to readers. I make no claim to have exhaustively researched primary sources. I conducted archival research in the Rutherford B. Hayes Papers in Fremont, Ohio, and the Samuel J. Tilden Papers in the New York Public Library, as well as the Library of Congress's collection of the papers of Manton Marble, a Democratic newspaperman who wrote the Democrats' national platform in 1876 as well as many of Tilden's public statements that year and who was deeply involved in the dispute over Florida's electoral votes. I also read daily issues of the *New York Times* from May 1, 1876, through March 4, 1877. But I relied primarily on printed primary sources and especially on secondary works. In short, I offer here my interpretation of the election of 1876. I make no claim that this interpretation is definitive. I do hope, however, that it is persuasive.

In closing, let me thank the individuals who helped me with this effort. I am indebted to the staffs at the manuscript divisions of the Library of Congress and New York Public Library and especially the staff at the Rutherford B. Hayes Presidential Center. My colleague Charles W. McCurdy loaned me materials on the work of the Federal Electoral Commission. Stumped by a critical aspect of the 1875 Ohio gubernatorial election that launched Hayes on the path to the presidential nomination, I called on the encyclopedic knowledge of my friend and former student Professor Mark W. Summers of the University of Kentucky. Almost instantly he inundated me with the necessary information. Finally, I benefited from suggestions from John McCardell, Mike Nelson, and Fred M. Woodward, the director of the University Press of Kansas.

REPUBLICANS' FALL FROM GRACE

To fully appreciate how unlikely the Republican Party's comeback was in 1876, one must understand how dramatically Republicans' fortunes had slumped between 1872 and the end of 1874. In November 1872 Republicans won the White House for the fourth consecutive time—and they won big. Incumbent President Ulysses S. Grant amassed half a million more votes than he had in 1868 and rolled up a plurality of 750,000 popular votes out of some 6.4 million cast. He crushed his Democratic rival in the electoral vote by a greater than four-to-one margin, 286 to 63. Altogether, Grant carried thirty-one of thirty-seven states, including every northern state, whereas he had lost New York, New Jersey, and Oregon in 1868. To boot, Republicans won 196 of the 281 congressional races contested that year (69.7 percent), including 43 of the 73 seats (58.9 percent) from former Confederate states that had been subjected to congressional Republicans' Reconstruction policies. Republicans' hold on power, in short, appeared unshakable.

The extent of the Republicans' victory in 1872 was deceptive, however, and their grasp on power soon stood in jeopardy. For one thing, the increase in Grant's national total between 1868 and 1872 disguised some substantial Republican defections among both leaders and voters in the North. Incumbent Republican U.S. Senators Carl Schurz of Missouri, Charles Sumner of Massachusetts, and Lyman Trumbull of Illinois, as well as Governor John M. Palmer of Illinois, former Indiana Congressman

George W. Julian, former Ohio Congressman James M. Ashley, Pennsylvania's Civil War Republican Governor Andrew Curtin, and incumbent Massachusetts Congressman Nathaniel P. Banks (a former Speaker of the House of Representatives and a three-term governor of the Bay State) all joined a political revolt against Grant known as the "Liberal Republican movement." Statistical analysis of the popular vote in Massachusetts suggests that one-tenth of that state's eligible voters left the Republican column in 1872, and most would never return. More remarkable, Grant received more than 250,000 fewer votes in the Midwest in 1872 than he had garnered in 1868. Obviously, Republicans did not need those voters to win in 1872; such would not be the case later.

Almost all the increase in Grant's national total between 1868 and 1872—440,000 votes, in fact—came from former slave states, and most of those new Republican votes undoubtedly came from newly enfranchised freedmen. In the late 1860s congressional Republicans had sought to build a biracial Republican coalition that could control state and local governments in the former Confederacy and use them to protect blacks' civil and political rights. Thus they had enfranchised blacks and temporarily disfranchised a fraction of white Confederate sympathizers in the Military Reconstruction Acts of 1867–1868. In 1869 they had extended black suffrage outside the former Confederacy by passing the Fifteenth Amendment, which won ratification by the end of 1870. Most southern whites had resisted this Reconstruction program from its outset in 1867, and between 1867 and 1872 the terrorist Ku Klux Klan had used violence and intimidation to drive Republicans from power in the South. Yet federal military intervention and prosecutions in federal courts, authorized by a series of Enforcement Acts in 1870 and 1871, had effectively suppressed the Klan and preserved Republican control in most former Confederate states by the end of 1872.

Republicans never dominated Virginia's state government, even though Grant carried it in 1872. In 1871 Democrats had retaken control of Georgia and were on the verge of retaking Texas in 1872, which Grant lost. By 1872, Tennessee as well as the new state of West Virginia had also fallen to the Democrats. Since the late 1860s, the most reliably Democratic states in the nation were the former border states of Missouri, Kentucky, and Maryland. Grant lost tiny Delaware in 1868 but won it in 1872. In sum, Grant's seemingly impressive victory in 1872 depended in part on Republicans' carrying nine of the fifteen former slave states. Yet Republicans' competitiveness in those states was precarious, indeed. By

1876, Republicans still dominated the governmental machinery in only South Carolina, Florida, and Louisiana.

A marked decline in normal levels of Democratic voter turnout in most states contributed even more significantly to the Republicans' cakewalk in 1872. The Democrats had, in fact, run no candidate of their own. Instead they had grudgingly endorsed Horace Greeley, the surprising choice of the Liberal Republican convention held in May 1872.[1] Since 1841 Greeley had edited the *New York Tribune,* the nation's leading Whig and then Republican newspaper. For years he had denounced Democrats as lawless, shiftless, drunken sots, and for years he had endorsed causes that Democrats, especially southern Democrats, considered anathema. It was little wonder, then, that hundreds of thousands of Democrats stayed home on Election Day rather than support this lifelong foe. Even with the support of Republican bolters, Greeley ran behind Horatio Seymour, the Democrats' 1868 presidential candidate, by 18,000 votes in the six New England states; 150,000 votes in the three mid-Atlantic states of New Jersey, New York, and Pennsylvania; and an astonishing 270,000 votes in the Midwest. He also ran behind Seymour in Delaware, Georgia, Kentucky, Louisiana, North Carolina, and South Carolina. (Mississippi, Virginia, and Texas did not participate in the 1868 election, and Florida cast no popular votes; hence it is impossible to draw comparisons with those four states.)

Nor was Greeley popular with all Republicans sympathetic to the Liberal Republican movement. Whereas Liberal Republicans demanded a sharp reduction of tariff rates, Greeley had been a lifelong proponent of high protective tariffs. Nor did Greeley seem sympathetic to the Liberals' other top priority—civil service reform that would destroy party politicians' control over the federal government's workforce. By 1872, Greeley had embraced Liberals' demand for an end to federal intervention in the South and a restoration of full political rights to those former Confederates still disqualified from holding public office by state laws and the third section of the Fourteenth Amendment. This stance, however, left him vulnerable to vicious lampooning by Thomas Nast, the widely read political cartoonist for *Harper's Weekly* who had recently played a central role in toppling New York City's hugely corrupt Boss William M. Tweed from power.

Whatever Greeley's liabilities as a presidential candidate, however, both Republicans and Democrats in 1872 recognized that Liberal Republicans had put their finger on a shift in the northern electorate's

"'Let Us Clasp Hands over the Bloody Chasm'—Horace Greeley." Several
cartoons drawn by Thomas Nast in 1872 mocked Greeley's call for
northerners and southerners to forget their sectional animosities. This one
shows Greeley reaching in vain across the graveyard of Union prisoners at
the notorious Andersonville prison camp. *(From Morton Keller,* The Art and
Politics of Thomas Nast *[New York: Oxford University Press, 1968].)*

mood. That shift would accelerate between 1872 and 1876. From the late 1850s to 1871, competition between Republicans and Democrats had centered on the racial and sectional issues associated with the Civil War and Reconstruction. Starting in 1866, Republicans had run as defenders of their Reconstruction policies. Democrats, in turn, had opposed the passage of Reconstruction legislation and the Fourteenth and Fifteenth Amendments in Congress. In 1868 they had promised to repeal the whole program should they win the election. That Democratic opposition had allowed Republicans to tar Democrats as Confederate sympathizers, just as they had during the war. This practice of "waving the bloody shirt" had proved spectacularly effective in most northern elections since 1866, and it would play a central role in the Republicans' victory in the presidential election of 1876.

Liberal Republicans wanted to shift the political agenda away from sectional and racial issues and to smash the monopoly that Republicans and Democrats had exercised over the nation's political life since the late 1850s. The new party sought "the break-up of old parties," boasted E. L. Godkin, editor of the *Nation,* in May 1872. "Reconstruction and slavery we have done with; for administrative and revenue reform we are eager."[2] By "reform," Liberal Republicans meant three distinct but related things. They sought an end to corruption and a restoration of honesty in government at all levels of the federal system. One disgusted Illinois Republican, for example, explained his support for the Liberals in the spring of 1872 as follows: "For the last four years everything in the political line has been run by *rings* and *favoritism* without regard to *qualifications* or *honesty.* And now we are tired of it." Because the incumbent Republicans had failed to clean their own house, "the time has come to bring the country back to first principles, which means *economy, honesty, and capability.*"[3] To achieve honesty and capability in government jobs, Liberals demanded a civil service system based on testable intelligence rather than partisan loyalty. They railed at the patronage system, under which the cronies of Republican (and, in some localities, Democratic) officeholders monopolized appointive government jobs, and those appointees were expected to contribute part of their salaries to the party during election season. Most important, Liberals insisted on a sharp reduction of government expenditures and tax rates at all levels of the federal system. At its core, liberalism and the Liberal Republican movement that embodied it in 1872 sought to reverse the growth of an active governmental state and the expenses it entailed, which had characterized

"It Is Only a Truce to Regain Power ('Playing Possum')." This Thomas Nast cartoon shows Horace Greeley and Senator Charles Sumner, another Republican who bolted to the Liberal Republican camp in 1872, urging a freedman to reach across the bodies of murdered blacks to shake hands with two stock Democratic characters: a southern member of the Ku Klux Klan and an apelike Irish thug of the type who murdered blacks during the New York City draft riots of 1863. (From Morton Keller, The Art and Politics of Thomas Nast [New York: Oxford University Press, 1968].)

Republican governance at the national, state, and local levels since the start of the Civil War in 1861.

In 1872 this call for governmental retrenchment and reform had considerable appeal in both the North and the South. It influenced almost everything both Democrats and Republicans did between 1872 and 1877. "Reform" became a mantra chanted by both parties, but especially the Democrats, in 1876. That year, both major parties identified the Liberal Republican bolters of 1872 as the key bloc of swing or independent voters on which victory hinged, and both orchestrated their campaigns to win them over. The Liberal Republican movement, in short, did not simply fade away after Greeley's crushing defeat in 1872. It persisted, even holding a much-publicized meeting in New York City in May 1876 to decide whether it should run its own candidate that year. The reason for the persistence of these dissident Republicans—who had supported Lincoln's administration and most of the Reconstruction legislation passed by congressional Republicans between 1866 and 1872—is quite clear. After Grant's overwhelming reelection, many of their demands went unmet. Instead, the extent of corruption among Grant's inner circle and many other Republicans was vividly exposed.

Even in 1872, however, the Liberal Republican program had considerable appeal, which both major parties clearly recognized. Why most white southerners, even those who refused to vote for the hated Greeley, welcomed a call to end federal intervention in the South and restore political rights to ex-Confederates is easily understood. Calls for retrenchment and tax relief, moreover, had nationwide salience. From the time Republicans began to take control of southern state governments in late 1867, white property owners had complained about wasteful expenditures and unprecedented tax levels on land. Hence, ostensibly bipartisan Tax Payers' Conventions of property holders had, since 1868, voiced white southerners' complaints against the new Republican regime. Many poorer whites, meanwhile, used violence rather than soapboxes to express their discontent at Republican governments that depended heavily on newly enfranchised black voters everywhere in the former Confederate states.

Many northern property holders empathized with these southern complaints. At the start of 1872, the federal income tax levied in 1862 and, much more important, the heavy federal excise taxes levied on almost every economic transaction and many consumer products remained on the statute books. Economic historians have demonstrated that these high federal tax rates, along with tariff duties, generated a substantial surplus of federal revenue over expenditures for years after 1866. The federal government used this surplus to buy back bonds issued during the Civil War and thus to reduce the government's debt. Such purchases undoubtedly benefited the holders of federal bonds, including, significantly, the many national banks organized under federal laws passed in 1863, 1864, and 1865. This new national banking system and the privileges it gave to its investors remained a bête noire of many midwestern Democrats throughout the 1870s. Not all northerners paying federal taxes owned bonds, however. More important, and less well known, during and after the Civil War, both local and state northern governments also increased their tax rates to pay the annual interest on bonds issued to raise money for bounties to volunteers during the war and subsidies to families of its northern casualties.

The incidence of local, state, and federal taxation in the North, in sum, was high—indeed, demonstrably higher than in the South after the war. Carping was inevitable, but then came numerous exposures of corruption at the local and state levels. Outright payoffs to state and local officeholders seemed to come directly out of abused taxpayers' pockets. The most notorious example was Boss William Tweed, who, along with his Democratic cronies, fleeced New York City taxpayers of millions of dollars in the late 1860s before the ring was exposed and prosecuted in 1871. But Republican local and state governments in Pennsylvania or Wisconsin, for example, were no less guilty of cheating the propertied. Graft and boodle appeared pervasive. Hence, Liberal Republicans' call for retrenchment and "financial reform," along with their demand for an end to federal interference in the South—which, after all, was expensive whether it involved prosecution in federal court or the insertion of federal troops—had considerable salience.

To propitiate the northern electorate's growing impatience with Reconstruction and the political warfare over it, Democrats in 1872 announced a "New Departure" by promising that they would no longer seek to repeal the Reconstruction program or the constitutional amendments. Echoing Liberal Republicans, Democrats said they wanted to move on to different issues. Republicans tried even harder to neutralize the Liberals' appeal. At Grant's urging, congressional Republicans in 1872 passed an amnesty act that removed political disqualification from all but a handful of former Confederate leaders, lowered tariff rates by 10 percent, and repealed the income tax and all excise taxes save for those on tobacco and alcohol. Even earlier, Grant had won authorization from Congress to appoint a civil service commission. In 1871 it reported rules concerning the hiring, firing, and qualifications of federal employees. Grant endorsed those rules in December 1871, and throughout 1872 he adhered to them.

However successful these moves may have been in limiting defections by normal Republican voters to the Liberal Republicans, after Grant's triumphant reelection, Republican fortunes plunged rapidly. Even before Grant's second inauguration in March 1873, hard evidence of elected Republicans' apparent corruption and greed appeared. In the winter of 1872–1873 some congressional Republicans' complicity in what became known as the Crédit Mobilier scandal was exposed.[4] Epitomizing how insiders during this era pillaged public funds through intentional cost overruns, the Crédit Mobilier was a construction company composed of the corporate directors of the Union Pacific Railroad. In their capacity as the railroad's directors, they hired the Crédit Mobilier (that is, themselves) to build the road and readily paid its padded bills with the U.S. bonds Congress had appropriated to subsidize construction. Then, through the agency of Massachusetts Republican Congressman Oakes Ames, the Crédit Mobilier supposedly bribed enough Republican congressmen by selling them its stock substantially below market value to delay a congressional investigation of the company's raid on the Treasury. Some historians have questioned whether the men receiving the stock were responsible for delaying an investigation. Nonetheless, the scheme smelled of influence peddling, all but one of the implicated congressmen were Republicans, and the Grant administration was tarnished with guilt by association. As if this exposure were not bad enough, that same winter Republicans in Congress enacted a law that raised their own salaries and that of the president retroactively. This so-called Salary Grab infuriated taxpayers and ignited increased calls for a reduction of federal expenditures.

During Grant's second term, further exposures of Republican corruption made "Grantism" a synonym for sleaze. One of Grant's in-laws had already been implicated in a scheme by Jay Gould and Jim Fisk to corner the New York gold market in 1869. Another belonged to a notoriously corrupt customhouse gang in New Orleans that helped prop up Louisiana's Republican administration. When Grant on two occasions between 1872 and 1876 sent troops into Louisiana to defend that regime against violent Democratic attempts to overthrow it, he seemed to be siding with his relative. Grant's second secretary of war, William Belknap, would be forced to resign to escape congressional impeachment on charges that he had accepted payoffs from Indian sutlers in return for granting them lucrative trading licenses. Grant's private secretary Orville Babcock was accused of attempting to delay federal prosecution of the so-called Whiskey Ring, in which revenue agents and distillers colluded to defraud the government of the taxes they owed. These were only the most prominent of the illegalities that further scandalized Liberal Republicans and gave Democrats potent ammunition between 1874 and 1876.

In 1873 itself, however, another development proved far more threatening to Republicans' political fortunes. In the fall of that year Jay Cooke & Company, the nation's largest bank, collapsed, igniting a financial panic across the country and launching perhaps the most severe economic depression of the nineteenth century. Hard times lasted until late 1878 in the North and much longer in the South.

Business after business closed its doors; workers for industrial, commercial, and transportation firms lost their jobs; and farmers faced plummeting prices for their agricultural products. Incumbent political parties often experience voters' wrath during depressions, as Democrats had during the late 1830s, and the "in" Republicans proved no exception to that rule. No seats in the House of Representatives were at stake in the fall elections of 1873, but the returns from state contests that year alerted Republicans to the fate that might await them in the fall of 1874. Democrats increased their vote in Pennsylvania, carried the Minnesota and New York state legislatures, and elected governors as well as legislatures in Connecticut, Wisconsin, and Ohio. In the South, meanwhile, Texas's state government permanently fell to the Democrats, and Democrats made gains in state legislative races elsewhere. With Greeley no longer heading the Democratic ticket, traditional Democratic voters proved ready and willing to support Democratic candidates.

If only because the state legislatures chose U.S. senators, Republicans in Washington could hardly ignore these setbacks. Yet the state elections of 1873 had another aspect that complicated Republicans' response to them. In many northern states, and especially in midwestern states, Democrats alone did not oppose incumbent Republicans. Instead, a raft of splinter parties cooperated with Democrats to oust Republicans or siphoned off sufficient Republican votes to allow Democratic candidates to win. These splinter parties offered a variety of economic panaceas to deal with hard times. Antimonopoly parties promised to open economic opportunities for individual entrepreneurs. Labor Reform parties sought state laws to help workers and, increasingly, provide public jobs for the unemployed. Greenbackers touted currency inflation to combat price deflation. Grangers demanded railroad regulation to cut shippers' expenses.

In 1874 these third-party movements continued to proliferate. In Indiana, for example, Antimonopolists and Grangers combined to run an independent legislative ticket pledged to lowering freight rates and reducing railroads' political influence. In other midwestern states such as Iowa and Illinois, so-called Independent Reform parties ran their own candidates for Congress or formed coalitions with Democrats.

This proliferation of dissident, economically oriented third parties in the Midwest posed both a problem and, paradoxically, an opportunity for Republicans, who faced a looming political catastrophe in the congressional elections of 1874. On the one hand, discontented voters in the Midwest who had supported Republicans since the Civil War because they considered Democrats Copperhead traitors were far more likely to support such third-party challengers than to defect openly to the hated Democrats. Thus Republican politicians from the Midwest needed some program or appeal that could bring discontented voters back home. On the other hand, the monetary inflationism touted by many of the midwestern independents was gall and wormwood to the Liberal Republican bolters of 1872, who demanded the fastest possible return to specie payments and a gold standard.

What is clear, if only by inference, is that Grant and most Republican congressmen believed that it was essential to bring as many Liberal Republican bolters as possible back to the party when the new Forty-third Congress opened in December 1873 and thus avert a Democratic rout in the 1874 congressional elections. To accomplish this goal, in 1873 and 1874 Grant appointed several new cabinet members whom Liberals admired. The most important of these men was Treasury Secretary Benjamin H. Bristow, who almost immediately set out to break up the Whiskey Ring.

More important, Grant's courtship of the Liberals had considerable consequences for the federal government's efforts to enforce Reconstruction in the South, that is, to protect black voters from white violence and Republican state governments from armed Democratic challenges. Liberal Republicans demanded not just an end to federal intervention in the South but also a sweeping retrenchment of federal expenditures. At the start of 1874, Republicans in Washington gave them just that. In

January, Grant announced to the press that it was "time for the Republican party to unload. . . . This nursing of [carpetbagger] monstrosities [in Louisiana, Texas, and Mississippi] has nearly exhausted the party. I am done with them, and they will have to take care of themselves." The *New York Herald* sang its immediate approval of this new course. "Reconstruction, the carpet-baggers, the usurpation of power supported by troops—all this is dead weight, a millstone, that if not speedily disengaged will carry republicanism to the bottom."[5] Other Republicans joined the headlong retreat from Reconstruction that winter. Congress slashed appropriations for the new Justice Department, thus curtailing new federal prosecutions of white terrorists in the South. Then, the attorney general announced in the spring of 1874 that the federal government had achieved all its goals there.

As the depression deepened during 1874 and a massive repudiation of Republicans at northern polls appeared more likely, however, Republicans reversed course in an effort to save southern Republican congressional seats by maximizing black turnout. By the fall, the same attorney general who had announced that federal enforcement efforts in the South were complete was urging federal attorneys in the South to "spare no effort or necessary expense" in prosecuting anyone who interfered with blacks' right to vote.[6] Months earlier, in May, Senate Republicans had attempted to increase black voter turnout in the South by passing a civil rights bill that required the integration of railroads, steamships, streetcars, schools, hotels, and restaurants. Although House Republicans refused to enact this measure until early 1875, its impending passage, and the dramatic change in race relations in both the North and the South it portended, clearly made it an issue in the 1874 elections.

The civil rights bill had long been the pet project of Senator Charles Sumner of Massachusetts, the foremost champion of black rights among elected Republican officeholders, who died on March 11, 1874. The civil rights bill also reflected a sea change that was occurring in internal southern politics by the spring of 1874. As historian Michael Perman has brilliantly demonstrated, between the end of 1868 and mid to late 1873, former Whigs led both the Republican and the Democratic (or Conservative) parties in most southern states. Both groups of Whigs sought to win converts from the other to strengthen their political position against factional rivals in each party—northern carpetbaggers and blacks among Republicans, and diehard pro-Confederate Democrats among Conservatives. The upshot was that both Republican and Conservative leaders sought to keep the race issue out of southern campaigns. This tactical stand-off clearly advantaged the Republicans in most states. Blacks loyally supported Republican candidates, while potential white voters for the Conservatives massively abstained. Over time, however, blacks and their carpetbagger allies among Republicans increasingly demanded more appointive and elective offices for their majority wing of the Republican coalition and a more affirmative pro-black legislative agenda. Simultaneously, onetime Democrats increasingly rankled at the racial cease-fire Whig leaders had imposed on the Conservative Party.

After 1873, former Whigs were ousted from the leadership of both parties, and the new leaders eagerly embraced the politics of race that the erstwhile Whigs had suppressed. To mobilize even more blacks for the Republican Party, Republicans passed civil rights laws in three states and gave far more elective and appointive political positions to blacks. In short, they intentionally portrayed the Republicans as the party of blacks. Democrats simultaneously took up the mantle of white supremacy. They called on whites to restore "home rule" by driving the now black-oriented Republican machines from power. In this new situation, Democrats clearly had the advantage. Although black turnout for the Republican Party did in fact increase in some southern states, previous white abstainers far outnumbered blacks who had hitherto failed to vote. Consequently, in 1874 most remaining Confederate states where blacks lacked a majority of the potential electorate—Alabama, Arkansas, and North Carolina—also fell to the Democrats. Undoubtedly, the impending civil rights bill in Congress helped spark the movement of racist whites toward the Democrats.

Regardless of how much a racist backlash might help northern Democratic candidates in the upcoming congressional elections of 1874, sitting northern Republican congressmen knew that their constituents' economic grievances posed their biggest hurdle. Something had to be done to prove that Republicans had a plan for economic recovery. Yet there were severe constraints on what they could do. The howls for retrenchment and tax relief precluded public works projects that might pump money into the economy and provide jobs for the unemployed. In 1874 midwestern Grangers' demand for railroad regulation seemed to be a subject for state, not federal, legislation. Republicans, who still controlled both houses of Congress, did raise tariff rates in 1874 by the same 10 percent they had lowered them two years earlier, promising that such increases would help protect rapidly disappearing manufacturing jobs. But that seemed just a drop in the bucket, especially to nervous midwestern Republicans who had seen the beginnings of a massive voter revolt against them in 1873.

This situation apparently left monetary policy as the only tool the federal government could use to address hard times. When policy makers looked at monetary policy, however, they confronted a bewilderingly complex conundrum that had divided interest groups and thus both political parties internally since the end of the Civil War. What historians call the post–Civil War "Money Question" involved several separate but related matters.[7] One was the staggeringly high bonded indebtedness the federal government had contracted during the war and the equally high annual interest rates it was required to pay to service that debt. A second was the high tax rates the government had levied, in part to meet those payments, for there was simply no way to lower federal taxes until the debt was eliminated or re-funded by substituting new bonds at lower interest rates. Selling new bonds, in turn, required the federal government to guarantee that both the principal and interest would be paid in gold specie, as it had done in the Public Credit Act of 1869.

That requirement brought two other wartime financial measures into play. During the war the United States had abandoned a specie standard by authorizing the issue of $450 million worth of legal tender notes known as greenbacks. By the end of the war, some $432 million worth of greenbacks were in circulation. Greenbacks produced at least three consequential economic effects: wartime price inflation in the North, which negatively affected most manufacturing employees, whose pay lagged behind prices; a differential between the value of gold and the value of greenbacks, which made gold itself an object of speculation; and enhanced tariff protection against foreign competition for northern manufacturers. The so-called gold premium operated because importing merchants had to pay for foreign goods in gold or its equivalent, raising the greenback price of what they sold relative to domestically priced goods. So it is little wonder that northeastern importing merchants and the bankers they dealt with led the postwar demand for an immediate resumption of specie payments on greenbacks that eliminated the differential in the value between gold and paper money.

Greenbacks were not the only form of new paper money the government had created during the war. It had also established a national banking system and passed laws forcing most private banks to jettison their state charters and join the new system. This system required banks to purchase a certain face value of federal bonds, which they could buy with depreciated greenbacks, and then deposit those bonds with a new Treasury Department official, the comptroller of the currency. The comptroller would issue the bank national banknotes worth 90 percent of the face value of the deposited bonds. The banks could circulate those banknotes as interest-bearing loans while still earning the annual interest payments on the bonds deposited with the comptroller. In short, bonds purchased with greenbacks, not specie, constituted the reserve behind the banknotes. For banks that entered this system, it provided extraordinarily lucrative possibilities, but there was a catch. The wartime legislation capped the total amount of banknotes in circulation at $300 million. Once that cap was reached, no new banks could be chartered. During the war, the system resulted in a severe maldistribution of banknotes to the advantage of northeastern states and at the expense of the Midwest and especially the South.

This congeries of laws immediately split both Democrats and Republicans into what were called hard- and soft-money camps after the war (in fact, there were three camps, as explained later). Significantly, the major divisions fell primarily, though not exclusively, along East-West geographic lines. As noted earlier, the federal government used its surplus revenues in the late 1860s and early 1870s primarily to buy back federal bonds and issue new lower-interest bonds to reduce federal expenditures on interest payments and thus federal tax rates. That policy raised the question of whether interest rates on old bonds and both the principal and interest on new ones should be paid in gold or greenbacks. On this question, eastern Republicans and Democrats, on the one hand, and western Democrats, on the other, assumed diametrically opposite positions.

Easterners insisted that the nation's credit required the payment of both interest and principal in gold. But they also insisted that the face amount of greenbacks in circulation be sharply reduced so that the country could use the foreign gold it earned from bond sales to resume specie payments as soon as possible. In contrast, midwestern Democrats insisted that there must be no contraction of the currency supply and that both the interest and principal on bonds must be paid in greenbacks. Some went even further, demanding that national banks and national banknotes be utterly abolished and that unbacked legal tender notes— that is, greenbacks—be made the nation's exclusive circulating currency. Here, Democrats' ancient hatred of bankers' privileges and their control over money supplies reared its head, even though prior to the Civil War, Democrats had demanded that government-minted specie, not paper dollars, serve as the country's currency.

Between these two groups stood the most important set of political actors—Republican congressmen and senators who represented manufacturing and other entrepreneurial interests in Pennsylvania, upstate New York, and the rapidly growing Midwest. They rejected bond payments in anything but gold as repudiation. But they also rejected any contraction of the circulating currency because it would raise the cost of credit necessary for their constituents' enterprises and eliminate the gold premium from which they benefited. These Republicans, however, were not necessarily averse to some contraction of the greenback supply if it were accompanied by an expansion of the national banking system and the amount of bond-backed banknotes it could issue to the areas they represented.

The outbreak of depression following the banking panic of late 1873 only intensified these positions. Midwestern Democrats, now joined by many labor unions and farmers, increasingly called for inflation of the currency with more greenbacks to raise prices and destruction of the hated national banking system. Midwestern Republicans, in turn, hardened their resistance to currency contraction and stepped up calls for an expansion of national banks. Insisting that the fluctuating price of gold and the uncertainties it produced among investors and other businessmen was the root cause of the panic and depression, eastern Republicans and Democrats ratcheted up demands for a contraction of the amount of greenbacks in circulation.

The upshot of this tug-of-war was that in April 1874 Congress passed what became known as the "Inflation Act," over the opposition of eastern hard-money men in both parties. Importantly, healthy majorities of Republicans in both the House and the Senate supported the measure.[8] It increased the amount of national banknotes in circulation by $46 million and the amount of greenbacks by $18 million. The title of the measure was premature, however. No congressional bill becomes an act unless the president accepts it, and on April 22 Grant ringingly vetoed it. His motives were clear. He desperately hoped to woo back the Liberal Republican bolters of 1872, most of whom were hard-money men. A subsequent measure shifting some banknotes from the East to the West failed to appease the inflationists. Nor did the support that the majority of Republican congressmen had given the April inflation bill. What mattered to them was that a Republican president had killed the only federal measure that seemingly offered relief from their economic ills. Thus Republican candidates stood naked before the wrath of angry voters when the polls opened in the fall of 1874.

Those elections produced one of the most stunning reversals in American political history. In 1872 Republicans had captured 196 House seats and the Democrats only 83, with 2 southern seats won by Independents. In 1874 Democrats won 167 House seats and the Republicans only 99; in addition, 8 anti-Republican Independents won election. The numbers could have been even bleaker for Republicans. In 1872 Republicans had won 8 of the 10 House seats filled from Mississippi and California, but both those states postponed the 1874 election to 1875, when the results stood at 7 Democrats, 2 Republicans, and 1 Independent. By mid-November 1874, in sum, Republicans knew that when the new Forty-fourth Congress met in December 1875, Democrats would control the House of Representatives for the first time since the mid-1850s.

As table 1 in appendix A reveals, the swing toward the Democrats was especially marked in the former Confederate states, but it was also substantial in the mid-Atlantic states and the Midwest. Nor was the anti-Republican landslide confined solely to congressional races. Democrats won the governorship and usually the legislative majorities as well in California, Missouri, New Jersey, New York, and, astonishingly, Massachusetts. Democratic gains in the states translated into Democratic gains in the Senate. Whereas Republicans had enjoyed a fifty-seat Senate majority over Democrats as recently as the Forty-first Congress (1869–1871), in the Forty-fourth their edge would be reduced to fourteen seats.

Democrats' white supremacist campaign in the South, fueled in part by anger at the impending civil rights bill, disgust at the corruption permeating the Grant administration—from Washington to local customhouses, navy yards, and Internal Revenue offices—and, most important, resentment of hard times, which found an obvious target in the incumbent majority party, all undoubtedly contributed to the Republicans' smashing defeat. But analysis of the popular vote in the congressional elections of 1874 and 1875, when Democrats won twelve of the seventeen seats at stake, compared with the returns in 1872, when Republicans rolled up a popular-vote majority of more than 750,000, reveals—as it did to politicians at the time—a crucial fact: disgust with Republicans' record since 1872 did not necessarily translate into voter affection for the Democratic Party. Between 1872 and the 1874–1875 congressional elections, the Democratic vote increased in every region of the nation except the border states, where Democrats registered their most crushing victories. Nationwide, this increase amounted to approximately 333,000 votes, which by itself almost halved the Republicans' 1872 majority. This increase in Democratic turnout undoubtedly reflected a return to the polls of many dissatisfied Democrats who had refused to vote for Horace Greeley. The Democratic vote in 1874 also clearly included Liberal Republicans who had voted for Greeley in 1872.

Far more important, however, between the presidential election of 1872 and the congressional elections of 1874–1875, the drop in the Republican vote was more than twice the increase in the Democratic vote (see table 2 in appendix A). Historians of Reconstruction have shown that in the South, this Republican decline after 1872 in part reflected the defection of white Republicans—or scalawags, as Democrats called them—to the Democratic Party once the race line was drawn in southern politics. Yet elsewhere the story was decidedly different. In once staunchly Republican New England, Republican losses exceeded Democratic gains by almost three to one; in the mid-Atlantic states of New Jersey, New York, and Pennsylvania, by almost two to one; and, most important, in the vote-rich Midwest, by a nearly four-to-one ratio.

In short, however calamitous the results of the 1874 elections were for the Republicans—and many feared they presaged an even worse catastrophe in the presidential election of 1876—Republicans' biggest problem was the refusal of their usually faithful voters to come to the polls at all. Abstention, not defection to Democrats or third parties, was the party's biggest headache in 1874 and 1875. For the Republicans, then, the question was whether they could bring those former supporters back to the polls and mobilize new ones. They had learned in 1860 and 1864 that they needed no electoral votes from the South to elect a president. Northern states were the key, and the figures in table 2 show that in every northern region of the country, especially in the Midwest, Republicans mobilized far more additional voters than did Democrats between the off-year congressional elections of 1874–1875 and the presidential and congressional elections of 1876. Table 3, in turn, vividly illustrates how that return of northern Republican voters affected congressional elections in 1876. What must be explained is how Republicans accomplished this remarkable turnaround in a region with a heavy majority of electoral votes—and a region still mired in exceedingly hard economic times.

A PIVOTAL CONGRESSIONAL
SESSION

To assert that the second session of the Forty-third Congress, sitting from December 7, 1874, until March 3, 1875, determined the outcome of the 1876 presidential election is an exaggeration. Nonetheless, the actions, and inactions, of this three-month session shaped much of the campaign's content and predicted the controversy over its results with uncanny accuracy. One action in particular denied Democrats a presidential victory that, otherwise, they clearly would have won. If one needs evidence that most U.S. presidential elections are not shaped exclusively by the candidates running or the events occurring in the election year itself, this congressional session provides it.

Upon their return to Washington for the short session, both Democratic and Republican congressmen, many of the latter now lame ducks, recognized that this would be the last session of Congress in which Republicans controlled both the House and the Senate. That awareness influenced almost everything they said and did. Given that fact, the gingerly nature in which the Republican majority handled the race and Reconstruction questions indicated that northern Republicans considered both issues deadweight that must be jettisoned if the party was to have a chance in 1876.

In the previous session, Senate Republicans had passed a civil rights bill mandating the racial integration of most public facilities, including public schools and colleges, but the House had not acted on it. Even so, many Republicans grumbled that a racist backlash against this impending measure, and especially its provision regarding schools, had contributed to the Republicans' rout in the 1874 elections in both North and South. Thus, as soon as the House took up the measure in February 1875, Samuel Kellogg, a Connecticut Republican who had only narrowly won election in 1873, offered an amendment deleting the school provision. This passed, despite the vigorous protests of several southern black Republicans. Some northern Republican champions of the amendment rationalized that mandatory school integration would prompt most southern states to shut down their public school systems entirely and thus sacrifice one of the genuine achievements of Republican Reconstruction in the South. In this form the measure passed the House and Senate on largely party-line votes. Significantly, it included no enforcement mechanisms other than the promise that federal courts would hear suits filed by freedmen. To the extent that this measure influenced results in 1876, it gave Democrats additional ammunition.

Far more telling was how congressional Republicans dealt with the enforcement of blacks' voting rights in the South and continued federal support for state Republican regimes. These questions had particular salience because of contemporaneous events in Louisiana, where politics during Reconstruction was more chaotic, corrupt, and violent than in any other ex-Confederate state. A brief recap of those events must suffice here. After the gubernatorial election of 1872, Democrats claimed that their candidate, John McEnery, had won rather than Republican William Pitt Kellogg, whom Grant's administration supported. When legal challenges of the results failed, many Democrats resorted to armed violence in the form of so-called White Leagues to drive state and local Republican officeholders from office. They massacred more than a hundred blacks in Colfax, Louisiana, in April 1873, and in August 1874, after Congress had adjourned, they executed six black Republicans in Coushatta. Then, in September, armed white militia, professing loyalty to the putative Democratic governor, seized the statehouse in New Orleans, forcing Kellogg to seek refuge in the federal customhouse.[1] Grant issued a proclamation ordering the rioters to disperse and dispatched federal troops to New Orleans. Order was restored, and Kellogg was reinstalled in the statehouse, but Grant kept the federal troops in New Orleans and other parts of Louisiana to protect black voters in the November 1874 elections. They were still in New Orleans on January 5, 1875, when Democrats tried to seize control of the new state legislature by force, only to be dispersed by federal troops that put Republicans in charge. Grant had sent Major General Philip Sheridan to New Orleans as an observer, and after the January fracas, Sheridan sent a widely publicized telegram describing Democrats as *banditti* who deserved execution. These events caused a sensation in the North and fueled demands, even among many Republicans, that Grant's military tyranny over the South must stop.

Grant, for one, did not back down. In a special message to the Senate on January 13, 1875, he admitted that the northern public was sick of federal intervention in the South and said he regretted having to order it. He also denied that he had directly commanded the federal troops to interfere with the organization of Louisiana's legislature on January 5. Nonetheless, he also rehearsed the gruesome history of white violence against blacks in Louisiana and reminded the Senate that he was under oath to enforce the Fifteenth Amendment and the enforcement acts aimed at protecting blacks' right to vote. So long as he was president, Grant declared, "Neither Kuklux Klans, White Leagues, nor any other association using arms and violence to execute their unlawful purposes can be permitted in that way to govern any part of this country." Grant concluded by asking Congress to pass a law clarifying his role in Louisiana.[2]

Congressional Republicans' response to this request was to send a House investigating committee to New Orleans chaired by New York Republican William A. Wheeler. It arranged a compromise by which Democrats were given control of the lower house of the Louisiana legislature and Republicans control of the senate, along with Democrats' promise that they would not attempt to impeach the Republican Kellogg. Congressional Republicans accepted the "Wheeler Compromise," despite Grant's protests against violent attempts to seize control of governments. Wheeler, the compromiser, would be the vice-presidential nominee on the Republican ticket in 1876.

In early February 1875 Grant sent another special message to the Senate, denouncing the current Democratic administration in Arkansas and the new state constitution adopted in 1874 as illegal usurpations of power from the rightful Republican governor. Congress, he insisted, must do something to right this egregious wrong. Again the House responded with an investigating committee, this time chaired by Vermont Republican Luke Poland. It subsequently accepted Poland's rosy report that all was well in Arkansas and that no changes were necessary.

Nothing, however, reveals congressional Republicans' eagerness to bury the issue of federal enforcement of Reconstruction in the South so well as their handling of Grant's request for a new enforcement act.

The provision of the 1871 Ku Klux Klan Act authorizing the president to suspend the writ of habeas corpus and declare martial law in areas suffering especially atrocious antiblack violence had expired at the end of 1872, and Grant wanted that authority revived. Republican Speaker of the House James G. Blaine, who hungered after the Republican presidential nomination in 1876, delayed any action on this request until it was too late in the session for the Senate to consider it. "If that bill had become a law the defeat of the Republican party throughout the country is a foregone conclusion," he later explained to John R. Lynch, an African American Republican congressman from Mississippi. "We could not have saved the South even if the bill had passed, but its passage would have lost us the North. . . . In my opinion, it was better to lose the South and save the North, than to try to save the South, and thus lose both the North and South."[3] Likewise, other Republicans had clearly concluded that Reconstruction was now an albatross that could only drag the party down to defeat. "The truth is," one northern Republican wrote, "our people are tired out with this worn out cry of 'Southern outrages'!!! Hard times & heavy taxes make them wish the 'nigger,' 'everlasting nigger,' were in _____ or Africa."[4]

While congressional Republicans rebuffed Grant's pleas for stronger enforcement of Reconstruction in the South, they heeded his advice on monetary policy, though they hardly needed it. Republicans knew that the depression had crippled them in the 1874 elections, in part because they had failed to enact a credible policy to provide relief from hard times. And they knew that their only chance of presenting a distinctively Republican policy lay in this session, while they still controlled both chambers of Congress. In his annual message of December 1874, Grant called on Congress to enact some measure to achieve the resumption of specie payments as soon as possible and another measure to establish free banking, that is, to remove the cap on the amount of national banknotes that could be circulated and thus on the number of banks in the national banking system. Laying out an argument that Republicans would repeat ad nauseam through November 1876, Grant claimed that only ending the fluctuating value of greenbacks by bringing them to par with gold could induce economic recovery, for businessmen refused to invest or engage in trade so long as that value fluctuated.

Republicans' problem, of course, was to contrive some compromise measure acceptable to both easterners, who believed that resumption depended on contracting the face value of greenbacks in circulation, and westerners, who opposed any currency contraction. A bill was hammered out in the Senate Finance Committee, which its chairman, Ohio's John Sherman, reported to the Senate on December 21, 1874. A caucus of all Republican members had discussed the bill to ensure party unity against any attempts to amend it on the floor. As a Kentucky Democrat accurately hooted during the Senate debate, "This bill . . . is a species of Janus-faced legislation, and should be deemed rather a measure of party policy, than of financial relief. The expansionists, by one construction, can claim it as their measure and give it their support, while the contractionists, by a different construction, can insist that they have triumphed, and the bill is one of contraction which commands their support."[5]

The Specie Resumption Act of 1875, which Republicans rammed through without amendment and which would become a major issue in the 1876 presidential race, had three sections. The first called on the government to start minting silver coins immediately to replace the fractional paper currency worth 10, 25, and 50 cents then in circulation. "It is a resumption of specie payments upon the silver standard for the fractional currency," Sherman boasted.[6] The second section merely called for the elimination of the small fees that government mints charged holders of gold bullion for converting that bullion into gold dollars, presumably to encourage such sales.

The third section, the longest and most controversial, was the heart of the bill. It called for free banking, which, Sherman gleefully told the Senate, was an antimonopoly measure—a clear attempt to appeal to the antimonopoly sentiment evident in 1874. The bill further provided that for every $100 of new national banknotes issued by the comptroller of the currency above the existing statutory cap, the secretary of the treasury must immediately redeem $80 worth of greenbacks in gold and withdraw them from circulation until the face value of circulating greenbacks was reduced to $300 million. Finally, the bill provided that on and after January 1, 1879, the Treasury "shall redeem in coin the United States legal-tender notes then outstanding" at its office in New York City "in sums not less than fifty dollars." To prepare for this mandatory redemption, on a fixed date, the secretary of the treasury was authorized to put aside any surplus federal gold revenues accumulated, as well as to sell bonds purchasable in gold at home and abroad for the exclusive purpose of achieving redemption.[7]

Free banking, which western Democrats hated, made the bill a Republican measure, but as some Senate Democrats immediately and angrily pointed out, it also made the bill a dubious method of achieving either resumption or economic recovery. For one thing, as Democrats charged and Sherman admitted, as of January 1, 1879, the government would need enough gold to redeem not just greenbacks but also national banknotes. For another, as Democrats railed and Sherman also admitted, the withdrawal of greenbacks down to the $300 million limit depended on the initiative of national bankers requesting new banknotes from the comptroller of the currency. As Sherman put it, free banking "provides for an enlargement of the currency in case the business of the community demands it, and in case any bank in the United States may think it advisable or profitable to issue circulating medium in the form of bank-notes." Thus, Sherman disingenuously maintained that his bill provided for neither the contraction nor the expansion of the currency, "but leaves the amount to be regulated by the business wants of the community."[8]

That method, Senate Democrats immediately and accurately retorted, was the rub. With business activity paralyzed by the depression, bankers lacked customers for loans and hence would not seek additional national banknotes. And until those notes were issued by the Treasury, no greenbacks would be withdrawn from circulation. "You will have no increased banking under this bill, if you pass it," thundered Ohio Democrat Allen G. Thurman, "until business begins to revive."[9] Far from promoting economic recovery, the success of the Specie Resumption Act depended on such a recovery.

Others voiced still more objections. Hard-money men noted that the bill was unclear whether greenbacks withdrawn from circulation would be permanently destroyed or held in reserve for possible reissue. Others complained that the bill was far too vague about how the Treasury was to accumulate gold prior to the 1879 deadline. Sherman could only confess that he had purposely left these matters vague so that future congresses could consider them.

Despite these penetrating Democratic shafts, Republicans fended off all proposed amendments. They passed the bill in the Senate in late December and in the House in early January, on almost strict party-line votes.[10] On January 14, 1875, Grant happily signed it into law. Yet the astonishing number of members of both chambers who failed to record a vote indicated considerable dissatisfaction with Sherman's slippery measure. It carried the Senate by a vote of 32 to 14, with 27 abstentions, and the House by a vote of 125 to 106, with 57 abstentions. Some of these men may have been out of town or paired with men who were, but others were clearly present. The nonvoters included hard-money eastern Democrats and Republicans who obviously considered the bill's hazy resumption provisions inadequate, as well as western and southern Republicans who may have worried about its contractionist implications. If we can infer their motives from their later actions, the two Nevada Republican senators who abstained may have been miffed that the bill did not call for the remonetization of silver dollars as well as small change. Indeed, they were already raising the cry that the removal of silver dollars from the coinage list by an act passed in early 1873 was the "Crime of '73." At this point, however, western inflationists, many of whom wanted to destroy the national banking system, looked to an expanded circulation of government-printed greenbacks, free of any specie backing, as a panacea for economic hardship. "Free silver" had yet to become westerners' monetary priority.

In short, Sherman's effort to rally Republicans around a compromise monetary measure that distinguished them from Democrats and might provide a compelling issue for the 1876 campaign did not fully succeed. Both parties remained badly divided internally over the money issue. Those divisions would influence both the selection of presidential candidates in 1876 and the campaigns they subsequently ran.

Thus, Republicans in this short congressional session enacted a controversial measure that became one of the two most important issues in the 1876 presidential election. They also, remarkably, predicted fully two years before the event the dispute over counting electoral votes that would make that election so notorious. Republican Senator Oliver P. Morton of Indiana took the lead here. On January 21, 1875, he reported a proposed constitutional amendment from the Committee on Privileges and Elections that would change the way presidents were elected. The debate on how to choose and count electoral votes would continue intermittently in the Senate for the remainder of this short session.

The gist of Morton's proposed constitutional amendment (which was later sent back to committee, where Morton himself buried it) was to have states elect all but two of their electors by congressional districts rather than by winner-take-all statewide slates. Many Americans today would find this proposal appealing. For years, as Morton carefully documented, the winning presidential candidate's margin in the electoral college was grossly larger than his margin in the popular vote. The minority party in any state went unrepresented under the existing (and current) system, Morton protested. It was undemocratic and unrepublican. A bare-knuckled partisan bruiser, Morton minced no words about his intentions. In 1868, he explained, massive and well-documented Democratic frauds in New York City had produced a huge majority for Horatio Seymour that exceeded substantial upstate Republican majorities for Grant, giving that state's entire electoral vote to the Democrats. Democratic frauds might do so again in 1876, especially if, as many predicted, New York's Democratic Governor Samuel J. Tilden (elected in 1874 by a comfortable, if suspicious, 50,000 popular majority) was the Democratic presidential candidate in 1876. Tilden himself was already straining every nerve and spending his ample personal fortune to achieve just that outcome.

But Morton's proposed amendment, and especially the Senate debate provoked by it, pinpointed another problem. How should Congress resolve cases in which states submit rival slates of electoral votes? This was no phantasm. In 1872 both Democrats and Republicans in Louisiana had submitted electoral votes (just as they had submitted rival totals of gubernatorial votes), and the Republican-dominated Congress had refused to count either slate. The same thing might happen in 1876 in Louisiana and other southern states, Morton hinted darkly. The existing language of the Constitution provided no help. The Twelfth Amendment merely said that electors in every state should meet on a day set by Congress, and after their votes had been certified by the state's governor, they should be sent under seal to the president of the Senate (normally the vice president), who would open them in February before a joint meeting of the House and Senate, "and the votes shall then be counted." But, as many senators asked in early 1875, counted by whom?

Morton stipulated that section 2 of his committee's proposed constitutional amendment had an answer. It stated, "The Congress shall have power . . . to establish tribunals for the decision of such elections as may be contested."[11] Morton noted that the majority of his committee members believed that the Supreme Court should be the tribunal that decided who deserved contested electoral votes. Other senators on the floor in January and February 1875 also urged that the Supreme Court decide disputed electoral votes. The start of the Forty-fourth Congress in December 1875 witnessed a flood of proposed constitutional amendments concerning presidential elections, based on the assumption that electoral votes from southern states would be in dispute, and many of them stipulated that the Supreme Court should be the tribunal that awarded any state's disputed electoral votes to one candidate or the other. These Senate discussions taking place in early 1875 provide a blueprint that reveals why Congress included Supreme Court justices in the tribunal it subsequently created to decide the disputed electoral votes in early 1877.

Nonetheless, Morton's chief focus in the debates over his proposed amendment and later in February, when he reported first a proposed rule and then a statute from his committee, was the existing arrangement by which Congress counted electoral votes. This was not a statute. Instead, it was the Twenty-second Joint Rule that the Republican-dominated Congress had adopted in February 1865.[12] This rule stipulated that when the House and Senate convened to watch the president of the Senate open the electoral votes, any representative or senator could object to the reception of any state's electoral vote, no matter how trivial the technical grounds for his objection. As soon as such an objection was raised, senators were to return to their chamber (joint sessions were held in the House) and, without any debate, members of the House and Senate would vote whether to sustain the objection. If either chamber did so, the state's electoral vote would be thrown out, no matter how the other chamber voted. This rule was outrageous, Morton initially protested, for it allowed a single house of Congress to disfranchise the voters of any (or every) state in a presidential election. And he had evidence. In 1872 Congress had refused to count the electoral votes from Louisiana and had come within a whisker of doing so in Texas, Mississippi, and Arkansas. But in 1872, Morton noted, those votes did not matter, for Grant had clearly won an electoral vote majority anyway. But what would happen, he ominously asked, if the electoral votes in question could determine the winner?

However high-minded Morton's initial rhetoric was, later, when he introduced a law stipulating that no state's electoral vote could be thrown out without the concurrence of both houses of Congress, he was more forthright. When electoral votes were counted in 1877, he warned, "the House will be Democratic and the Senate will be Republican." House Democrats were certain to reject enough electoral votes from Republican states so that no one had a majority. Then, according to the Constitution, the decision would be thrown into the Democratic House, which "will elect a Democrat for President." His warning culminated with the following rant:

It will be in the power of our friends on the other side in the next House of Representatives . . . to throw the election into the House no matter what the votes may be. Under the rule the Republican party cannot elect a President. Why? Because it is in the power of the House of Representatives, . . . to throw out the vote of every Republican State. . . . The result would be that the election would go into the Democratic House.[13]

Morton's nakedly partisan fear-mongering was sufficient to arouse the Republican majority of the Senate to pass a law that required the concurrence of both houses of Congress before any state's electoral votes were voided. But it was passed so late in the session that the House never acted on it. When the session closed on March 3, 1875, the odd Twenty-second Joint Rule remained the only existing provision for deciding disputed electoral votes.

At the tail end of the session, Republicans in the Senate (on February 26) and then in the House (on March 1) frantically passed a measure that, arguably, did more than anything else to determine the outcome of the 1876 presidential election. This was a bill authorizing the residents of Colorado Territory to apply for admission to statehood by adopting a constitution and sending it to the president. No previous study of Reconstruction or the presidential election of 1876 adequately explains the admission of Colorado as the "Centennial State" on August 1, 1876. Yet it is a tale that cries to be told.

Congress first offered statehood to the residents of Colorado in 1863, at the same time the offer was made to Nevadans. The latter accepted the offer, but at the time and on several subsequent occasions, the voters of Colorado—most of whom were silver miners—nixed statehood and chose to remain a federal territory. Their apparent antipathy to statehood is an important background to this story.

Then, on June 8, 1874, at the urging of Jerome Chaffee, the Republican representative of Colorado Territory (who would be one of the two U.S. senators first elected from Colorado), House Republicans again passed a bill authorizing statehood for Colorado. There is no evidence from the debates that congressional Republicans had any idea that Colorado's admission might affect the outcome of the 1876 presidential election. Still, their motives can be readily inferred. Republican losses in the state elections of 1873 accurately heralded a Republican disaster in the congressional elections of 1874. Admitting Colorado as a state might shore up Republican strength in the Senate by adding two new Republican members. Should this Congress fail to act, Republicans suspected, Colorado statehood would be a dead issue, for the new Democratic House would never allow it.[14]

The House bill contained a number of provisions giving the new state generous federal land grants to entice residents to accept statehood, as well as provisions regarding the schedule for calling, holding, and ratifying the work of a constitutional convention that seemed to assure statehood by early 1875 at the latest. The bill also contained wording of great partisan significance, although, astoundingly, no Democrat ever complained about it.[15] It stated that if the new constitution was ratified by a majority of the territory's voters, the territorial governor should certify that ratification and send his certification, along with a copy of the new constitution, to the president, "whereupon it shall be the duty of the President of the United States to issue his proclamation declaring the State admitted into the Union on an equal footing with the original States, without any further action whatever on the part of Congress."[16] This language was retained in the Senate version of the bill that became law. Here, then, is the answer to why the Democrat-controlled House in the new Forty-fourth Congress did not prohibit Colorado's admission in the summer of 1876. The preceding, Republican-controlled Congress had neutered it. Once the bill passed in 1875, Democrats' hands were tied.

Initially, it appears, some Democrats failed to recognize the partisan implications of Colorado statehood. Chaffee's bill passed the House by a margin of 171 to 66, with 52 members not voting. The majority included 139 Republicans and 32 Democrats; 43 Democrats and 23 Republicans constituted the minority. Because the bill passed under a rule that required a two-thirds majority, Democrats could have killed it had they united against it. More intriguing are the negative Republican votes. Not all Republicans welcomed the prospect of two more western Republican senators, especially New England and other northeastern Republicans who, one can infer, had no wish to provide allies to the two Nevada Republican senators who were already clamoring for the minting of silver dollars.

This regional dimension of the Republican vote became clear in the Senate on June 23, 1874, the last day of the session, when Nevada's William M. Stewart called on his colleagues to pass the House's Colorado bill. Both Republican senators from Rhode Island immediately sought to quash Stewart's motion, and William Sprague's motion to table it carried 33 to 20. Twenty Republicans and 13 Democrats voted to kill Colorado statehood; 17 Republicans and only 3 Democrats voted to keep it alive. Thus Senate action was postponed until the second session.

By the time the Senate took up the Colorado statehood bill in February 1875, its partisan implications were far clearer. As a result, Democrats unanimously supported motions to adjourn and thus prevent action on it, and the vast majority of Republicans opposed those motions. Still, when Phineas Hitchcock, the Nebraska Republican who was now managing the bill, urged the Senate to enact it on February 24, he met considerable opposition from a minority of Republicans as well as from Democrats. Hitchcock pleaded with his colleagues not to amend the House bill, lest the House fail to enact it during the few remaining days of the session. Republicans and Democrats alike roared that Hitchcock was seeking to subvert the Senate's rights as an independent chamber, and both offered numerous amendments, which the hapless Hitchcock eventually accepted without the need for a roll-call vote.

For our purposes, the most important amendments were demanded by Vermont's crotchety Republican George Edmunds, who had already clashed during this session with Sherman over the terms of the Specie Resumption Act and with Morton over his attempt to replace the Twenty-second Joint Rule. Edmunds, the chairman of the Senate Judiciary Committee, openly admitted that he wanted to delay Colorado's admission, and it seems likely that he wanted to kill it outright. His key amendment would delay any meeting of a constitutional convention in Colorado until the winter of 1875–1876, a full year later than the original House bill had contemplated. Equally important, it specified that no popular referendum on a Colorado constitution could be held prior to July 1876. This amendment passed by a vote of 27 to 22, with 12 Republicans, including 6 New Englanders, joining 15 Democrats in the majority; Republicans cast all the negative votes.

Edmunds argued disingenuously that the purpose of his amendment was to give the residents of Colorado, who had already rejected three offers of statehood, ample time to decide whether they wanted to enter the Union under their new constitution. But then he immediately offered another amendment clearly aimed at dissuading those residents from doing so. This poison pill would have drastically reduced the land grants offered to Colorado in the enabling legislation. It went down to defeat 22 to 28. Edmunds and 7 other Republicans, including 4 other New

Englanders, joined 14 Democrats in the minority; 26 Republicans, who were clearly fed up with Edmunds's obstructionism, and 2 Democrats constituted the majority. When Edmunds then tried to shut down the consideration of Colorado statehood by moving to executive session, 32 Republicans voted against him. Later that day, when the Senate finally passed the measure and sent its revised bill back to the House, Republicans had restored a semblance of party unity: 41 Republicans and 2 Democrats supported its adoption; no Republicans and 13 Democrats futilely opposed it.

The Senate bill reached the desk of the Speaker of the House on February 26. Normally, such an amended bill would have been printed so that members could read it and compare it with the original. But time constraints in the dwindling days of the session precluded that. House members had been so preoccupied with their close-of-session duties that few, if any, knew precisely what the Senate amendments entailed. A few gleeful Democrats shouted on the House floor that the Senate had postponed Colorado's admission as a state until 1877. Unnerved, some Republicans called unsuccessfully for an instantaneous vote rejecting the Senate's amendments. Another Republican moved to suspend the rules to allow selected Republicans to approach the Speaker's desk and read what the Senate had done to their bill, but this motion failed to achieve the two-thirds majority necessary to pass. Finally, on March 1, after the Speaker had read the gist of the Senate's amendments to nervous House Republicans, the House voted to adopt the Senate version of the Colorado statehood bill under a rule that again required a two-thirds majority to suspend the House's normal order of business. This motion carried 164 to 76. Now, in contrast to June 1874, only 15 Democrats joined 149 Republicans in the majority; only 7 Republicans, rather than 23, joined 69 Democrats in opposition. Nonetheless, if those few Democrats who supported the bill had joined the majority of their colleagues in opposition, Colorado statehood would have failed by a vote of 149 to 91. Even if it had been a strict party-line vote, the bill would have failed by a vote of 156 to 84.

What is the relevance of this tale? an impatient reader might ask. This book is supposed to be about the presidential election of 1876, not what Congress did in the winter of 1874–1875 with regard to Colorado or anything else. The answer is this: George Edmunds's hostile amendments succeeded in delaying the entry of two Republican senators from Colorado until December 1876. But once President Grant proclaimed

Colorado's admission as a state on August 1, 1876, it was entitled to participate fully in the presidential election in November of that year. The new Republican state legislature, citing the expensive arrangements to hold a referendum on the new state constitution in July as an excuse, refused to allow a popular vote for president and cast the state's 3 electoral votes for the Republican ticket. Something else, however, was much more important. Prior to Colorado's admission as the Centennial State on August 1, the total number of electoral votes was 366, meaning that a majority—one vote more than half—was 184 electoral votes. But with the addition of Colorado's 3 electoral votes, the total stood at 369, making 185 electoral votes the necessary majority. Only later would rueful Democrats learn that their failure on two separate occasions to bury the Colorado statehood bill in the House had been an egregious blunder.

3

PREVIEWS

Between early March 1875, when the Forty-third Congress adjourned, and the meeting of the new Forty-fourth Congress in December, at least three additional developments with great significance for the 1876 presidential election occurred. One, concerning incumbent President Ulysses Grant, had crucial implications for Republicans' presidential nomination and the kind of campaign Republicans could run. The second was a series of state elections, starting in March and extending to November, a few weeks before the new Congress assembled. Previous historians have properly noted the importance of two of those contests, Ohio's and Mississippi's, but others also set patterns repeated in 1876. One such pattern is the striking extent to which Democrats and Republicans took similar—indeed, almost identical—positions on the issues debated in 1875. That congruence reappeared in 1876. In addition, the results of those elections shaped calculations—and, for both parties, some miscalculations—about which states each might carry in 1876 and the kind of nominee most likely to do so. Third, and perhaps most important, 1875 witnessed the emergence (or reemergence) of anti-Catholicism as a potent Republican campaign issue, one that many Republicans expected to be a lethal anti-Democratic weapon in 1876 as well.

From the moment of Grant's triumphant reelection in 1872, rumors, usually instigated by Democrats, circulated that he would seek a third term in 1876. Democrats cited the administration's frequent insertion of federal troops in the South and its posting of federal marshals at the polls in northern cities to deter immigrant voting as evidence that Grant intended to deploy federal power to hang on to the White House. Democrats, indeed, charged Grant with "Caesarism," or plotting to undermine republican self-government. As Grant later wrote, he found these inflammatory charges "beneath the dignity of [his] office" to answer. By early 1875, therefore, cries about a third Grant term had reached a crescendo.[1] Those cries clearly embarrassed Republicans who had no wish to defend Grant's increasingly besmirched record in 1876. Thus, in state platforms adopted in early 1875, they had little choice but to echo Democrats' vehement opposition to the very idea of a third term for anyone. No official Republican statements, however, matched some Democrats' demands that all presidents be limited to a single term and that the president's salary be rolled back to the $25,000 from which it had been doubled by the Republicans' notorious Salary Grab Act of 1873. In sum, the longer the third term question lay open, the greater the advantage Democrats seemed to have.

Finally, after Pennsylvania Republicans pronounced themselves "unalterably opposed" to a third presidential term for "any person" at their May 26 state convention, Grant wrote a public letter to that convention's chairman, General Harry White, renouncing his intention of seeking one. Dated May 29, 1875, Grant's letter was hardly Shermanesque, and it hardly quieted Democratic fear-mongering about a permanent military dictatorship on the horizon. Only an amendment to the Constitution, Grant insisted, could prevent a president from seeking a third term, and no such amendment had yet been adopted. Nonetheless, he wrote, "I am not, nor have I ever been, a candidate for renomination. I would not accept a nomination if it were tendered, unless it should come under such circumstances as to make it an imperative duty—circumstances not likely to arise."[2] However ambivalent, Grant's letter sufficed to open the Republican presidential nomination to other aspirants. And some of those aspirants would seek to use the issues debated in the minority of states holding elections in 1875 to forward their prospects. The ultimate Republican nominee would, in fact, emerge from one of those state races.

The main reason why the prospect of a third Grant term so unnerved Republicans in 1875 was that in most state elections that year, as would be the case in 1876, both Democrats and Republicans avidly wooed Liberal Republicans and, in midwestern and West Coast states, other independent parties that had emerged in 1873 and 1874. This competitive courtship affected how most Republican and Democratic state parties dealt with specific policy questions concerning corruption, reform, specie resumption and monetary policy, and Reconstruction.

Democrats, at first blush, clearly seemed to have an edge in this competition. A state convention of New York's Liberal Republicans in September, for example, insisted that all future presidents be limited to a single term, a stand that only Democrats took in 1875. More important, Democrats had cooperated with Liberals in 1872 against Grant, and they were determined to preserve that alliance, no matter how heavy-handed their tactics might strike the modern observer. Connecticut's Democratic state convention, for example, claimed to represent "the Democratic and Liberal Republican Electors of Connecticut," while in the Bay State they called themselves "the Democrats and Liberal Republicans of Massachusetts assembled."[3] Iowa's Democrats asserted that their June state convention gathered "the Democrats, Liberal Republicans, and antimonopolists of the State of Iowa assembled." New York's Democratic convention in September invited the cooperation of "every true Democrat, every Liberal Republican and all our fellow citizens of whatever party name . . . to unite with us in supporting reform candidates on a reform platform." Pennsylvania's Democrats "cordially" asked "Liberal Republicans and all other men" to help them evict Republicans from office.[4] Finally, in Wisconsin, where Democrats had allied with a People's Reform Party in 1873 to take the governorship from Republicans, Democrats in 1875 labeled their convention "representatives of the Democratic and Liberal Reform and Independent Electors of Wisconsin" who would "abide by the principles of political reform adopted by the People's Reform Convention of 1873."[5]

The effectiveness of these blatant blandishments, however, can be questioned. In 1875 Democrats decisively carried Connecticut in April, but Republicans recaptured governorships in Massachusetts, New Hampshire, Ohio, and Wisconsin and retained the statehouse in Iowa, Maine, Vermont, and Pennsylvania. Aside from Ohio's, the results in New York were most pertinent to developments in 1876. There, Democrats carried the only important statewide race at stake, although by a considerably smaller margin than Samuel J. Tilden had won the governorship the preceding year. Meanwhile, Republicans regained control of both houses of the state legislature. Equally important, although the Liberal Republicans' state convention rejected a call by some delegates for a formal merger with the Democratic Party, it resoundingly applauded Governor Tilden's record as a reformer. In conjunction, these developments enhanced the argument of Tilden and his friends that only he could carry New York in 1876 and that, without New York, Democrats had no prayer of retaking the White House.

One reason for Republicans' resurgence in 1875 may have been their skill in neutralizing Democrats' appeal to Liberal Republicans and other independent parties on specific issues. Take, for example, Liberals' concern with corruption in government and their demands that rascals be thrown out; that government expenditures, payrolls, and taxes be slashed; and that civil service reform be instituted. Because of the increasingly malodorous reputation of Grant's administration, Democrats seemed to hold the high cards on the corruption and reform issue. As they would even more stridently in 1876, therefore, every 1875 Democratic state platform from California and Oregon to Maine, New Hampshire, and Massachusetts blasted the administration for its appointment of corrupt party hacks and its bloated federal budget that bled hapless taxpayers. "There can be no reasonable hope of reform and a restoration of prosperity under a Republican Administration controlled by a ring of officeholders who are eating out the substance of the people to enrich themselves and their servile retainers," Maine's Democrats fulminated. "In contempt of every pledge, they have gone from bad to worse until the extravagance, profligacy, and corruption that mark their course are viewed with astonishment and alarm. We believe the people demand a change."[6]

Democrats elsewhere rang changes on these themes that would constitute the heart of their 1876 presidential campaign. Copying an omnibus plank adopted by Democrats in Iowa and Ohio, for example, Pennsylvania Democrats in September "arraign[ed] the leaders of the Republican party for their extravagant expenditures and profligate waste of the people's money, for their corruption, for their peculation, for their contempt of constitutional obligations, for their extortionate increase of the salaries of our public officers, for their oppressive, unjust, and defective system of taxation, finance, and currency, [and] for their continuance of incompetent and corrupt men in office."[7]

Democrats' most important and effective portrayal of their commitment to Liberal Republicans' reform agenda, however, came in New York. There, they had won the governorship and control of the state legislature in 1874 and could actually do something to pursue reform. Tilden, who had won in 1874 in part because of his reputation for helping to bring down Boss Tweed in 1871, enhanced his reputation by prosecuting the so-called Canal Ring in 1875. This was a group of contractors and state employees who for years had fleeced the state government by submitting or paying padded bills for repairs and skimming toll revenues on the Erie Canal and its tributaries. Democrats' platform praised their "honest and fearless" governor for leading this clean-government crusade and, Democrats contended, reducing state expenditures by $3 million in a single year. As noted, the Liberal Republican state convention praised Tilden by name for his reform efforts.[8]

Though clearly at a disadvantage, Republicans refused to concede the good-government label to Democrats without a fight. Across the nation in 1875, as they would again in 1876, they correctly pointed out that Grant's administration had substantially reduced the federal debt accumulated during the Civil War and thus the government's annual expenditures on interest payments. Virtually every northern Republican state platform in 1875 explicitly praised Grant's administration (i.e., Treasury Secretary Benjamin Bristow) for prosecuting the Whiskey Ring and seeking the collection of tax revenues of which the government had been defrauded. "We demand honesty, economy, and efficiency in every branch of the state and national administrations, prompt investigation of all charges of wrong-doing, and summary exposure, prosecutions, and punishment of wrong-doers," declared New York's Republicans. "We therefore heartily commend the action of all officers, whether of the State [i.e., Tilden] or national Government, in their honest efforts for the correction of public abuses." Pennsylvania Republicans shamelessly averred, "The Administration of President Grant has in six short years steadily and unbendingly reformed every known abuse, and is today relentlessly on the track of wrong-doers." They insisted on "honest men in office—men with brains enough to know dishonesty when they see it and courage enough to fight it whenever they find it."[9]

Republicans hardly stopped with their commitment to the equivalent of motherhood and apple pie. Where Democratic state administrations seemed vulnerable to charges of malfeasance and profligacy in spending taxpayers' money, as in New Hampshire, Connecticut, and Oregon, Republicans drew up rhetorical bills of indictment. Kentucky Republicans singled out Bristow, Liberal Republicans' favorite cabinet member and first choice as Republican presidential nominee in 1876, as Kentucky's gift to the American people. In New Hampshire they explicitly praised the state's Republican voters for helping to evict from office Republican congressmen who had supported the notorious Salary Grab Act of 1873. And Maryland's outnumbered Republicans in 1875 openly allied against the incumbent Democratic state administration with a Citizens' Reform Party that, among other things, sought "an honest and economical administration of the government, both State and National."[10]

The 1875 state races, in sum, ensured that in 1876 both parties would portray themselves as good-government men, as reformers committed to honesty, competence, and efficiency. No disagreement existed on this professed goal; the question was which party could be better trusted to achieve it. It is little wonder that Republicans were so relieved when Grant disclaimed any designs on a third term or that they ultimately nominated a candidate who might appeal to Liberal Republicans.

Significantly, the September convention of New York's Liberal Republicans, the only such statewide gathering held in 1875, began its platform with a warning that "national disaster threatens" without a speedy resumption of specie payments. Just as significantly, it condemned Grant's administration "for its shifting and unstable policy in the administration of the finances" and "for its inflation of the currency, its fraudulent pretenses to the contrary notwithstanding."[11] Northeastern Liberal Republicans clearly found the Republicans' Specie Resumption Act inadequate, if not downright fraudulent, presumably because it delayed resumption until 1879 and made that goal more difficult by expanding the amount of national banknotes in circulation. Just as clearly, wooing Liberals' support required the affirmation of a commitment to resumption, if not to the law Republicans had hoped would resolve the matter.

Unlike the unanimous condemnation of governmental corruption and profligacy and the interparty consensus that federal enforcement of Reconstruction must be abandoned (discussed later), no regionwide agreement emerged between northern Republicans and Democrats on financial issues or on the related matter of what had caused the depression and thus how to remedy it. Instead, with a few important exceptions, both major parties split along East-West sectional lines. Within those sections, nonetheless, the two parties often offered essentially identical nostrums on the money question. What is equally striking is the scarcity of direct or indirect allusions by either party to the Specie Resumption Act itself. On this matter the 1876 campaign would differ dramatically from that of 1875.

With the glaring exception of Pennsylvania—where Republicans endorsed free banking but ignored specie resumption altogether, and Democrats condemned the contraction of greenback circulation and the expansion of the national banking system called for by the Specie Resumption Act—Republicans and Democrats in the Northeast, as well as in the West Coast states of California and Oregon, took almost identical stances on the money question. Echoing New York's Liberal Republicans, both parties demanded a return to specie payments as fast as possible and utterly condemned any increase of the paper money supply, presumably including national banknotes, as inimical to that goal and to the restoration of prosperity. To be sure, occasional partisan differences appeared. Some Democrats condemned Republicans' law as a sham and faulted it for delaying specie resumption, while some Republicans cited Democrats' votes against the act in Congress as giving the lie to their professed commitment to resumption. Nonetheless, the absence of partisan differences on the money question is far more striking.[12]

Outside of Pennsylvania, easterners of both major parties condemned inflation of the money supply as the ultimate evil. Their denunciations of it were stunningly similar. In Maryland, for example, Democrats "protest[ed] against any increase in the circulating currency, but demand[ed] that such measures be adopted by Congress as will result in the resumption of specie payments at the earliest possible moment," whereas Republicans "earnestly" favored "the return to specie payments at the earliest practicable moment, and the cessation of all further expansion of the currency." Maine's Republicans declared that "a sound currency based on coin, and redeemable in coin, is essential to the prosperity of the people. We therefore approve all judicious legislation [i.e., the Resumption Act] looking to that end." Maine's Democrats echoed that "a sound currency, coin or its equivalent, [is] essential to stability in business and a restoration of prosperity." Hence they demanded "steps toward specie payment and no steps backward." In Massachusetts, similarly, both parties stressed the harm that greenback inflation did to "the earnings of labor." "We favor a speedy return to specie payments," intoned Democrats, "as essential to the revival of the commerce, business, and credit of the country, and to the welfare of the laboring masses."[13]

From Pennsylvania westward to Ohio, Iowa, and Minnesota, the position of both parties on the money question differed markedly from that of their eastern counterparts. There, contraction of the existing currency supply, not its inflation, was identified as the archevil. Democrats and Republicans alike regarded specie resumption as an obstacle to, rather than a necessity for, economic recovery. When Democrats or Republicans allowed that specie resumption was ultimately desirable, therefore, they always added the crucial caveat that it must be achieved at a gradual pace that did no further economic harm. Iowa Democrats, for example, favored specie resumption "as soon as the same can be done without injury to the business interests of the country, and in the meantime a sufficient supply of national currency [greenbacks] for business purposes." Kentucky Republicans called for "resumption of specie payments at the earliest date consistent with the business interests of the country." Those in Wisconsin "advocate[d] the gradual resumption of specie payments by continuous steps, in such manner as to disturb the business interests of the country as little as possible." And Ohio Republicans, rather than praising John Sherman for devising a law that fixed January 1, 1879, as the date for resumption and established free banking, recommended that a "policy of finance should be steadily pursued which, without unnecessary shock to business, or trade, will ultimately equalize the purchasing capacity of the coin and paper dollar."[14] Quite unlike northeastern Liberal Republicans and the Democrats and Republicans who courted their support, no party in the Midwest demanded resumption "as soon as possible."

There was one other dramatic difference between Democratic platforms in the West and those in the East. In Oregon, Iowa, Ohio, and Pennsylvania, where Democrats copied the economic planks of Ohio's Democratic platform virtually word for word, Democrats denounced the national banking system as an egregious monopoly that fattened greedy bankers and oppressed the working class. They also usually demanded its immediate abolition and the substitution of more greenbacks for the national banknotes then in circulation. In short, western Democrats demanded precisely the expansion of greenback currency that northeastern Republicans and Democrats alike condemned as an obstacle to specie resumption and economic recovery. In turn, the large gains Democrats had made at Republicans' expense in the Midwest's congressional elections of 1874 help explain Republicans' tepid endorsement of specie resumption and their silence about the free banking provision of Sherman's law.

A geographical disparity in financial resources, especially of national banknotes available to businessmen, if not the incidence of economic hardship among the working class during the depression, explains in part this sectional divide on the money question. But the main reason was probably political. In the Northeast, wooing hard-money Liberal Republicans dictated the economic platforms of both parties. Pennsylvania may have been an exception to this rule in 1875 simply because the unemployed mill and mine workers targeted by both parties significantly outnumbered Liberal Republicans in that state. Certainly Pennsylvania Republicans' full-throated endorsement of high protective tariffs to restore jobs to the unemployed suggests that reassuring Liberals on economic issues was not their top priority. In the Midwest and on the West Coast, in contrast, the independent parties courted by both Republicans and Democrats—parties that had often allied with Democrats to oust Republicans from office in 1873 and 1874—sought more than clean government or specie resumption. They also demanded abolition of corporate monopolies such as national banks, inflation of the currency supply to raise the prices farmers received for their crops, and forceful state regulation of railroads and other corporations.

Thus, just as both Republicans and Democrats in those states touted their commitment to railroad rate regulation and free, open access to water supplies for irrigation, both had to shun any forced contraction of the money supply that, as Democrats tellingly and repeatedly charged in 1875 and again in 1876, was entailed in fixing a precise date for specie resumption. Such a date, Democrats iterated and reiterated, would require the federal government to save, rather than recirculate, the specie it garnered from tariff revenues for the next four years. It would also cause businessmen and other wealthy individuals to hoard, rather than spend, the greenbacks in their possession as they awaited the future bonanza when greenbacks came to par with gold. According to western Democrats, in short, mandatory resumption at a fixed date would smother the flow of cash and credit necessary to rejuvenate business, put the unemployed back to work, and save farmers from losing mortgaged land. In the face of that withering critique, midwestern Republicans dared not fully embrace Sherman's handiwork—or at least so it seemed for most of 1875.

Going into the 1876 presidential campaign, both Republicans and Democrats remained internally divided over economic policy and the best response to the ongoing depression. Nonetheless, the sectional chasm separating Democrats was far deeper, and it would play a much greater role in complicating the selection of a national ticket and the adoption of a national platform in 1876, than would be the case among Republicans. The depth and breadth of that sectional chasm is readily apparent in the sharply contrasting Democratic platforms adopted in Ohio and New York in 1875, both of which put forward contenders for the 1876 presidential nomination.

On June 17 Ohio's Democrats (later copied by Pennsylvania's) declared that "the contraction of the currency heretofore made by the Republican party, and the further contraction proposed by it, with a view to the forced resumption of specie payment, has already brought disaster to the business of the country, and threatens it with general bankruptcy and ruin." Democrats therefore demanded "that this policy be abandoned, and that the volume of currency be made and kept equal to the wants of trade, leaving the restoration of legal tenders to par with gold to be brought about by promoting the industries of the people, and not by destroying them." By "abolishing legal tenders and giving national banks the power to furnish all the currency," Democrats added, Republicans sought to "increase the power of a dangerous monopoly, and the burdens now oppressing the people." In contrast, Democrats "demand[ed] that all national-bank circulation be promptly and permanently retired, and legal tenders issued in its place." Indeed, greenbacks should be accepted for payment of tariff duties, a step that would cripple the federal government's accumulation of gold necessary for specie resumption (Democrats did not point this out). The national banking system must be abolished and replaced by state-chartered banks of deposit and discount, with no power to issue banknotes, Democrats insisted. During the fall campaign, Democratic speakers and newspaper editors fleshed out this case. Because national banks had to deposit federal bonds with the Treasury to belong to the system, the expansion of the system called for in the Specie Resumption Act would necessitate an increase in the national debt and retention of the oppressive federal taxes necessary to pay the annual interest on that debt.[15]

In September New York's Democrats adopted a platform that flatly—and, one suspects, intentionally—repudiated the handiwork of their Ohio party brethren. It began by denouncing "repudiation in every form and guise" and demanding "a speedy return to specie payments," an explicit rejection of Ohio Democrats' insistence in the late 1860s that bondholders be paid in greenbacks rather than gold. Whereas the Ohioans blamed the depression on the contraction of currency in circulation, the New Yorkers cited inflation as the root cause. "The present depression of business is caused by reaction from the unhealthy stimulus of an excessive, depreciated, and irredeemable currency," as well as by enormous local, state, and federal taxes and "extravagance, waste, and peculation in the administration of public affairs." Further currency inflation, as called for by western soft-money men, would only worsen the depression, not cure it. Because "the existing volume of currency is greater than can be absorbed by business," and because "the recent fall of prices has followed repeated inflations," declared New York Democrats, no attempt "to increase the currency" could "revive prosperity." Instead, it would only "interrupt the healing processes of industry . . . create distrust and new uncertainties in business, paralyze beginnings of enterprise," and "rob labor of its too scanty employment."[16] Left unsaid, but clearly impelling this vigorous rejection of western Democrats' monetary nostrums, was the fact that any endorsement of them would fatally undermine eastern Democrats' courtship of Liberal Republicans.

The Liberal Republican movement, at least in the border states, had originated in the late 1860s behind a call to end federal enforcement of Reconstruction in the South. In 1875 and 1876 Liberals' continued antipathy to federal intervention clearly influenced the stand taken by both Democrats and Republicans on Reconstruction. Grant's dispatch of federal troops to Louisiana in late 1874, their role in ousting Democrats from the Louisiana legislature in January 1875, and Grant's request to Congress for authority to intervene in Arkansas and suspend habeas corpus elsewhere clearly left Republicans vulnerable on this matter. During 1875 Democrats from the West Coast to New England bellowed their outrage at the president's actions. Democrats in Maine, for example, declared "that the conduct of the Administration in setting up by the bayonet in a sovereign State a government having no title to authority and in entering a legislative hall with armed soldiers and dragging out members elected by the people, is a daring outrage that should unite every patriot in the land in the common effort to drive from power the actors in so dangerous a crime against civil liberty."[17] Indeed, in a display of fervid imagination, Maine's Democrats even blamed the economic depression on Reconstruction in the South. By their analysis, corrupt carpetbagger regimes in the former Confederacy had so stunted the postwar South's economic recovery that northern manufacturers were deprived of a market crucial to their own prosperity. The route to economic recovery in the North, in short, lay in driving Republicans from power in the South.

By 1875, of course, Republicans were well aware of Liberal Republicans' and other northern voters' disenchantment with further federal intervention in the South. That is why, in the second session of the Forty-third Congress, they rebuffed Grant's call for additional action in Arkansas and Louisiana and quashed his request for renewed authority to suspend habeas corpus. In 1875, as they would again in 1876, they were just as cautious in their platforms. Only Connecticut and Iowa Republicans praised Grant's tough response to Louisiana's White Leaguers. Others ignored Reconstruction entirely or merely expressed a commitment to blacks' civil and political rights, a stance that several northern Democratic platforms, reembracing the New Departure of 1872, echoed.

Some northern Republicans openly, or at least indirectly, criticized the administration's southern policies. Those in Maine insisted that "local self-government in all matters that are local must be strictly adhered to" and stated, "there can be no legitimate conflict between the powers of the nation and the powers of each state." New Hampshire Republicans condemned "all rapacity and mal-administration on the part of any Republican officials [in the South], whether white or black," and demanded that Louisiana be given "a republican form of government [i.e., one free from military interference] . . . without further delay." Republicans in New York declared that "the welfare of the country requires a just, generous, and forbearing national policy in the Southern States" and demanded "a firm refusal to use military power, except for purposes clearly defined in the Constitution."[18] Nonetheless, Republicans' apparent about-face on Reconstruction was most remarkable in Massachusetts.

In no northern state had the radical wing of the Republican Party exercised more power during the 1860s than in Massachusetts. Also, no other northern state had seen such a significant fraction of Republican voters defect to the Liberal Republican column in 1872, voters who apparently helped Democrats carry the state's governorship, legislature, and the majority of the state's congressional seats in 1874. Democrats were determined to hold those Liberal Republicans in 1875 and 1876. Their 1875 state convention not only claimed to represent Liberals in "the great work of political reform" but also reembraced the Cincinnati Liberal Republican platform of 1872 that had accepted the Thirteenth, Fourteenth, and Fifteenth Amendments "as a full, final, and permanent adjustment of political controversies incident to the late war."[19]

Republicans skillfully parried this Democratic appeal to Liberals when their own state convention met a week after the Democrats'. From start to finish of the balloting, one-fifth of the Republican delegates supported Charles Francis Adams, a leading contender for the Liberal Republican presidential nomination in 1872, as the party's gubernatorial nominee. Democrats also believed that having Adams on a ticket could lure Liberal Republicans, and in 1876, at the insistence of the party's presidential nominee, Bay State Democrats *themselves* would run Adams for governor. More important in 1875, Republicans' platform mocked Democrats' acceptance of the Reconstruction amendments as a final settlement of sectional issues. Republicans correctly insisted that Democrats had fought those amendments tooth and nail in the 1860s. Hence, as Republicans smugly read it, the new Democratic platform represented "both the most humiliating confession of past folly ever extorted from a political organization and a signal tribute to the righteousness of Republican principles."[20]

Lest anyone—and especially Liberals—interpret this boast as signaling Massachusetts Republicans' support for continued federal intervention in the South, they instantly tacked in a new direction. "The accusation that the Republican party seeks to keep alive old issues in order to avoid new ones, is unwarranted," the platform averred. "Our past, at least is secure. Able to review the record without remorse, we cheerfully commit it to history, and with the courage inspired by our success in a noble cause we address ourselves to the new duties of a new era of the nation." It then went on to endorse virtually everything Liberal Republicans wanted: only honest men as public officials, civil service reform, punishment of "official malfeasance" wherever found, retrenchment of governmental expenditures, and tax relief. As for the benighted South, Republicans cheered "the many evidences of reconciliation in spirit and purpose, as well as peace in fact," and wished that southerners of both races could now enjoy the "inestimable blessings" of prosperity "under local self-government, without the necessity of any interference from abroad."[21] Thus did Bay State Republicans further repudiate federal enforcement of southern Reconstruction. Thus did this convention held at the end of September turn a blind eye toward what Republicans well knew was going on in Mississippi at the time, for neither "reconciliation" nor "peace in fact" reigned in the Deep South states still controlled by Republicans. But—and this is the point—wooing Liberal Republicans absolutely necessitated ignoring the evidence of anti-black atrocities in Dixie.

Events in Mississippi in late 1874 and the first two-thirds of 1875 not only belied the rosy language of the Massachusetts Republicans' 1875 state platform. They also portended the use of intimidation, violence, and murder by gangs of heavily armed whites in the Deep South to frighten blacks away from the polls and thus topple Republicans from power in the 1876 presidential election. Starting in 1874, Mississippi's white Democrats launched a ruthless terrorist campaign to disrupt, decimate, and depose the state's Republicans. In broad daylight, rifle clubs composed of Confederate veterans disrupted Republican meetings and campaign rallies. If physical scuffles broke out, as they often did, whites seized the opportunity to gun down blacks in the street, pursue terrified black Republican supporters into the surrounding countryside, and murder them in cold blood. In July 1874 the white Democrats seized control of Vicksburg's city government by armed force and took over the surrounding county government in December. (Similar slaughters occurred in 1875 in Clinton, Yazoo City, and other places.) Local Republican officials, blacks and whites alike, fled to the state capital at Jackson in fear for their lives. Scores of terrified blacks called on Republican Governor Adelbert Ames (the son-in-law of Massachusetts Republican Ben Butler, who had managed the civil rights bill in the House during the second session of the Forty-third Congress) to protect them with the state militia. Aware that no whites would serve in the militia and that arming blacks risked all-out race war, Ames in September wired authorities in Washington to send in federal troops to protect black voters in the upcoming November 1875 state and congressional elections.

Grant was on vacation at the New Jersey shore when Ames's desperate request arrived, but in telegraphic exchanges, Attorney General Edwards Pierrepont persuaded Grant to turn Ames down. Current federal law, Pierrepont advised Grant, forbade the insertion of troops in any state until after the state government had tried and failed to enforce the law. Ames had made no such attempt. Pierrepont then informed Ames that no federal troops would be sent to Mississippi until it was clear that the state militia could not restore order. Thus Ames reluctantly organized a few black militia units but later disbanded them when Democratic leaders at a conference at the governor's mansion promised—falsely, as it turned out—to cease the violence and intimidation. No troops were sent, and the result was exactly what Ames had predicted. In November 1875 black turnout for Republican candidates plummeted drastically in a number of counties. As a result, Democrats won control of both houses of the state legislature as well as four of the state's six congressional seats, whereas they had won only one seat in the previous congressional election.

As soon as the new state legislature met in January 1876, it impeached and removed from office the African American Republican lieutenant governor and filed impeachment charges against Ames himself. To escape certain conviction on those charges, Ames, a native of Maine, resigned the governorship; he left Mississippi in March 1876 and never returned. Thus Democrats seized control of the entire state government, virtually guaranteeing that their party's presidential candidate would carry it in 1876. This so-called Mississippi Plan deeply impressed Democrats in the southern states where Republicans were still in control going into that campaign—Florida, Louisiana, and South Carolina, each of which would elect a governor on the same day as the presidential election. If rhetorical calls in defense of white supremacy did not suffice to mobilize whites behind the Democratic ticket and carry those states in 1876, public threats by white rifle clubs to murder any black man who dared to vote Republican might do the trick.

The lessons from the sickening episode in Mississippi did not end there. Grant later told Mississippi's black Republican Congressman John R. Lynch, the only incumbent Republican from that state to survive the 1875 debacle, that upon his return from vacation in September he had been prepared to issue the proclamation dispatching federal troops to Mississippi, as Ames had requested. But then a delegation of Ohio Republicans had come to the White House and warned him that such an order would doom Republicans' chances of winning Ohio's gubernatorial election on October 12, 1875. And if they failed to regain the governorship in 1875, these men insisted, Republicans had no chance to carry Ohio in the 1876 presidential election. Mississippi had eight electoral votes, but Ohio had twenty-two. Given Democrats' statewide majorities in New York in 1874 and 1875, Republicans seemed to have no chance of retaining the White House in 1876 without Ohio. Ohio was thus a pivotal state in politicians' calculations for amassing electoral vote majorities long before the end of the twentieth century.

That political reality was dispositive. As Lynch later recalled, Grant admitted putting the welfare of his party ahead of what he considered the right thing to do for the party's loyal black supporters in Mississippi. Lynch's recollection of his conversation with Grant cites the president's desire to help Ohio Republicans in a close election rather than any attempt to mollify Liberal Republicans. Nonetheless, Grant's earlier attempts to do the latter on civil service reform and monetary policy suggest that Grant still recognized the importance of that effort.

The need to woo Liberal Republicans and other independent parties in 1875 produced congruence between Republican and Democratic stances on Reconstruction, monetary policy, and reform. On two other matters, however, Republicans and Democrats stood sharply at odds. These differences also help account for the Republican comeback that began in the North in 1875, and they would continue to play a significant role in 1876. As they would far more zealously and relentlessly the following year, Republicans waved the bloody shirt in 1875. It would be disastrous, Republicans warned again and again, if the national government fell completely into the hands of the Democrats—the party of wartime Confederates, who were clearly returning to power in the South, and of their traitorous northern sympathizers. That horrific prospect, Republicans hoped and Democrats clearly feared, would bring erstwhile Republican voters, who had defected in 1872 or sat out the elections of 1873 and 1874, back home.

Democrats might allege, as did Minnesota's in July 1875, that the three constitutional amendments adopted since 1865 had "closed a great era of our politics" by settling forever all questions growing out of slavery. Because they were "accepted in good faith by all political organizations and the people of all sections," the Democrats contended, "our politics must turn upon the questions of the present and future, and not upon those of the settled past." When it came to turning power over to Democrats in Washington, as opposed to protecting black voters or propping up Republican governments in southern states, however, northern Republicans had no intention of burying wartime sectional animosities. "Prudence and patriotism alike," declared Maine's Republicans, "demand that the administration of the Government [i.e., the national government] should be kept in the hands of the political organization which has always been true to it, and not given to the Democratic party which sought to destroy it." Echoed Massachusetts Republicans, "It would be the height of imprudence to commit all that has been achieved for union, freedom, and human rights, to a party that has no heart in the work and no stake in the glory." Iowa Republicans "cordially invite[d] all who are opposed to the restoration of the Democratic party to power to forget all past political differences and unite with the Republican party in maintaining the cause of true reform."[22]

The bloody shirt would help Republicans across the North in 1875 and even more so in 1876. This was also true in California and Oregon, the states most geographically remote from the bloodletting between 1861 and 1865 and from Reconstruction afterward. In these two West Coast states, based on the results of the 1875 elections, Democrats expected (mistakenly, as it turned out) to win their electoral votes in 1876. In many ways, the politics of Oregon and California were sui generis. In both, independent, state-oriented reform parties had eroded Republicans' support since 1872. The central issue in California's September 1875 election for governor, the state legislature, and four congressional seats, as it had been for several years, was which party was the more authentic foe of the state's monopolies—firms that supplied water and natural gas to San Francisco or water for irrigation to the state's farmers and, above all, the Central Pacific Railroad. Because the regular Republican Party was deemed the pawn of the Central Pacific, dissident Republicans, led by Newton Booth, formed a People's Independent Party in 1873 that, with the aid of California Democrats, elected Booth governor and then sent him to the U.S. Senate. In 1875 Democrats ran on their own, but Republicans remained divided between regulars and Independents. As a result of three-way races, Democrats captured the governorship and three of the four House seats, causing Democrats on the East Coast to consider California a sure thing in the 1876 presidential race.

They should have read the returns and the parties' platforms more carefully. Although the Democratic gubernatorial candidate won a 500-vote majority over the Republican and People's Independent candidates combined in 1875, the Republicans and Independents, most of whom were former Republicans, had an 11,000-vote statewide margin over the Democratic candidates in the House races. To no avail, California Republicans had used their pledge to regulate railroads and other monopolies, not the bloody shirt, to reach out to Independents in 1875. Pregnant with implications for 1876, however, the People's Independent platform vowed "that the vote of any citizen for the nominees of the People's Independent party of California in 1875, does not foreshadow or have any manner of significance or bearing on the question of national politics or the contest for President."[23] Indeed, in 1876 Newton Booth personally called on independent voters in California, as he had earlier in states such as Ohio, Indiana, Illinois, and Iowa, to return to the Republican fold in order to keep the party of Confederate and Copperhead traitors from capturing the White House. His appeal brought enough erstwhile Republicans home to give California's six electoral votes to the

Republican presidential candidate. Had those electoral votes gone into the Democratic column, as eastern Democrats fully and mistakenly expected, the outcome of the 1876 presidential election would have been very different indeed.

In 1876 eastern Democrats also counted on Oregon's three electoral votes, based on a misreading of the results in 1875. Democrats, with the help of independents, had won Oregon's governorship in 1874. The 1875 election featured a four-way contest for the state's lone congressional seat among a Democrat, a Republican, an Independent, and a prohibitionist. The Democrat won the seat by edging out his Republican competitor 9,373 to 9,106; nonetheless, the 837 voters, most of whom were former Republicans, who supported the Independent candidate clearly held the balance of power.[24] Oregon's Republicans had appealed to those Independents in 1875 by inviting "all persons opposed to the restoration of the Democratic party to power in the nation to forget all past political differences, and unite with the Republican party" for "true reform."[25] In 1875 that appeal had narrowly failed; in 1876, with control of the White House at stake, it would not.

Yet something else of enormous significance may account for the difference between Oregon's results in 1875 and 1876. One plank of the Independents' state platform in 1875 declared, "we oppose any division of the public school funds for sectarian purposes." The Oregon Republicans did not address this question in 1875, but like Republicans in virtually every state, they surely did in 1876. Across the country, in September 1875, New York's Liberal Republicans also vowed that "appropriations of the people's money to sectarian uses [must] cease." Here, then, was another way that Republicans might woo Liberals and other independents. By September 1875, Republicans in California, Iowa, Wisconsin, Ohio, New Jersey, and New York had also vowed, in the words of the Californians, "that any effort to divide the school fund for the purpose of supporting sectarian schools with a portion thereof shall be met with all the resistance in our power."[26]

Everyone knew that "sectarian uses" and "sectarian schools" meant Roman Catholic institutions and parochial schools. Because the Democratic Party was widely and correctly recognized as the political agent of the Catholic Church, exploiting anti-Catholicism seemed another way to bring defectors back to the Republican Party. Nor, in 1875, were Republicans simply creating a straw man to beat for partisan purposes. By the count of one historian, in the mid-1870s Catholics in seventeen northern states petitioned local and state officials to recognize, charter, or fund Catholic institutions such as charities, hospitals, colleges, and, most important, schools. Elementary school funding was the flash point because, since the 1850s, when this question had also emerged, opponents of Catholics' purported assault on the public school system had contended that public schools were vital to the preservation of republican self-government. Republicanism, so the argument went, depended on the choices of an informed citizenry at the polls, and only public schools, not Catholics' parochial schools, could provide the necessary education. Equally if not more important, politicians who championed Catholics' petitions were almost always Democrats. Certainly that was the case in 1875 in New Jersey. There, Republican charges that Catholic Democratic state legislators had launched an assault on the state's public schools fueled Republicans' recapture of both houses of the state legislature. It was also crucial to Republicans' recapture of New York's state legislature that year. The Democratic legislature elected in 1874 had passed, and Tilden had signed, the so-called Gray Nuns Act, which allowed Catholic nuns to teach in the state's public schools.

Ulysses S. Grant, whom Henry Adams, in his masterfully written autobiography, famously mislabeled "a baby politician," certainly recognized what a weapon anti-Catholicism could be for Republicans. In late September 1875 he told a reunion of the Army of the Tennessee in Davenport, Iowa, that the next crisis to face the country would not be along sectional or class lines. Rather, it would be "between patriotism and intelligence on the one side, and superstition, ambition, and ignorance on the other." "Not one dollar" raised for public schools, he continued, should "be appropriated to the support of any sectarian schools." The preservation of republican self-government itself required that all children have a public school education, "unmixed with sectarian, pagan, or atheistical dogmas." Catholic and other "private" schools must be "supported entirely by private contributions."[27]

As soon as Thomas Nast, a ferocious anti-Catholic bigot, read Grant's speech, he drew an approving cartoon for *Harper's Weekly* that was published on October 23, 1875. Entitled "The Plank—Hitting the Nail on the Head," it pictured Grant nailing a plank on the school question into Republicans' national platform for 1876. But he was also penning in and thus preventing the Catholic Church, portrayed as a huge, engorged serpent with a bishop's miter on its head, from swallowing up a nearby public school.

"The Plank—Hitting the Nail on the Head." This Thomas Nast cartoon
portrays Grant adding a plank to the Republicans' 1876 national platform,
which called for protecting the public schools from the Catholic menace.
Here, he is penning in the Catholic Church, portrayed as a voracious
serpent. *(From Morton Keller,* The Art and Politics of Thomas Nast *[New
York: Oxford University Press, 1968].)*

In September, before leaving for the army reunion in Iowa, Grant had decided against sending troops to Mississippi in order to aid Ohio Republicans in the October 12 gubernatorial election. It is likely that his fulminations against superstitious and ambitious Catholics had the same purpose, for in no state in 1875 was the Catholic school issue so central or did it generate so much national resonance beyond its borders as in Ohio. Moreover, Republicans had good reason to believe that retaking Ohio from the Democrats was absolutely essential if they were to retain the White House in 1876. For these reasons, and because the Ohio story introduces us to the man Republicans would nominate for president in 1876, that story merits a separate chapter.

4

THE EMERGENCE OF A REPUBLICAN CONTENDER
Ohio's Crucial Election of 1875

In the last two decades of the twentieth century and the first decade of the twenty-first, carrying Ohio has been absolutely critical to Republicans' chances of winning the presidency. And so it seemed to Republicans in 1875 and 1876 as well. Ohio's location, size, and political history made its 1875 gubernatorial election pivotal. The nation's third most populous state, it possessed twenty-two electoral votes, more than any other state in the Midwest, where Republicans had suffered their most disastrous losses in 1873 and 1874. Ohio Republicans shared those defeats, which marked a stark reversal from the state's political past. Republicans had carried its biennial gubernatorial election every year from 1855 through 1871. Similarly, they had carried Ohio in every presidential election from 1856 through 1872. With New York tilting Democratic in 1874, keeping the presidency in Republican hands in 1876 seemed inconceivable without carrying Ohio once again.

In 1873, however, Democrats narrowly captured the governorship and both houses of the state legislature, in part because separate prohibitionist candidates cut into the Republican vote. The real plunge in Republican fortunes came in 1874. Whereas Republicans had won fourteen of Ohio's nineteen congressional seats in 1872, they carried only seven of twenty in 1874. Whereas fewer than 900 votes had separated the Democratic and Republican gubernatorial candidates in 1873, Democrats' statewide margin in 1874 ballooned to almost 24,000 votes, an enormous gap by Ohio standards. It is true that Republicans performed just as dismally in 1874 in neighboring Pennsylvania, whose twenty-nine electoral votes were even more crucial to Republicans' chances in 1876. But popular incumbent Republican Governor John Hartranft would head the 1875 ticket in that state. In Ohio, Republicans would have to take on the Democratic incumbent William Allen.

Allen's nomination and election in 1873, the year he turned seventy, marked a miraculous political resurrection. He had served two terms in the U.S. Senate between 1837 and 1849, only to be dumped by Ohio's Democratic state legislators in the winter of 1849 in a deal they cut with Free-Soilers to send Salmon P. Chase to the Senate. Allen had then retired to a farm, where Democrats found him in 1873. Once an orthodox hard-money Jacksonian, Allen had morphed by the 1870s into a fan of greenbacks and a ferocious foe of currency contraction and national banks. That stance earned the septuagenarian such favor that, in an act of huge significance and monumental political stupidity, Ohio Democrats would name him the state's favorite son for the presidential nomination in 1876. Defeating this popular titan's reelection as governor in 1875 proved no easy task for Republicans.

Reviving Republicans' morale and remobilizing Republican voters who had sat out the elections of 1873 and 1874 in disgust was the initial reason Republicans inside and outside Ohio assigned so much significance to the October 1875 gubernatorial contest. Illinois, Indiana, and Michigan held no significant elections that year. Iowa, Minnesota, and Wisconsin, which did, collectively had only four more electoral votes than Ohio alone. Thus Ohio's contest seemed critical, especially because the chief job of gubernatorial candidates was to arouse the party faithful by speaking at as many campaign rallies around the state as humanly possible between their nomination and election day. As one Republican state legislator wrote on March 31, 1875, "If Ohio should be able . . . to elect a Republican governor, I am sure the 'tidal wave' of Democratic success will be shattered and the next President will be a Republican. If she fails in this hour," however, the Democrats would win the White House. In June a New Jersey Republican told the party's gubernatorial candidate that "you and our Republican friends in Ohio are to fight *the* battle that must decide the fate of the Republican party in the Nation. I cannot contemplate a national triumph of Democrats with feelings less than those akin to horror." "The Republicans of Ohio are already on the advanced skirmish line in the great battle about to be fought on the national field," echoed another Republican. "And the great issue is—Shall the Democratic party with its bad history, and . . . unrepentant of its terrible sins, be permitted to win the victory and conduct the affairs of the country? Do the people desire this?"[1]

Democrats in Ohio also accorded the 1875 election immense national significance. They viewed it, however, primarily as a referendum on the Specie Resumption Act, which they hated. If they won, they believed, they could commit the national Democratic Party to repeal of that law, regardless of the wishes of northeastern Democrats. By the last weeks of the campaign, eastern Republicans, such as the editors of the *New York Times*, believed that Ohio's election provided the clearest referendum in the country on specie resumption. Both parties, in short, saw the stakes in Ohio as enormous.

For that reason, most Ohio Republicans hoped that former Governor Rutherford B. Hayes would take on Allen in the gubernatorial race, and in March, April, and May, scores of them pleaded with him to do so. From the start, many tried to lure the reluctant Hayes to undertake another grueling statewide canvass with the promise that if he ran and won, "you will be the most prominent and unexceptionable [Republican] candidate for President in 1876."[2] "How wild!" Hayes noted about these spring 1875 predictions in his diary. "What a queer lot we are becoming! Nobody is out of the reach of that mania."[3]

So who was Rud Hayes, as his friends called him, and why were Ohio's Republicans so desperate to reenlist him for the 1875 campaign? Hayes's parents had roots in New England, but he was born in Delaware, Ohio, in October 1822, a few months after his father had died. His father's death made his mother's brother, Sardis Birchard, by far the most important older male figure in Hayes's life. Hayes would correspond with Birchard constantly throughout the remainder of his uncle's life. His children would spend their summers at Birchard's house in what is now Fremont, Ohio, a few miles south of Lake Erie along the Sandusky River. Hayes would move to that house in 1873 and inherit it after his uncle died in 1875. And the beautifully landscaped property surrounding it would become the site of the Hayes Presidential Library.

With Birchard's financial aid, Hayes attended and graduated from Kenyon College in an age when the number of college graduates remained minuscule. At Kenyon he developed a lifelong interest in buying and reading books. He also made several lifelong friends who aided his subsequent political campaigns, including future Supreme Court

Justice Stanley Matthews, who served with Hayes during the Civil War. Hayes also attended three semesters of law school classes at Harvard before passing the Ohio bar exams. By the early 1850s he had hung his shingle in Cincinnati, Ohio's largest city, where his practice apparently flourished. Hayes supported the Whig Party and then the Republicans after its demise, but he sought no significant political office prior to the Civil War.

His stellar service in that war launched Hayes's political career. A few months after the firing on Fort Sumter, Hayes accepted a commission at the rank of major in Ohio's Twenty-third Regiment of U.S. Volunteers. Standing about five feet, nine inches tall and with a robust physique when he enlisted at age thirty-eight, Hayes, like the new Republican president, was just beginning to grow a beard. Like so many Union army officers during the war, he lacked any previous military experience. Nonetheless, his Civil War service was the transforming event of his life, even though his regiment spent most of the war in what is now West Virginia, hardly the epicenter of the conflict. It is clear from his later correspondence that Hayes earned the ferocious loyalty of the men in his regiment because of his fair treatment and personal courage in battle. Hayes was always at the front of his troops during charges. He was wounded four times, most seriously in an assault on Confederate lines at South Mountain, prior to the battle of Antietam. Hayes also led his troops during the battles in the Shenandoah Valley against Jubal Early's Confederate forces in 1864. His senior officers admired him as much as his troops did, and he rose through the military hierarchy, ending the war at the ranks of brigadier general and brevet major general. Of great importance, Hayes served with a number of other Ohio Republicans, and for the remainder of his life he would address them, and they him, by the rank they had earned in the war.

In 1864 Cincinnati Republicans nominated Hayes for Congress, but in a masterful public letter that paid huge political dividends then and later, Hayes refused to leave the front to campaign as long as the fighting lasted. Nonetheless, he carried Ohio's Second Congressional District in October 1864 with almost 59 percent of the vote and again in 1866 with 56 percent. Hayes never served a day of that second term, however, for in the summer of 1867 he was nominated for governor. That year, in a campaign dominated by Reconstruction, Republicans' endorsement of a state constitutional amendment enfranchising Ohio's blacks, and monetary issues, he narrowly defeated Ohio's most able Democrat, Allen G.

Thurman, by about 3,000 votes, even though Democrats won control of the legislature and black suffrage was crushingly defeated. Running for reelection in 1869, he doubled his margin of victory over Democrat George H. Pendleton, author of the notorious "Ohio Idea" that called for paying off bondholders in greenbacks, not gold, and the Democratic Party's vice presidential nominee in 1864. In 1871 Hayes announced his retirement from office and was succeeded by his fellow Civil War veteran and friend, Republican General Edward F. Noyes.

Hayes, in short, had defeated the two most prominent Democrats in Ohio in his two runs for governor. He obviously possessed both political and legal talent, even though his interests were primarily scholarly. He had an especially deep interest in Ohio's natural resources and its early history. His personal collection of books and pamphlets on those subjects, along with his personal papers, would form the initial collections of the library dedicated to him. In 1876 some eastern Democrats would cite Hayes's supposed intellectual inferiority to their own presidential candidate, Samuel J. Tilden. (Democratic mockery of Republicans' brainpower hardly began in the twentieth century.) Yet in this judgment of Hayes they erred egregiously.

Any perusal of Hayes's letters and diary belies the charge. Though few historians have attributed to Hayes the eloquence of an Abraham Lincoln or a Woodrow Wilson, he in fact wrote with great clarity, force, and pith. One of his favorite phrases, for example, was "Otherwise, otherwise."[4] Or consider his trenchant evaluation of Salmon P. Chase, one Ohio Republican whom Hayes despised, after Chase's death in 1873: "Chase possessed noble gifts of intellect, great culture, and a noble presence. When this is said, all that is favorable has been said. He was cold, selfish, and unscrupulous."[5]

Hayes's response to the Ohio Republicans who implored him to run for governor in the spring of 1875 was that he would not do it. The reason he initially gave was that he could not afford to run because he needed to earn money to pay off bank loans he had taken to invest in urban real estate. After his refusal to run had been published in Republican newspapers, Judge Alphonzo Taft of Cincinnati, founder of the famous Taft political dynasty, entered the race for the Republican nomination. Hayes then emphatically and repeatedly told Republicans that he would never compete against Taft, whom he genuinely admired and believed would make an excellent candidate.

Rutherford B. Hayes. (Courtesy of the Library of Congress. LC-USZ62–13019.)

In his diary, however, Hayes listed other reasons for his initial refusal to run. The size of the Democrats' margin in 1874, the appeal of Democratic greenbackism to many Ohio Republicans during the depression, the expectation that Democrats would race-bait in reaction to the new Civil Rights Act of 1875, the loathsome corruption of Grant's administration, and Democrats' exploitation of the third-term bogeyman (Grant did not issue his letter renouncing any third-term plans until late May, four days before the Ohio Republican state convention was scheduled to meet) all seemed to doom Republicans to defeat in 1875. Yet Hayes told his diary that he was willing to run even if he faced sure defeat. What really stopped him was that there seemed to be no issue or "cause," as he put it, that engaged his interest in 1875. He knew that the Republican candidate would be required to defend the party's stand on specie resumption and against currency inflation. He had in fact done so ably in his two earlier campaigns, yet the financial question bored him. Indeed, after his nomination he admitted to John Sherman that he had never read the Specie Resumption Act.

By the time Ohio Republicans met on June 2, however, a potential question had appeared that deeply engaged Hayes. Nonetheless, he still refused to block Taft's bid for the nomination because he believed Taft to be perfectly sound on this issue too. "Are we ready for the Catholic question?" he asked one correspondent on April 7. In a letter written three days later he told the same man, "if there was an issue that I felt interested in, I might be led to reconsider [his refusal to seek the nomination]." "But," he wrote in May, "the Catholic question is not yet up; it may never be."[6] This question was also the reason that most Republican delegates to the state convention ignored Hayes's wishes and gave him the gubernatorial nomination over Taft by a vote of 396 to 151.

The issue arose out of proceedings in the Ohio legislature that spring, followed by the stupendously maladroit responses of a few Catholics to those proceedings. In March, on a party-line vote, the Democratic majority passed a bill championed by a Cincinnati Democrat named John Geghan. Neither the bill that was passed nor, apparently, a longer version Geghan had introduced in February said anything about public schools or Catholic demands for a portion of public school funds to support parochial schools. It simply said that freedom of conscience required that Catholic priests have access to prisons, reform schools, orphanages, insane asylums, and other state institutions to minister to the religious needs of their Catholic inmates. In a public letter to a Catholic constituent, however, Geghan portrayed the bill as a debt owed by the Democratic Party to its loyal Catholic supporters. Cincinnati's *Catholic Telegraph* then poured gasoline on the flames Geghan had ignited. "Catholics in the state . . . exercising their rights of suffrage," it warned, "have a very strong claim upon a political party, which it will not be safe for political leaders or aspirants to political office to ignore or despise." If Catholics withdrew that support, the Democratic Party would "fall in this city, county and State. . . . That party is now upon its trial; Mr. Geghan's bill will test the sincerity of its professions."[7]

Here was a smoking gun. In Republicans' eyes, the unanimous Democratic support for Geghan's bill proved that the Democratic Party was the subservient toady of the Roman Catholic Church. And if Democrats supported this bill, Republicans predicted, their next step would be aiding a Catholic assault on the public school system by drawing monies from publicly raised tax revenues to support Catholic parochial schools. "We stand by free education, our public school system, the taxation of all for its support, and 'no division of the public school fund,'" vowed Republicans in their June state platform. The charge that Democrats supported such a division was sheer demagoguery, Democrats accurately but futilely retorted in their own platform. Because the state constitution explicitly prohibited any such division, the Republican platform was "an insult to the intelligence of the people of Ohio, and a base appeal to sectarian prejudices."[8]

Indeed it was, but the Republicans were not about to abandon so potent an appeal, regardless of the provisions of the state constitution. Charges that Democrats were helping Catholics obtain public funding for parochial schools had fueled massive defeats of Democratic candidates in the 1850s. Now such accusations appeared available to the Democrats' political foes once again. "The interesting point," Hayes wrote in his diary the day after receiving the gubernatorial nomination, "is *to rebuke the Democracy by a defeat for subserviency to Roman Catholic demands.*"[9] "The secret of our enthusiastic convention is the school question," he later wrote to James G. Blaine. "The Democrats take the hint, and are in retreat." Still, "we shall down them on the school and other State issues."[10]

Hayes and other Ohio Republicans continued to believe in the potency of attacking Catholic Democrats' purported threat to the public school system until the end of the campaign. He ordered the state party chairman to distribute a tract in both English and German "on the

Geghan and school question" as soon as possible. "Nothing is so much desired and needed."[11] "We must not let the Catholic question drop out of sight," he urged a Republican editor. "We can't, I think, do better than stick to the texts, *honest money*, and *no sectarian interference with the schools.*"[12]

Democrats, in contrast, hardly wanted the Ohio campaign to focus on public tax support for Catholic schools. As noted earlier, they deemed the money question and the Specie Resumption Act the central issues in 1875. In a state still racked by depression, they believed that denouncing currency contraction would be a winner. In his many campaign speeches, Hayes had to defend hard money and the law Republicans had passed to achieve it against Democrats' withering attacks, even though he knew that such a stand would offend those Republicans enthralled by greenback inflation. There seems little question, however, that he initially identified anti-Catholicism as the biggest gun in Republicans' arsenal. Thus he preferred to let other Republican speakers carry the ball on financial questions.

Both Senator John Sherman, who accompanied Hayes on his first campaign swing, and Republican Congressman James A. Garfield in fact balked at the Republican platform's evasive plank on resumption and demanded a vigorous defense of the Specie Resumption Act. We must press "our views of finance boldly and aggressively, against the wretched and dishonest scheme of the Democracy," Garfield instructed Hayes from Washington in late June. "I think now, is the time for us to cripple the Democracy for next year. Even if they should win this campaign, it will hopelessly divide them in next year's Presidential Campaign."[13] Ohio Republicans did not carry the assault against Democrats' greenbackism alone. By the end of the campaign, out-of-state speakers were imported to defend the Specie Resumption Act and attack the purported horrors of monetary inflation. By far the most important of these speakers, in terms of both his impact in Ohio and the significance of what his aid to Ohio Republicans meant, was the nation's most prominent Liberal Republican, Carl Schurz, whose term as U.S. senator from Missouri ended on March 3, 1875. That the Democrats' increasingly strident demands for repeal of the Specie Resumption Act could drive Schurz into the Republicans' camp in 1875 spoke volumes about the latter's ability to compete for Liberals' support in 1876. Put another way, no matter how much eastern Democrats echoed Liberals' stance on the money question, western Democrats' opposition to resumption and calls for increasing the greenback circulation by abolishing national banks could negate anything the easterners said.

There is no question that in the last four weeks of the Ohio campaign the money issue rivaled and perhaps surpassed the Catholic school issue as the focus of partisan debate. As noted, eastern Republican newspapers such as the *New York Times* certainly pronounced it the central issue by late September. Nonetheless, there can be no question that Hayes, like many other Ohio Republicans, believed that the Catholic school issue would provide the key to success. Hayes's obsession with this issue raises an obvious question about his personal prejudice against Catholics. Some hints of such a bias appear in his valuable diary.

In 1854 Hayes expressed awe at the depth of anti-Catholic hatred exploited by Know-Nothing candidates that year, but he himself never joined the Know-Nothings. In 1873, however, Hayes angrily protested on two occasions when Catholic priests opposed a proposal by Hayes and his uncle Sardis that town authorities in Fremont appropriate funds to build a public library. "It is said the Catholics opposed because they hate libraries," he noted on September 13.[14] For an avid reader and bibliophile like Hayes, this belief could have spawned a supposition that the Catholic hierarchy sought to gut the public school system to save Catholic schoolchildren from having to read books in public schools. Nonetheless, it is more likely that he and other Ohio Republicans stressed the Catholic question because they believed it was a winner.

One reason was its appeal to non-Catholic Germans, especially the large German community in Cincinnati that remained Liberal Republicans. Hayes had readily supported Alphonzo Taft's potential nomination because of Taft's popularity among Liberal Republicans in Cincinnati. Another reason was the school issue's ability to mobilize other Protestant Republicans who had sat out the elections of 1873 and 1874, which the Republicans lost. As early as June 8, for example, future President William McKinley, one of the many Ohio Republicans who had served with Hayes during the Civil War, wrote from Canton that "the leading topic with us will be the school question. We have here a large catholic population which is thoroughly democratic, a large protestant german element that hitherto have been mainly democratic, [but] they hate the Catholics—their votes we must get."[15] "*Harp on the Romanists,* and bring out the *whole vote* and you will have 40,000 majority," advised a Columbus Republican in early August.[16] Hayes never believed that wild prediction, but later that month he informed Minnesota's Republican governor that "the vote will be out in larger force than for many years at a State election." Although mining and manufacturing districts might go Democratic because of the depression, "we gain heavily by returning Germans & Liberals, by the waking of lazy Republicans, & somewhat by anti-Catholic Democrats. . . . We may not have a large majority, but I think we shall pull through."[17]

And so Republicans poured it on, and nowhere more so than in Cincinnati, the source of the anti-Catholic campaign and the site of the largest concentration of Liberal Republican Germans in the state. "The Democratic party . . . by its alliance with the Roman Catholic priesthood . . . is committed to the policy of that Church, which is to shiver the free schools to pieces," ranted the Republican *Cincinnati Daily Gazette* a few days before the election. "It only remains for us to say to the friends of free schools, and the opponents of a union between Church and State, to go to the polls and vote for Hayes." On election day itself the *Gazette* iterated, "The Roman priesthood . . . has declared its determination to break up the Ohio public schools, and has made the subserviency of the Democratic party to its demands the price of the Catholic vote."[18] Thus did the hapless John Geghan, who failed to win reelection to the legislature that October, define the central issue of Ohio Republicans' campaign.

Hayes proved correct about a massive increase in voter turnout and his own narrow margin of victory. Whereas some 69 percent of Ohio's potential electorate turned out in 1874, 87 percent voted in 1875, and Republicans' share of that turnout soared from 32.5 to 43.8 percent. Nonetheless, Hayes defeated William Allen by only about 5,500 votes out of some 593,000 cast. The closeness of the result, even though Republicans swept both houses of the legislature as well as every statewide office at stake, testified to the effectiveness of the Democrats' attack on the Specie Resumption Act. A Hayes victory, warned Cincinnati's leading Democratic newspaper the day before the election, would be read across the country "as a verdict in favor of specie resumption." Such a verdict would ruin "businessmen, mechanics, and laboring men" alike. "Men would hoard their money instead of investing in business, for who would take the risks and chances of business when greenbacks would appreciate sixteen percent if locked up in a safe to wait for specie redemption." Republican success, in short, would produce a "grand army of the unemployed."[19] Yet just as surely, Hayes's narrow victory attests to the wisdom of Republicans' emphasis on the Catholic school issue, as well as to the skill with which Republican speakers, including Hayes, defended the necessity of specie resumption.

Hayes wrote in his diary on election day that, "if victorious, I am likely to be pushed for the Republican nomination for President."[20] Within a week of Hayes's triumph, indeed, Republican newspapers across Ohio were plumping him for president. Nor were Ohioans the only Republicans who touted Hayes's nomination. After his inauguration as governor in January 1876, Hayes reported to his beloved wife, Lucy, who had remained in Fremont with the youngest of their eight children, that General Philip Sheridan, under whom Hayes had served in the Shenandoah Valley in 1864, had written that his preferred 1876 Republican national ticket was "*Hayes and Wheeler.* I am ashamed to say," Hayes sheepishly added, "Who is *Wheeler?*"[21] Wheeler, of course, was New York Republican Congressman William A. Wheeler, who had arranged the compromise between Republicans and Democrats over control of the Louisiana legislature in January 1875 when Sheridan was still stationed in New Orleans.

Sheridan's prediction of the Republican national ticket in 1876 proved remarkably prescient. Nonetheless, that ticket was not chosen until after a herculean fight over the presidential nomination. And one of the things that shaped the intraparty jousting was that Rud Hayes and his Ohio Republican allies were not the only ones who sought to exploit the Catholic school issue, especially after Grant, with an assist from Thomas Nast, had nationalized it in his speech to Union army veterans in late September 1875. Of the other men mentioned as possible Republican nominees in late 1875, Senator Roscoe Conkling of New York was considered Grant's preferred candidate, while his Treasury Secretary Benjamin Bristow, the darling of Liberal Republicans, was the man Grant most wanted to prevent from getting the nomination. Nonetheless, the nominal front-runner by late 1875 was the former Republican Speaker of the House, James G. Blaine of Maine. And it was Blaine who sought to seize the apparent momentum of the anti-Catholic initiative launched by Hayes and Grant to advance his own prospects.

Shortly after Hayes's victory in October, Blaine sent a public letter to the Ohio Republicans' state chairman. In it he asserted that the only way to settle the school question and prevent further Catholic assaults on public school funds was to adopt an amendment to the U.S. Constitution. That amendment, wrote Blaine, must stipulate that "no money raised by taxation in any State, for the support of public schools or derived from any public fund therefore, shall ever be under the control of any religious sect, nor shall any money so raised ever be divided between religious sects or denominations."[22]

Dated October 20, 1875, Blaine's letter first appeared in an Augusta, Maine, Republican newspaper that Blaine himself had once edited. Its current editor accompanied the letter with a warning shot across the bow of the incoming House Democratic majority. "The issue is now before the country. There is no question about that. It is better that it should not be a party issue, and the Democratic Congress can keep it out of politics by adopting and acting upon the suggestion which Mr. Blaine has made." Should the Democratic House fail "to show a sufficient patriotism to propose an amendment making a final disposition of the danger, then the Republican party will no longer hesitate to add this to the other boons it has conferred upon the American people, and it will be a conspicuous issue of the Presidential campaign of 1876."[23]

Buoyed by their Ohio victory in 1875, Republicans, especially Blaine and Hayes, had no intention of dropping the Catholic school issue in 1876. Instead, they intended to pillory Democrats as a pro-Catholic party in the presidential campaign. They were as good as their word. In his annual message in December 1875, Grant called on Congress to pass the kind of amendment Blaine envisioned. That amendment, argued Grant, should require "each of the several States to establish and forever maintain free public schools adequate to the education of all the children [i.e., including Catholics] . . . irrespective of sex, color, birthplace or religion." It should forbid "the teaching in said schools of religious, atheistic, or pagan tenets" and prohibit "the granting of any school funds or school taxes, or any part thereof, either by legislative, municipal, or other authority, for the benefit or in aid, directly or indirectly, of any religious sect or denomination."[24]

If Grant intended his message as a hint to Conkling to seize the issue in the Senate, which the Republicans still controlled, Conkling failed to do so. Instead, Blaine almost instantly introduced his amendment in the House, which the Democrats ruled. The ball was now in the Democrats' court. The race for the Republican presidential nomination and the general election itself had begun in earnest. And the starting gun was the Catholic school issue.

REPUBLICANS' NOMINATION

At least one Democrat wanted to pick up the gauntlet Blaine had thrown down regarding a constitutional amendment to protect the public schools. "I wish to make prominent, Democratic authority on the subject of public schools," former U.S. Senator William M. Gwin wrote to the editor of the *New York World,* the most influential Democratic newspaper in the country, in early January 1876. "That will take the wind out of the sails of the Grants & Blaines, who wish to make this school question an issue against the Democratic party in the approaching Presidential election."[1] House Democrats, however, did not see the matter's urgency. They would stall serious discussion of any constitutional amendment until the summer, after Republicans and Democrats had nominated their tickets.

At the start of the congressional session, Democrats, with the impending presidential campaign much on their minds, had other priorities. One was to launch investigations of almost every department in the executive branch to document Republican corruption, which they intended to make the focus of the presidential race. To Republicans' deep embarrassment, they netted some big fish. Secretary of War William W. Belknap, whose wife had accepted payments from a sutler at Fort Sill in return for getting him a government contract, was impeached by the House and escaped conviction in the Senate only because he had resigned moments before the House acted. Even so, the heavily Republican Senate voted 37 to 24 for Belknap's conviction. Another House committee recommended that the secretary of the navy also be impeached for accepting payoffs from a Philadelphia contractor, but Congress adjourned before Democrats took any action on that recommendation. Along with the forced resignation of Grant's personal secretary, Orville Babcock, for complicity with the Whiskey Ring, Democrats had ample ammunition for the fall campaign.

Democrats' second priority was to replace the Republicans on the House staff with Democrats. That staff, along with the House payroll, had ballooned considerably since prewar days. Republicans had filled many of those jobs with wounded veterans of the Union army. Now those northern heroes were sacked and replaced, in many instances, by wounded veterans of the Confederate army. A large number of southern Democrats elected to the House in 1874 and 1875 had in fact worn Confederate uniforms during the war, and they may have simply wanted to help their comrades in arms. But this was a public relations blunder of the first order. It gave Republicans hard evidence for the bloody-shirt rants they would make the centerpiece of their own presidential campaign. Beginning with state platforms adopted in the spring, such as Missouri's and Iowa's, and then in the national platform drafted in June, Republicans charged Democrats "with sending Union soldiers to the rear, and promoting Confederate soldiers to the front."[2]

This was not the only gift House Democrats gave to Republicans and to their most ambitious aspirant for the presidential nomination that winter. In an obvious effort to woo white southerners, as if any more wooing were necessary, Samuel J. Randall, a Philadelphia Democrat, introduced a bill in January to remove the disqualification from holding political office from the handful of ex-Confederates still disbarred under the Fourteenth Amendment. Blaine rose immediately with an amendment to Randall's bill that would exclude Jefferson Davis from the pardon "on this ground, that he was the author, knowingly, deliberately, willfully and guiltily, of the gigantic murders and crimes at Andersonville."[3] Blaine then delivered a long speech about northern sacrifices and southern treason during the war that would eventually fill five full newspaper columns. To boot, he eviscerated Georgia Democrat Ben Hill, a former Confederate senator who protested Blaine's attack on alleged Confederate atrocities. Blaine, in short, had seized the lead in waving the bloody shirt, just as he had on the Catholic school issue. Evidence abounds that this speech helps explain why midwestern Republicans in particular demanded his nomination. They deemed Blaine the Republicans' strongest potential candidate by far.

James G. Blaine, front-runner for the Republican nomination in 1876.
(Courtesy of the Library of Congress. LC-DIG-cwpbh-03700.)

At least one very savvy Democrat, who expected Blaine to win the Republican nomination, agreed. During the 1840s Edwin Casserly had edited the Albany organ of Martin Van Buren's wing of the New York Democratic Party. In the 1850s he had moved to San Francisco, where he still resided in 1876. "I feel a presentiment of defeat in the contest this year," he wrote to a New York editor and friend on May 5. "The rag-baby lunacy of Democrats would have given us a hard fight at best, but with the Pope & Jeff Davis piled on that, I fear that we are fatally handicapped for the race."[4]

If these actions confirmed Blaine's status as the Republicans' front-runner, they do not fully account for it. Blaine was enormously popular among his Republican colleagues in the House, who had elected him Speaker in three straight congresses. Most of those men worked diligently and enthusiastically to commit Republicans in their home districts and states to Blaine's nomination. By the time the Republican national convention met in June, Blaine would have more delegates than any other contender.

Not all Republicans loved Blaine, however, and at least three other Republican officeholders in Washington also sought the Republican nomination, if only to deprive Blaine of it. One was Indiana Senator Oliver P. Morton, who at the start of the Forty-fourth Congress renewed the cries he had made during the second session of the Forty-third of an impending crisis in the counting of electoral votes. Indeed, he would persuade his Senate Republican colleagues to repeal the Twenty-second Joint Rule. Without the concurrence of the Democratic House, however, it was unclear what effect that action had. Aside from his service as Indiana's wartime governor, Morton was known primarily for endlessly and ruthlessly waving the bloody shirt. For this reason, whatever support he had outside of Indiana came almost exclusively from southern Republicans, especially black southern Republicans. Yet Morton also had liabilities. Like so many Republican senators, he had used a vise-like grip on federal patronage in his state to build a machine, and he seemed sympathetic to western soft-money men, who were numerous in Indiana. Thus he was anathema to Liberal Republicans and other civil service reformers. Morton had also suffered a severe stroke in 1865 that left him crippled for the remainder of his life. If Republicans sought a hale and hearty candidate, he was not their man.

New York's Senator Roscoe Conkling, whom many Republicans believed was Grant's favorite for the nomination, was a spoilsman

Indiana Senator Oliver P. Morton, a contender for the Republican presidential nomination in 1876. Morton had warned as early as January 1875 that there would be a crisis in counting the electoral votes because of Congress's Twenty-second Joint Rule. In February 1877 he served on the Federal Electoral Commission. (Courtesy of the Library of Congress. LC-DIG-cwpbh-03624.)

New York's flamboyant Republican Senator Roscoe Conkling. A bitter foe of Blaine and unsuccessful aspirant for the Republican nomination in 1876, Conkling would participate on the Senate committee that devised the Federal Electoral Commission of 1877. (Courtesy of the Library of Congress. LC-USZ62–79522.)

extraordinaire. His power in New York and his ultimate control of that state's convention, which would nominate him over the protests of reformers such as George William Curtis, editor of *Harper's Weekly,* stemmed from a machine composed of federal appointees. A flashy dresser with flaming red hair, Conkling detested Blaine, and he seems to have entered the race primarily to keep New York's delegates to the national convention out of Blaine's column. This hatred stemmed from an incident in the House some years earlier when both Conkling and Blaine had served there. What provoked Blaine is unclear, but he denounced Conkling's "haughty disdain, his grandiloquent swell, his majestic, super-eminent, turkey-gobbler strut."[5] Conkling never forgot or forgave that withering insult. As a newspaper correspondent later reported from the national convention in June, Conkling's supporters bent "their sole and individual energies to the defeat of Blaine."[6]

Aside from these two worthies, Pennsylvania's Republican Senator Simon Cameron, long notorious for his shady political dealings and discredited for his bumbling record as Lincoln's first secretary of war, did not seek the nomination himself, but he too sought to keep Blaine from getting it. Also the beneficiary of a state machine manned by federal appointees, Cameron rigged Pennsylvania's 1876 Republican convention, which named Governor John Hartranft, a loyal member of Cameron's machine, as the state's favorite son and ordered delegates to stick to him. It also imposed a unit rule on those fifty-eight delegates to prevent any of them from bolting to Blaine at the national convention.

Despite their rivalries, Blaine, Morton, Conkling, and Cameron all agreed that the third Washington officeholder who sought the nomination must not get it. This was Treasury Secretary Bristow, the darling of reformers inside and outside the party because of his prosecution of the Whiskey Ring. Of all the contenders, Bristow seemed most likely to support civil service reform, a prospect poisonous to the men whose power rested on their control of patronage. Bristow's chances for the Republican nomination seemed so slim that Liberal Republicans such as Carl Schurz, who had called a meeting for May 15 in New York City, sought in vain to persuade him to accept an Independent nomination.

However long the odds against Bristow appeared, he had supporters on the Republican National Committee that met in Washington on January 13 to issue the call for the national convention. Blaine wanted it held in Philadelphia, but Bristow's supporters, along with Morton's, persuaded the committee to schedule the convention for June 14 in

Cincinnati, close to both Kentucky and Indiana. No one at the time thought that this site might help Rutherford B. Hayes, whom Republican editors in Ohio—and only in Ohio—were already touting for the nomination.

Hayes's visibility soon increased markedly, however. On January 21 Senator John Sherman issued a widely printed public letter endorsing Hayes for president. "The Republican party in Ohio, ought in their State Convention to give Gov. Hayes a united delegation instructed to support him in the National Convention," wrote Sherman. "In Genl. Hayes we honestly believe that the Republican party of the United States will have a candidate for President who can combine greater popular strength and greater assurance of success than other candidates, and with equal ability to discharge the duties of Presd't of the U.S. in case of election."[7] Federal officeholders in Cleveland, for unspecified reasons, openly rejected this pro-Hayes advice. Considerable sympathy for Bristow existed in southern Ohio, especially among Cincinnati's influential bloc of Liberal Republicans. And Morton's Indiana friends made strenuous efforts to marshal support for him in several western Ohio congressional districts. Nonetheless, when the Republican state convention met in Columbus on March 29, with more than 700 delegates in attendance, Hayes was its choice for president, and delegates to the Cincinnati national convention were instructed to support him with rocklike solidarity.

By then, Hayes himself no longer thought the prospect of his nomination so far-fetched. "Both parties are injured by what is going on at Washington," Hayes wrote to a Civil War comrade on March 9. "Both are, therefore, more and more disposed to look for candidates outside that atmosphere." Two days before the state convention met, an Ohio Republican in Washington sent Hayes's secretary news that must have thrilled the governor. "There is a feeling here that if Morton carries and holds a good slice of the South and Conkling gets up any strength outside N.Y., that the race will be between Hayes & Bristow, with chances in favor of the Gov."[8]

Aside from this enthusiast's mistaken prediction about what would happen at the Republicans' nominating convention, the obvious question is why he omitted Blaine from his list of possibilities. That question is addressed later; here, one other action—or nonaction—by the Ohio state convention deserves attention. On March 18 Sherman fervently urged Hayes to make sure that the Republican state convention strongly endorsed specie resumption and Sherman's Specie Resumption Act.

Neighboring Indiana's Republicans, raged Sherman, had waffled on the currency issue. "We can't afford to demagogue with the Democracy on this question."[9] Whether Hayes attempted to influence the convention is unknown. What is clear is that the platform adopted on March 29 said absolutely nothing about greenbacks, national banks, or specie resumption. Furthermore, the gathered Republicans selected ex-Senator Ben Wade as an at-large delegate to the national convention and shunned the sitting Republican senator, a studied slight that deeply rankled Sherman. In sum, while sectional disagreements over the money question racked Democrats in 1876, Republicans were hardly free of them, as the weasel-worded plank on money in the Republicans' national platform would soon demonstrate.

Sherman's exclusion from the Ohio Republican delegation is more understandable than the glaring omission of Blaine's name from the letter sent to Hayes's secretary on March 27. We have no idea who Z. F. Miller was or which Republicans in Washington he was talking to. He may have been simply uninformed. After all, the Republican state conventions that sent delegates pledged to Blaine to Cincinnati almost always met in April or May, after he wrote. Conversely, he may have been very well informed. Since January, rumors had been circulating in Washington, especially among newspaper correspondents assigned to the capital, of a story that might blow Blaine's candidacy out of the water.

As early as January, Henry Van Ness Boynton, the Washington correspondent of the *Cincinnati Gazette,* informed that paper's editor that he had evidence about Blaine's railroad dealings. Democrats, who also knew the story, he warned, could use it to defeat Blaine should he be the Republican nominee. Actually, Boynton's information was less damaging than that possessed by an Indianapolis editor who was also Morton's brother-in-law; that editor passed his information on to William Henry Smith, president of the Western Associated Press headquartered in Chicago and a close personal friend of Hayes. The information shared by the midwestern Republican newsmen involved complex transactions, but the essential details are as follows.

In the early 1870s Blaine had helped defeat a House bill that would have harmed the interests of the as-yet-unbuilt Little Rock and Fort Smith Railroad. He subsequently made a deal with that company's president, a Boston financier named Warren Fisher, to market $130,000 worth of the firm's bonds to his Maine friends for an equal amount of bonds as a commission. The bonds soon proved worthless, and Blaine sought to save his friends who had purchased them from total financial ruin. He approached the government-subsidized Union Pacific Railroad, whose interim president was then Tom Scott, president of the Pennsylvania Railroad. Blaine sought a $64,000 cash loan using $75,000 of the worthless Little Rock and Fort Smith bonds as collateral. Scott ordered that the "loan" be made. As of 1876, not a penny of it had been repaid. The deal, which the current directors of the Union Pacific had only recently discovered, thus stank of influence peddling by Blaine, first at the Little Rock and Fort Smith and then at the Union Pacific, or, more precisely, to Scott. Every informed political observer in 1876 knew that Scott was avidly seeking government subsidies for yet another proposed railroad, the Texas and Pacific.

The three midwestern editors possessed most of these details by March, but they were at a loss what to do with them. They feared that Blaine's friends would blame the men whose nominations they sought—Hayes, Morton, and Bristow, respectively—for releasing them. Thus a Democratic paper, the *Indianapolis Sentinel,* first broke the story on April 11. Smith blamed Morton for leaking the information, while Blaine blamed Bristow's backers. But the damage was done. The Democratic chairman of the House Judiciary Committee immediately appointed a subcommittee of two southern Democrats (one an ex-Confederate soldier) and one Republican to investigate the ex-Speaker's railroad affairs. Gleeful Democrats smelled blood in the water.

On April 24 Blaine took the House floor on a point of personal privilege and flatly denied having any dealings with the Union Pacific Railroad, a denial supported by a letter he had coaxed from Scott. He admitted that he had *purchased* some Little Rock and Fort Smith bonds at market price and had effectively lost his shirt in that unwise investment. That denial seemed so convincing that a host of states—Delaware, Maryland, New Jersey, Minnesota, Wisconsin, Illinois, Iowa, Kansas, Nebraska, California, and Oregon—all sent delegates pledged to Blaine to the national convention in May. For many of those men, that commitment was unshakable. As the chairman of the Wisconsin delegation later announced upon his arrival in Cincinnati, "We are for Blaine, first, last, and all the time."[10]

The two Democrats on the subcommittee appointed to investigate Blaine remained unconvinced, however. On May 15—coincidentally, the very day that Liberal Republicans were meeting at New York's Fifth

Avenue Hotel—they took testimony in Washington from two directors of the Union Pacific who had discovered the so-called Blaine bonds on the company's books, as well as from Scott. The two directors professed an inability to remember who had told them the bonds were Blaine's. Scott simply lied, stating that he, not Blaine, had deposited the bonds as collateral for prepayment of part of his salary as the Union Pacific's interim president. The *New York Times*'s Washington correspondent immediately telegraphed a report to that paper declaring that Blaine had been completely exonerated.[11]

Nonetheless, the two southerners on the subcommittee remained skeptical. On May 31 it heard testimony from James Mulligan, the former bookkeeper for Warren Fisher. He testified about Blaine's deal to market $130,000 of Little Rock and Fort Smith bonds and the extravagant commission Blaine had earned for that service. He also claimed to have, in his hotel room, a bundle of letters between Blaine and Fisher that could prove it. Blaine, who attended the hearing, immediately asked the lone Republican on the subcommittee to call a recess. That night Blaine visited Mulligan's hotel room and demanded to see the letters. When Mulligan eventually produced them, Blaine snatched the bundle from the startled bookkeeper, pocketed it, and fled the room. The next morning, when Mulligan told the subcommittee what had happened, it demanded that Blaine turn over the letters. Blaine refused.[12]

News of Blaine's apparent intention to hide or destroy incriminating evidence against him was quickly telegraphed around the nation. "Blaine is now out of the question in my judgment," wrote one of Hayes's Ohio supporters on June 3. "Blaine's Nomination Now Out of the Question," echoed a headline in the *New York Times* that very day.[13]

Yet the resourceful and brazen Blaine was not finished yet. On Monday, June 5, just nine days before the Republican convention was to open, he again took the House floor on a point of personal privilege. First he attacked the two southern Democrats on the subcommittee for pursuing a partisan witch hunt to avenge his crushing humiliation of Ben Hill in January. Then he threw the letters down on his desk and huffed: "I am not afraid to show the letters. Thank God Almighty! I am not afraid to show them. There they are. There is the very original package."[14] Blaine then proceeded to read passages from various letters, apparently chosen randomly but obviously carefully selected to conceal any incriminating evidence. Furthermore, he accused the Democratic chairman of the full Judiciary Committee of concealing what Blaine called an exculpatory telegram on his behalf, reducing that gentleman to stammering apologies. This bravura performance, one of the most sensational ever witnessed in the House of Representatives, produced ecstasy among his friends in Washington and around the country. Once again, Blaine had taken the attack to the ex-Confederates in the House. The nomination still seemed to be Blaine's to lose.

The following Sunday, June 11, as Republican delegates streamed into Cincinnati, Blaine and his wife, on a typically hot and humid Washington day, walked the mile from their home to church. On ascending the steps to the church entrance, Blaine passed out and fell into his wife's arms. Friends helped her get him home. Some Democrats believed this incident had been carefully staged to delay the ongoing committee investigation and earn Blaine public sympathy. "Blaine Feigns a Faint," headlined the story sent by one Democratic correspondent from Washington.[15] Whether Blaine had suffered a sunstroke or a seizure is unclear, but he remained unconscious for two full days while rumors spread that he would die or be permanently blinded. He awoke on Tuesday, June 13, with his mental faculties fully intact, news that was instantly telegraphed to Cincinnati. But other telegraphic dispatches also arrived there from Washington. When Benjamin Bristow learned of Blaine's collapse on Sunday, he had immediately rushed to the Blaine home to check on the congressman's condition. Blaine's wife had stopped him at the door and refused to let him in. That widely reported rebuff mortified Bristow and infuriated his supporters, who renewed their determination to prevent the recovered Blaine from grasping the presidential nomination.

Among those Bristow supporters were some of the men who had attended the conference of Liberal Republicans at New York's Fifth Avenue Hotel on May 15. This was not a convention but a private, invitation-only gathering of leading academics and professional men. Henry Adams, then a history professor at Harvard, and Carl Schurz had hatched the idea for this conclave. Invitations went out over the names of Schurz; William Cullen Bryant, editor of the *New York Evening Post*; Theodore Dwight Woolsey, former president of Yale; Alexander H. Bullock, former Republican governor of Massachusetts; and Horace White, editor of the *Chicago Tribune*. Henry Cabot Lodge, future Republican senator from Massachusetts but then Adams's doctoral student at Harvard, served as corresponding secretary. Some 200 distinguished men attended, including the former and current presidents of Williams College, an Amherst College professor then sitting in Congress, William Graham Sumner of Yale, Frederick Law Olmsted, well-known civil service reformer Dorman B. Eaton, and David A. Wells, the equally well-known proponent of tariff reduction. The influential Democratic *New York World* mocked this highly educated assemblage as "'a select company of self-appointed political apostles' assembled in a 'back parlor' 'to work out the regeneration of the country."[16] But these blue bloods had agendas—and the plural is important, for if the short speeches delivered on the first day are an accurate indication of the general sentiment among this extraordinary body of intellectuals, priorities differed. One former Republican thought the primary goal was irrefutably to condemn the corruption of Grant's administration. A New Haven minister declared guaranteeing specie resumption the central issue of the 1876 race. Still another contended that civil service reform that would strip congressmen and senators of their control over patronage appointments was, by far, the most important objective. Finally, one midwestern attendee declared that he was fed up with abstruse dithering about abstractions. What the meeting must do, he said, was to work as hard as possible to secure Benjamin Bristow's nomination at the upcoming Republican national convention.[17]

Largely because Bristow had refused to accept an Independent nomination (by 1876, many Liberal Republicans preferred that nomenclature), but also in part because some attendees supported the Democrat Tilden, no attempt to nominate a presidential candidate occurred. Instead, the meeting, which carried over to the morning of May 16, endorsed an address drafted primarily by Schurz that was clearly intended as a warning to the Republican convention.

As expected, Schurz's address lambasted the corruption of Grant's administration. It called for civil service reform and then declared that "at the coming Presidential election we shall support no candidate who in public position ever countenanced corrupt practices or combinations, or impeded their exposure and punishment, or opposed necessary measures of reform."[18] The "Best Men," as one historian labeled them, at the Fifth Avenue conference thus did not explicitly endorse Bristow. Instead, they made it crystal clear that his leading opponents—Blaine, Morton, and Conkling—were beyond the pale.

From the published reports of this gathering, no one even mentioned Ohio Governor Rutherford B. Hayes as a possible Republican nominee. By mid-May, Blaine, Bristow, and Morton had all sent him feelers about accepting a vice presidential nomination on a ticket with them instead. Among most eastern Republicans, however, Hayes remained a virtual nonentity. Going into the national convention, Hayes appeared to many Republicans to be one state's favorite son, similar to Pennsylvania's Hartranft and Connecticut's Marshall Jewell, Grant's former postmaster general. Though perhaps estimable men, they had no chance of winning the nomination against the big four—Blaine, Morton, Conkling, and Bristow.

Rumors abounded among the Republicans in Cincinnati even before the convention opened. "You are pretty much the unanimous second choice of the Convention so far as I can learn, and they all want you for second place," A. E. Lee, Hayes's secretary, wrote to the governor on June 12. To deprive Blaine of any Ohio support, "New York delegates have hinted again and again as broadly as they could that they wanted us [Ohio's delegates] to stand by you to the last."[19] M. F. Force, who had spoken with the pro-Bristow Massachusetts delegation, wrote on the same day that they would swing to Hayes if Bristow faltered. "The candidate nominated by the convention cannot be elected unless he be a person who will draw at least a large part of what may be called the Bristow element," which would vote for no one whose character did not give "assurance of an administration strong enough in its purity to insist on a correction of abuses."[20]

This opinion seemed to rule out Conkling, Morton, and Blaine, and on June 14, the convention's opening day, Hayes's secretary wrote to him that "the vast majority of the cool, thinking men of the Convention are manifestly against Blaine and regard his nomination as exceedingly unwise."[21] Hayes himself, however, believed that Blaine would win. That very day, June 14, he wrote to another Ohio delegate that should Blaine be nominated, he wanted his name withdrawn as a vice presidential nominee. "I have the greatest aversion to being on a ticket headed by a man whose integrity in public life will be constantly and seriously questioned."[22]

Blaine clearly had a plurality of delegates, but not a majority. That was the central fact of the convention. Republicans awarded two delegates for every senator and representative a state possessed, as well as two delegates each to the nine federal territories that had nonvoting representatives in the House and to the District of Columbia. The total was 756, making 379 votes the necessary majority for nomination. Estimates among reporters in Cincinnati gave Blaine between 270 and 300 votes on the first ballot. Blaine's friends boasted that he would pick up enough additional votes on the second and third ballots to win the prize. The question was where he might get them. Certainly they would not come from Conkling's vindictive minions in the New York delegation, nor from the Indiana Republicans who had vowed to stand by Morton until the bitter end. The Ohioans had caucused the day before the convention opened, chosen ex-Governor Edward F. Noyes as delegation chairman, and pledged once again to stand by Hayes. Bristow's reforming friends would never back Blaine. Southerners might, once they determined that Morton had no realistic chance, but they seemed just as likely to switch to Conkling or especially to Bristow, whom they saw as a fellow southerner. Everyone expected Connecticut's delegates to be up for grabs after a complimentary vote for Marshall Jewell on the first ballot, yet they seemed to be leaning toward Bristow as their second choice. Besides, there were far too few of them to put Blaine over the top.

That left Pennsylvania, which astute newspapermen in Cincinnati quickly identified as the convention's pivotal delegation. Pennsylvania had 58 votes that were pledged to Hartranft, so long as he remained a candidate. In the weeks leading up to the convention, most Republicans believed that they would ultimately be delivered to Conkling as a unit because of a reshuffle of Grant's cabinet in mid-May. At that time, he announced that Attorney General Edwards Pierrepont would leave to become minister to Great Britain and that Ohio's Alphonzo Taft, who had replaced the disgraced Belknap as secretary of war, would move to the Justice Department. The new war secretary would be Don Cameron, Simon Cameron's son and leader of the Pennsylvania delegation to Cincinnati. To Blaine's outraged supporters, especially in the Midwest, this appointment seemed like a blatant intervention by Grant to hand Pennsylvania's votes to Conkling, his favorite. As one correspondent reported from the Illinois Republican state convention in Springfield on May 23, Illinois Republicans thought that Cameron's appointment "meant the sale and delivery of the Pennsylvania delegation to Senator Conkling."[23] One result of that belief was that Conkling had absolutely no hope of adding midwestern votes to his own column. "There are no Conkling men in the Northwest," William Henry Smith wrote to Hayes from Chicago on May 27.[24]

When the Pennsylvania delegation reached Cincinnati, however, it became clear that many of its members were chafing under their instructions and that as many as half the delegation, if not more, favored Blaine. Cameron knew it, and at an exceedingly fractious caucus before the convention, he sought to reimpose the unit rule adopted at the earlier state convention. But that rule could hold only as long as Hartranft remained in the race. "It has become clear that any attempt to turn Pennsylvania to Conkling will nominate Blaine," wrote one shrewd newsman on the night before the convention opened. "The only interest that any candidates except Blaine can now have in Pennsylvania is that it should adhere constantly to Hartranft."[25] To ensure that that happened, others correctly reported, a deal had been cut among the Morton, Conkling, and Bristow forces to add some of their delegates to Hartranft's column on each succeeding ballot so that there would be no excuse for the Pennsylvanians to withdraw him.

But even if the supporters of the leading anti-Blaine candidates—Morton, Conkling, and Bristow—could stop or at least delay Blaine's nomination, it seemed clear that none of those men had a prayer of amassing the necessary majority. Thus they began to think of a possible compromise candidate. As one Associated Press reporter wired on the night before the convention opened, "there would be a consultation" that night or the following morning "of the Conkling, Bristow, and Morton leaders to see if they cannot agree to unite upon Hayes in case it becomes apparent that Blaine's defeat can be accomplished in no other way." Meanwhile, the Ohio delegation had, "with shrewd audacity," determined that day "to stick solid to Hayes until a majority of delegates decide that it is useless to continue the struggle."[26] The Ohioans, in short, expected a stalemate among the front-runners that would give their governor the prize. And they played their cards with exceptional skill.

Not a single ballot on the nomination took place until June 16, the convention's third day. Other matters occupied the first two days. As was customary, the opening day was devoted primarily to the appointment of committees on credentials, rules, permanent organization, and resolutions. A string of speeches entertained delegates as they waited for those committees to report. Blaine's forces gained an early advantage on organizational matters. One of them proposed, and the convention voted to accept, a resolution that would allow territorial as well as state representation on all the committees. Since Blaine controlled all the territorial delegations except Wyoming's, this gave Blaine's forces a majority on all the committees. That coup paid dividends by the end of the first day, when the committee on organization named Edward McPherson of Pennsylvania, the longtime Republican clerk of the House of Representatives and an ardent Blaine supporter, as the convention's permanent president. Prior to the announcement of his selection, McPherson had proposed that the convention move immediately to balloting for the nominee the next morning, but Connecticut's Joseph R. Hawley, a Bristow man, immediately and successfully demanded that the proposal be sent to the rules committee without a vote. As one shrewd newspaper correspondent reported, Blaine's friends "want to vote immediately and recognize the danger of delay. The opposition to Blaine have an interest in postponing action as long as possible."[27]

The reaction to the first day's many speeches revealed the mood of the delegates and the divisions among them. Calls for specie resumption evoked loud applause, as did calls for a continued commitment to the rights of southern blacks. Civil service reform was another matter entirely. According to reporters, George William Curtis (one of two New York delegates who refused to vote for Conkling), speaking on behalf of the Republican Reform Club of New York City, which had sent nonvoting observers to the convention, drew applause from Bristow men and the spectators' gallery. In contrast, voting delegates who supported Morton, Conkling, and Blaine reacted to Curtis's speech with stony silence or hisses, evidence that a majority of delegates would never accept Bristow.[28]

Adoption of committee reports, including the national platform drafted by the resolutions committee, and nominating speeches constituted the second day's agenda. The rules committee reported first, and at least two of its rules marked a setback to the Blaine forces, which wanted to vote on the nomination as quickly as possible. One rule, passed over the protests of the chairman of Maine's delegation, required adoption of the platform before a consideration of candidates. Another stipulated that during the roll call of states on nominations, no delegates could change their votes after the state's vote had been announced by the chairman until the entire roll call was completed. Its purpose, according to one reporter, was "to prevent a stampede to Blaine on the first ballot, and it was, of course, warmly opposed by the friends of the gentleman from Maine."[29] Yet a third rule adopted by the convention would prove even more important. This required that once a roll call on the nomination had been completed without any clear winner, the next roll call would begin immediately, without any recess during which delegates could consult with one another. In effect, this rule meant that the various anti-Blaine forces had to agree on a strategy during the night of June 15.

The credentials committee next reported its decisions on the disputed delegations from Florida, the District of Columbia, and Alabama. The first two occasioned little controversy, although the rejection of a District delegation associated with "Boss" Alexander Shepherd prevented Frederick Douglass, who had addressed the convention on its first day, from taking a seat as a voting delegate. One of the contesting delegations from Alabama was headed by the notoriously corrupt carpetbag Senator George Spencer; it supported Morton but was also considered willing to truck with the Conkling men. The other was uninstructed but was thought to be leaning toward Bristow. On a close vote of 375 to 354—the convention's first roll call—the committee's recommendation to reject the pro-Morton Spencer delegation prevailed. There is no breakdown of how individuals voted, but Bristow—and Hayes—men were elated.

Connecticut's Joseph R. Hawley, whom one reporter called "the most pronounced hard money man in America," next presented the platform drafted by the resolutions committee. Its contentious deliberations had taken most of the night. Western delegates, it was reported, wanted to "temporize" on the party's commitment to specie resumption. The financial plank alone apparently took more than three hours to hammer out.[30] Hawley admitted that his committee "constituted men of somewhat differing sentiments and widely separated localities, and mostly strangers to each other."[31] The Republican platform, in short, represented an uneasy compromise.

The seventeen-plank platform reiterated Republicans' commitment to restoration of the Union, pacification of the South, southern blacks' rights, a protective tariff, and generous treatment of Union army veterans. It declared that congressmen should have no control over federal patronage appointments, that most offices should "be filled by persons selected with sole reference to efficiency of the public service," and that Republicans would "hold all public officers to rigid responsibility, and engage that the prosecution of all who betray official trusts shall be speedy, thorough, and unsparing." Here were echoes of the state platforms Republicans had adopted in 1875 and 1876, aimed at bringing Liberal Republicans back into the party's fold. Even so, the absence of any explicit reference to civil service reform is noteworthy.[32]

Five planks deserve closer scrutiny. According to newspaper reports, the plank that aroused the most enthusiasm among the delegates and spectators—so much enthusiasm, in fact, that the crowd demanded that Hawley read it twice, igniting rounds of prolonged cheering—was the seventh. Obviously inserted by Blaine men on the resolutions committee, this demanded a constitutional amendment that blocked Catholics from diverting public school funds to parochial schools. House Democrats may have thus far quashed consideration of Blaine's amendment, but Republicans clearly believed that anti-Catholicism could still be a powerful weapon in the presidential campaign.

Similarly, two other planks clearly indicated Republicans' intention of waving the bloody shirt for all they were worth in the fall. Democrats, one averred, counted on carrying every southern state "through the efforts of those who were recently arrayed against the nation." A Democratic "success thus achieved would reopen sectional strife and imperil the national honor and human rights." The second, an omnibus plank copied almost word for word from various state platforms, starkly warned northern voters what was at stake in the election by forcefully reviving partisan hatred of Democrats. It merits quotation at length:

> We charge the Democratic party as being the same in character and spirit as when it sympathized with treason, and with making its control of the House of Representatives the triumph and opportunity of the nation's recent foes; with reasserting and applauding in the national Capitol the sentiment of unrepentant rebellion; with sending Union soldiers to the rear and promoting Confederate soldiers to the front. . . with deliberately proposing to repudiate the plighted faith of the Government; with being equally false and imbecile upon the overshadowing financial question; with thwarting the ends of justice by its partisan mismanagement and obstruction of investigation; with proving itself through the period of its ascendancy in the lower house of Congress utterly incompetent to administer the Government.

This ringing omnibus plank contained a bone for virtually every presidential aspirant in the party, and it was warmly applauded.

Two planks, in contrast, provoked controversy on the convention floor. Clearly adopted to meet the demands of West Coast delegates, the eleventh plank urged Congress "to fully investigate the effect of the immigration and importation of Mongolians on the moral and material interests of the country." As soon as Hawley finished reading the platform, Edward L. Pierce, the Massachusetts representative on the resolutions committee and a close friend of the deceased Charles Sumner, arose to protest that this plank outrageously violated Republicans' commitment to racial equality. He, all the other New Englanders, and the lone black on the resolutions committee had voted against it, he declared, and the full convention must reject it. In response, western delegates on the committee, though intriguingly not those from California or Oregon, contended that its purpose was to protect white workers in the West from unfair coolie labor and the immoral temptation of Chinese prostitutes. Pierce demanded a roll call on his motion to expunge the plank from the platform, and the motion went down to defeat, 532 to 215. As the subsequent campaign would reveal, however, West Coast Republicans hardly considered this toothless plank sufficient to parry Democrats' flagrant exploitation of anti-Chinese sentiment in their states.

Far more important was a floor challenge to the financial plank that had tied the resolutions committee in knots because so many western Republicans refused to commit themselves to Sherman's Specie Resumption Act. That plank, indeed, utterly ignored the 1875 act. Alluding instead to the Public Credit Act concerning the repayment of bonds in gold, which Republicans had adopted in early 1869, it stated that at that time Republicans "had solemnly pledged" the government's "faith to make provision at the earliest practicable period for the redemption of United States notes in coin. Commercial prosperity, public needs, and national credit demand that this promise be fulfilled by a continuous and steady progress to specie payment." In short, there was no fixed date for specie resumption; this was a waffle akin to that adopted by midwestern Republican state platforms in 1875 and 1876. One member of the resolutions committee protested this plank "as a step backward" on specie resumption, as indeed it was, because "it is uncertain and vague in its promise, leaving the time of resumption unsettled, and being thereby calculated to further disturb public confidence." He proposed a substitute plank declaring "that it is the duty of congress to provide for the carrying out [of] . . . the Resumption Act of congress, to the end that the resumption of specie may not be longer delayed."[33] Surprisingly, this totally justified protest came not from a northeastern Republican but from Edward J. Davis, the former governor of Texas.

Hawley responded to Davis on behalf of the rest of the committee. He opposed the substitute plank on two grounds. First, he averred, party platforms should announce general principles rather than endorse specific pieces of legislation. Second, he considered the Specie Resumption Act worthless, since it delayed resumption until 1879. He had voted against it in the House, and he would never accept a platform that endorsed it. Hawley carried the day. By voice vote, the convention shouted its approval of the original plank and of the entire platform. Time would soon show that this was a grave mistake. The Republicans had opened up room for the Democrats to argue plausibly that they were just as committed to specie resumption as the Republicans were, even if they called for repeal of the Specie Resumption Act, which the Republicans themselves had refused to endorse. Thus, in the bidding war between Republicans and Democrats for Liberal Republican support, the Republicans had seemingly surrendered their advantage on the money question.

It was nearly three in the afternoon when debate on the platform ended. The 7,000 people squeezed into the hot convention hall had sat for four straight hours without a break. Some delegates called for an adjournment until the following morning, but convention president McPherson insisted on moving immediately to the nomination of candidates. The roll of states was called alphabetically, and when a state had a candidate, nominating and often seconding speeches were made. Hence the order of nominations proceeded from Connecticut's Jewell to Indiana's Morton to Kentucky's Bristow to Maine's Blaine to New York's Conkling to Ohio's Hayes to Pennsylvania's Hartranft.

On behalf of Morton, Indiana's Richard W. Thompson, a former Whig congressman, stressed Morton's devotion to the rights of southern blacks; notably, P. B. S. Pinchback, the black lieutenant governor of Louisiana, seconded the nomination. John M. Harlan, chairman of the Kentucky delegation and future Supreme Court justice, emphasized Bristow's bona fides as a genuine Republican. He had fought in the Union army, voted to ratify both the Thirteenth and Fourteenth Amendments as a state senator, prosecuted the Ku Klux Klan as a U.S. attorney, and courageously advocated equal funding for black schools in Kentucky, exalted Harlan. Yet Harlan also noted Bristow's prosecution of the Whiskey Ring as evidence of his devotion to "honest government." He concluded by urging the convention to make Bristow "our leader in this contest for Republican principles against corruption and fraud."[34]

The seconding speeches for Bristow proved as significant as Harlan's effort. Luke Poland of Vermont maintained that the Democratic victories in 1874 and 1875 "grew out of doubt and distrust and dissatisfaction in our own party," in short, from massive Republican abstention. Bristow, Poland insisted, could end that internal dissatisfaction better than any other candidate. Claiming to speak for those Republicans "who have seen that reform is possible within the Republican party," New York's George W. Curtis portrayed Bristow "as the embodiment of government purification." As if these remarks did not suffice to offend party regulars, Richard Henry Dana of Massachusetts outraged them by asserting that Bristow was the only possible Republican candidate who could carry Massachusetts in the fall.

Dana was followed to the podium by Robert G. Ingersoll of Illinois, who made the nominating speech for Blaine. A lawyer from Peoria with a wide practice across the state and the most famous avowed atheist in the land, Ingersoll was probably the most powerful public speaker in the United States. His stem-winding speech aroused such paroxysms of enthusiasm among Blaine men in the spectators' galleries that many feared the convention would be stampeded for Blaine. Ingersoll began by mocking Dana. If any Republican candidate failed to carry Massachusetts, he sniffed, Republicans in the Bay State should disband. The question was who could carry more closely contested states, and Blaine was the man for the job. Republicans wanted a real leader, sang Ingersoll, a man familiar with foreign affairs and the duties of every branch of the federal government (a transparent contrast to Treasury Secretary Bristow), a man committed to specie resumption and to protecting "every citizen at home and abroad." Republicans, continued Ingersoll, demanded "a man who believes in the eternal separation and divorcement of church and school." Republicans demanded "a man whose political reputation is spotless as a star; but they do not demand that their candidate shall have a certificate of moral character signed by the Confederate congress." That man was "the grand and gallant leader of the Republican party, James G. Blaine."

Ingersoll had used up his allotted ten minutes, but the enthralled audience insisted that he be allowed to continue. Alluding to the centennial of the Revolution to be celebrated that year, Ingersoll called 1876 "a year in which the people call for the man who has preserved in congress what their soldiers won on the field . . . who has snatched the mask of Democracy from the hideous face of rebellion." "Like an armed warrior," Ingersoll thrilled, "like a plumed knight, James G. Blaine marched down the halls of the American congress and threw his shining lance full and fair against the brazen forehead of every traitor to his country and every maligner of his fair reputation. For the Republican party to desert that gallant man now is as though an army should desert their general upon the field of battle."

Robert Ingersoll of Illinois. Ingersoll's stem-winding nomination speech for Blaine almost stampeded the Republican convention. (Courtesy of the Library of Congress. LC-DIGcwpbh-05180.)

The enthusiasm ignited by Ingersoll's speech made the task of New York's Stewart L. Woodford, who nominated Conkling, doubly difficult. Woodford, however, was up to the task. "Let us not nominate with our hearts, but with our heads," he warned the convention. Republicans had carried New York by 50,000 votes in 1872, but the Democrat Tilden had carried it by 53,000 votes in 1874 (Woodford here inflated Tilden's 1874 margin by 2,700 votes). With Connecticut, New Jersey, Indiana, and Oregon apparently securely in Democratic hands, Republicans needed a candidate who could compete with Tilden for New York in the fall. Mindful of the anger provoked by Dana's speech, Woodford declared, "I do not claim that Roscoe Conkling is the only Republican who can carry the state of New York. I believe he can. . . . I plead that you to-day give us a candidate with whom and under whom we can achieve, not personal ambition, but a victory."

On behalf of Hayes, ex-Governor Edward F. Noyes, chairman of the Ohio delegation, stressed his military service during the war, "when those who are invincible in peace and invisible in battle were uttering brave words to cheer their neighbors on." Republicans needed a candidate who could carry contested states such as Indiana, Ohio, and New York, not just reliable Republican strongholds, Noyes continued. Hayes had carried Ohio against the state's three most prominent Democrats and would certainly do so again if he headed the ticket in November. Most important, however, Noyes characterized Hayes, "a scholar and a gentleman," as the perfect compromise nominee. Ohio Republicans would manfully support whomever the convention chose, he said. "But we beg to submit that in Governor Hayes you have those qualities which are calculated best to compromise all difficulties, and to soften all antagonisms. He has no personal enmities. His private life is so pure that no man has ever dared to assail it. His public acts throughout all these years have been above suspicion even." With Hayes at the top of the ticket, Republicans would carry Ohio's state election in October, and that would determine which presidential candidate won the state a month later. Is it "not worth while to see to it that a candidate is nominated against whom nothing can be said, and who is sure to succeed in the campaign?"

By the time a perfunctory nominating speech for Pennsylvania's Hartranft concluded, it was almost 6 PM, and delegates, alternates, and spectators had been jammed into the hot hall for seven straight hours without a break. It was also growing dark. Nonetheless, Blaine's friends, still flushed with enthusiasm from Ingersoll's rousing speech, pressed for an immediate vote on the nomination. The hall had gaslights that could be lit to provide illumination, they insisted. Friends of Morton, Conkling, Hayes, and Bristow all protested this move and demanded an adjournment until the following morning. Blaine supporter McPherson, as president of the convention, had to make the call. Announcing that he had been told the gaslights did not work, he adjourned the convention until ten o'clock the following morning.[35] Everyone regarded this decision as a severe setback for Blaine.

Later that night one of several *New York Times* reporters in Cincinnati wired the following dispatch: "The events of the day have given confidence to those who hope to save the Republican Party from James G. Blaine, and they have been engaged all evening, and are yet at work, in arranging to consolidate their strength, at the proper moment, upon some one candidate." He was sure that man would be Hayes.[36] Hayes's friends were equally confident. The biggest threat to his nomination, they now believed, was that someone else would get Hayes on the ticket as his running mate. "Don't permit your name to be used for the Vice Presidency under any circumstances," ex-Governor William Dennison telegraphed Hayes from Cincinnati.[37] Meanwhile, Hayes's friend M. F. Force met privately with Bristow, Morton, and Conkling men to tout Hayes as a compromise choice. The two latter groups, he later wrote to Hayes, opposed both Blaine and Bristow. At some point on the night of the fifteenth, "they finally agreed that it would be easier for Conkling and Morton to unite on you, a third party, than for either one to give up to the other."[38] One postconvention report from a *Times* correspondent, however, strenuously denied that any deal had been finalized that night. Only events during balloting on the sixteenth, according to him, decided the outcome.

As expected, on the morning of June 16 Blaine led on the first ballot with 285 votes. His support was far more broadly distributed among various state and territorial delegations than that of any other candidate.[39] Morton ran second with 124 votes, Indiana's 30 and all the rest from the South and the District of Columbia. Alabama, Missouri, North Carolina, Virginia, and West Virginia, however, preferred Blaine to Morton. Bristow ran a surprisingly strong third with 113 votes. Conkling garnered 99, including 69 of New York's 70 votes. Hayes ran fifth with 61 votes, followed closely by Hartranft's 58, exclusively from Pennsylvania. Between them, Michigan and New Jersey gave Hayes 9 votes, and he also picked up a scattering of votes from Alabama, Illinois, Nevada, Vermont, and West Virginia. Finally, Jewell's 11 complimentary votes marked the end of his candidacy.

On the second ballot Blaine picked up 11 additional votes, both Conkling and Morton lost a few, and Hayes added 3 to his total. The big news, however, concerned Hartranft. Following the prearranged deal to keep Pennsylvania's unit rule in force, nine delegates from Nevada and North Carolina shifted to the Hartranft column. More important, after Don Cameron, the chairman of the Pennsylvania delegation, again cast the state's 58 votes for Hartranft, four delegates protested that they wanted to vote for Blaine, but Cameron refused to allow it. They demanded a ruling from convention president McPherson on the legitimacy of Pennsylvania's unit rule. The pro-Blaine McPherson announced that all delegates could vote freely, despite state rules, thus rejecting the unit rule. One Pennsylvanian protested and demanded a vote on whether McPherson's ruling should be sustained by the delegates. On a voice vote, it was. McPherson then ordered that the four Pennsylvania votes be recorded for Blaine but added that once the roll call, which had been interrupted, was finished, the convention could debate and vote on his ruling.

As soon as the roll call ended, a motion was made to reconsider the voice vote sustaining McPherson's decision. Since virtually everyone interpreted that decision as an attempt to break up the Pennsylvania delegation to Blaine's advantage, a roll-call vote was taken, and the motion to reconsider carried 381 to 359. Most Blaine men voted against reconsideration, and most Morton, Bristow, and Conkling men, as well as, surprisingly, all 58 Pennsylvania delegates, voted in favor.[40] There were other anomalies. Twelve New Yorkers voted against reconsideration—that is, in favor of Blaine. Ohioans, who were instructed to support Hayes, split 24 to 20 in favor of reconsideration.

Before the new vote on McPherson's ruling occurred, Ingersoll gave a blistering speech against unit rules, and the chairman of the Indiana delegation ably defended them. No delegate, he protested, had a right to violate the instructions of the state convention that chose him. To the extent that these brief speeches changed any minds, Ingersoll was more persuasive. McPherson's ruling against unit rules was sustained by a vote of 395 to 353, with 15 New Yorkers and 14 Ohioans joining Blaine's friends in the majority. Had they joined the other anti-Blaine men in voting against McPherson, Blaine's hopes would have been dashed.

Yet, unexpectedly, the ruling did not send Pennsylvanians rushing pell-mell toward Blaine. On the third ballot, only 3 Pennsylvanians supported Blaine, and 55 clung to Hartranft. On that ballot, Blaine, Morton, and Conkling all lost a few votes, while Bristow's total increased to 121, Hayes's to 67, and Hartranft's to 68. No one was remotely close to the necessary majority. Nor did many votes shift on the fourth ballot.

The first big change occurred on the fifth ballot, which began immediately after the results of the fourth were announced. When Michigan was reached in the alphabetical roll call of states, chairman William A. Howard, one of the founders of the state's Republican Party in 1854, announced: "There is a man in this section of the country who has beaten in succession three Democratic candidates for President in his own state, and we want to give him a chance to beat another Democratic candidate for the Presidency in the broader field of the United States." To the cheers of Ohioans in the spectators' gallery, Howard then cast all 22 of Michigan's votes for Hayes. Nonetheless, no landslide toward Hayes occurred. At the end of that ballot, Hayes's total had climbed to only 104, 10 votes fewer than Bristow received and far behind the leader Blaine, with 286. Still, Hayes now led Conkling, Morton, and Hartranft.

The sixth ballot commenced immediately, squelching attempts by some delegations to call a recess for "consultations." On this ballot 14 Pennsylvanians voted for Blaine and only 44 for Hartranft. Blaine's total ballooned to 308, his strongest showing yet, while Hayes finally edged ahead of Bristow, 113 to 111. The convention's secretary immediately began to call the roll for the seventh ballot, again squelching attempts to call a recess. Here McPherson adamantly enforced the convention's rules.

The stalemate finally broke on the seventh ballot. When Indiana was reached, Will Cumback withdrew Morton's nomination and cast 25 votes for Hayes and 5 for Bristow. Iowa and Kansas stuck by Blaine. Harlan of Kentucky then unexpectedly withdrew Bristow's name and cast all 24 of the state's votes for Hayes. When Cumback then tried to switch Indiana's 5 votes for Bristow to Hayes, Ingersoll won a ruling that the convention's rules forbade such a switch until after the roll call was completed.

Harlan's swing to Hayes proved decisive in the delegations still in play. New York, whose delegates had left the floor for a hurried consultation, cracked next. Its chairman cast 61 votes for Hayes and 9 for Blaine. Pivotal Pennsylvania then decided the outcome. Cameron finally withdrew Hartranft's name and cast 28 votes for Hayes and 30 for Blaine. As Hayes's secretary wrote to him from Cincinnati that night, had Pennsylvania's unit rule still been in effect, all 58 votes would have gone to Blaine, who would have won the nomination with 379 votes. Instead, the final totals listed Bristow with the 21 votes he had received before Harlan withdrew his name, Blaine with 351, and Hayes with 384.

The staunchness of Blaine's supporters merits comment. "You have no idea of the feeling for Blaine," one Ohioan wrote to Hayes after the decision had been made. "I could not have believed it possible."[41] The Iowa, Kansas, Maine, Maryland, Minnesota, and Wisconsin delegates had stood by him almost to a man on all seven ballots; Illinois gave him 38 votes on the first ballot and 35 on the last. Nonetheless, the aborted plan among the anti-Blaine men to concentrate behind Hayes if that were the only way to prevent Blaine's nomination had finally reached fruition. Here, the Ohio delegation's solidarity behind Hayes and its refusal to allow his consideration for vice president were all-important. In a subsequent letter to Hayes, William Henry Smith credited Ohio's performance to chairman Noyes's skill. "Better management I never saw," gushed Smith. "He was able, judicious, uniting, unselfish, inspiring, adroit. . . . The General seemingly never slept. His eyes were everywhere and discipline was preserved with as much rigor as on the field of battle."[42]

The selection of a running mate for Hayes was anticlimactic. Several states had favorite sons, but New York's William A. Wheeler, who had received a few votes for president on several ballots, was the clear favorite. The Republicans knew they needed a New Yorker on the ticket to have any chance of carrying the Empire State. After a few votes were cast on the first roll call, the convention named Wheeler by acclamation. Phil Sheridan's prediction six months earlier had proved correct.

Telegrams of congratulation with predictions of victory poured into the governor's office in Columbus from Bristow, Conkling, Blaine, and Grant. "You have secured victory for us in November by giving us a true man for whom every Republican can vote," Bristow wired to Kentucky's Harlan. "Our grand old party has done itself high honor in the choice it has made," echoed another Republican from Washington.[43] Two other themes, however, dominated the messages that flooded Hayes immediately after his nomination. The first was that it gave Republicans a fighting chance to bring back the Liberal Republicans who had bolted in 1872. The second was that it was up to Hayes personally to seal this deal in his letter of acceptance, for Liberals and other Independents had expressed great dissatisfaction with the platform's flabby planks on specie resumption and civil service reform.

Nonetheless, on the day after Hayes's nomination, Democratic Speaker of the House Michael C. Kerr of Indiana (who was mortally ill and would not live out the year) worriedly warned Manton Marble that "Hayes and Wheeler is a ticket with which we cannot afford to trifle. It invites us to a trial of our best metal."[44] The question now was whether Democrats would in fact choose their own party's "best metal" at their national convention in St. Louis in the last week of June.

6

DEMOCRATS ARE FORCED TO STRADDLE

Fierce competition among bitter rivals generated the drama of the Republicans' nomination process. For the Democrats, in contrast, the real suspense involved how eastern hard-money men could be reconciled with westerners who hated compulsory specie resumption on a fixed date, currency contraction, and, especially, the national banking system. That chasm had somehow to be bridged. Realistic Democrats understood that they had no chance of capturing the White House unless they carried New York. Precisely for that reason, the odds-on favorite for the party's nomination by the start of 1876 was New York Governor Samuel J. Tilden, a renowned hard-money man. As early as January of that year, correspondents were sending Tilden the names of midwestern Democrats as potential running mates to balance his ticket.

A lifelong Democrat, Tilden was born in the Hudson Valley in 1814. His father was a personal friend of Martin Van Buren, who also resided in New York's Columbia County and became Tilden's political hero. Pale and sickly as a youth, Tilden read voraciously while other boys his age played outdoors. He also developed a lifelong passion for mastering and manipulating numbers. That talent later paid huge dividends. Because of it, Tilden could accurately calculate election returns; swap corporate bonds with dramatically disparate market values to finance, refinance, and merge railroad companies; and unravel the extraordinarily complex money trail in Boss William M. Tweed's books, a feat that ultimately led to Tweed's downfall.

Even in his youth Tilden displayed remarkable political precocity. Before adolescence, he had absorbed the states' rights tenets of the Jeffersonian faith. He participated in political conversations among men gathered in his father's store and, as a teenager, began writing newspaper articles defending Andrew Jackson and his policies.

Tilden's political proclivities and his uncertain health—he was an inveterate hypochondriac—rendered his formal education episodic. After attending a New England academy, he entered Yale College as a twenty-year-old freshman. He withdrew during his first year, however, because the food served at Yale played havoc with his chronically nervous stomach. In 1835 Tilden began to take classes at New York University, but he also took long leaves to campaign for Van Buren in 1836 and 1840 and to defend his hard-money policies. It is unclear whether he ever earned a degree, but the clearly brilliant Tilden learned enough at NYU and from clerking with a judge to pass the bar exam and begin practicing law in New York City after Van Buren's defeat in the 1840 election.

During the 1840s Democratic Party activism and his law practice absorbed Tilden's time and attention. As a lawyer obsessed with details, he worked long hours, often for meager pay. But he also helped New York Democrats elect a governor in 1842, for which he was appointed New York City's corporate counsel in 1843. After James Polk's election in 1844, Tilden visited the new president to try to obtain federal patronage appointments for New York's Van Buren men, but to no avail. In 1846 he served as a hard-money Democratic delegate to New York's constitutional convention. In 1848 he joined the Van Burenite Democrats' bolt to the Free-Soil Party, and he drafted the public statement justifying that bolt. Like Van Buren himself, he quickly returned to the Democratic fold after the 1848 election and never left it again.

During the 1850s Tilden abstained from Democratic presidential campaigns. Instead, he devoted himself primarily to his law practice, now housed in a handsomely furnished suite of offices on Wall Street. Starting in the late 1840s Tilden became involved in refinancing and merging failing midwestern railroad lines. These transactions involved the transfer of bonds worth millions of dollars at face value, some of which Tilden earned as a legitimate fee. In 1876 Republican newspapers repeatedly charged that Tilden, as a trustee for bonds held in escrow for pending deals, had illegally sold them for his personal profit. No historian has ever confirmed the veracity of those partisan charges. What is undeniable, however, is that during the 1850s and 1860s Tilden became a millionaire several times over, in an age when the president of the United States still earned the grand salary of $25,000 a year. His new-found wealth allowed him to purchase an elegant town house in New York City's exclusive Gramercy Park, where much of the Democrats' 1876 presidential campaign would be managed.

In 1860 Tilden predicted but was still appalled by Lincoln's election. The southern response to that victory inaugurated the most controversial chapters of Tilden's political career. In January 1861 he signed an address issued by an Albany Democratic meeting calling for compromise with southerners to avert a civil war. In contrast, after the firing on Fort Sumter, he notably shunned an invitation to attend a mass Union rally in New York City. Unlike the hale and hearty Rutherford Hayes, who volunteered at the age of thirty-eight, the sickly Tilden, then in his mid-forties, never considered military service. Instead, he joined other Democrats in carping at the centralization of power that Washington Republicans deemed necessary to win the war. In 1862 he managed his friend Horatio Seymour's successful campaign for governor, just as in 1868 he would manage Seymour's unsuccessful race against Grant for president. In 1864 Tilden attended the Democrats' national convention and served as New York's representative on the all-important resolutions committee. That service later proved to be an albatross. In 1876 Republican newspapers would repeatedly, and falsely, charge that Tilden had written the notorious peace plank in the 1864 platform. In fact, Tilden had unsuccessfully opposed in committee Clement Vallandigham's denunciation of the war as a failure. Once the platform was adopted, moreover, he immediately urged Democratic nominee George B. McClellan to publicly repudiate it in his letter of acceptance.

In 1865, after the sudden death of his predecessor, Tilden became chairman of the Democratic Party's state committee. He held that post until his nomination for governor in 1874. It was then that Tilden's political career became entangled with that of his fellow New Yorker Boss Tweed. Tilden, by then a member of New York City's exclusive Manhattan Club, and Tweed, trained as a chair maker (like his father) and a street brawler as a youth, haled from vastly different social milieus. Yet Tilden, whose responsibility as state chairman was to win elections for the Democratic Party, knew that Tweed, as commander of New York's legendary Tammany Hall, could deliver the votes—whether legal, illegal, or entirely fictitious—of Irish Catholics in New York City necessary to offset the usually heavy majority of Republican votes cast in upstate New York.

Mutually suspicious, the two warily cooperated for half a decade. Tilden did not start the public campaign in 1871 against Tweed's phenomenal looting of New York City's treasury and his systemic corruption of the state's legislature and judiciary. That honor belonged to the Republican *New York Times* and *Harper's Weekly*, whose run of anti-Tweed cartoons by Thomas Nast undoubtedly qualifies as the most effective political lampooning in American history. Nonetheless, in the fall of that year, contrary to the *Times*'s later gibes that he was a sham reformer, Tilden played a crucial role in toppling Tweed. Gaining access to Tweed's books, which the *Times* had published earlier, he traced the money trail from kickbacks on grotesquely padded city construction contracts to the bank accounts of Tweed and his cronies. Tilden helped organize the famous Band of Seventy and an anti-Tweed slate of Democratic legislative candidates in New York City, and in a dramatic state convention in October, he publicly announced that he would never vote for Tweed's minions. In November Tilden's reform ticket carried every assembly and state senate seat, save Tweed's own, in the metropolis. In sum, Tilden helped break Tweed's grip on the legislature. Meanwhile, Tilden had privately exerted pressure on Democratic Governor John Hoffman to appoint the special prosecutor who would convict Tweed and force him to flee the country to escape imprisonment. Tilden's role in smashing the Tweed Ring clearly helped him win election as governor in 1874, although the Democrats probably would have won that year no matter who their candidate was.

From the moment of his election, Tilden set his eyes on the White House. He devoted significant portions of his annual messages to the state legislature in 1875 and 1876 to criticism of Grant's administration. He especially savaged Republicans' purported financial mismanagement: huge and, according to Tilden, wasteful federal expenditures; crushing taxes; and a failure, despite annual promises, to resume specie payments on the greenbacks first authorized in 1862. Reform of the national government, he maintained, was imperative to restore honesty and efficiency to Washington and to inaugurate an economic recovery.

Tilden differed strikingly from the Republican Rutherford Hayes in a number of ways, aside from their experiences during the Civil War. The robust Hayes looked taller than his actual height; eight years older than Hayes, the pale and wizened Tilden, whose expensive suits always looked a bit baggy, appeared shorter than he actually was. The outgoing Hayes had many close friends. Shy and aloof, Tilden won many admirers but few friends. Most Democratic legislators in Albany found the governor to be the coldest of cold fish. Happily married, Hayes had sired eight children. Tilden was a lifelong bachelor whom some historians have described as utterly asexual.

Nonetheless, Tilden possessed a number of assets as he sought the Democratic presidential nomination—and he sought it more overtly than any other man in previous American history. First and foremost, he had carried New York's governorship by more than 50,000 votes in 1874, a Democratic margin that had sunk to 15,000 votes in the election of 1875, when Tilden himself was not on the ticket. By far the biggest weapon in the arsenal of those who touted Tilden for the nomination was the warning that no Democrat could win the presidency without New York's thirty-five electoral votes, as well as those of its neighbors. The East, not the West, they insisted, held the key to victory. "The argument that we must carry New York, New Jersey, and Connecticut" and that only Tilden can do so "has an all-potent influence," one Detroit Democrat wrote to his congressman in mid-May.[1]

Second, his reputation as a political reformer and a hard-money man made him the Democrat most likely to get the backing of Liberal Republicans. Tilden dearly coveted Liberal Republican support. For that reason, he had insisted that Liberal William Dorsheimer run with him as lieutenant governor in 1874, and in 1876 he made sure that Dorsheimer chaired New York's delegation to the Democratic national convention.

Third, Tilden had earned a reputation as an organizational wizard who could mobilize every possible vote for his party. During his stint as chairman of the Democratic state committee, he had built county organizations that canvassed potential voters' preferences so thoroughly that he came within 300 votes of predicting his winning margin in 1874, months before the election occurred. Many Democrats anticipated that he could perform the same wonders nationwide, were he the nominee.

Fourth, as noted earlier, Tilden had amassed a considerable fortune as a Wall Street lawyer—money he was willing to spend in his relentless pursuit of the nomination. Throughout the spring of 1876, Republican newspapers charged that Tilden was trying to buy the Democratic nomination. They were right. In the spring of that year, paid agents who reported directly to Albany crisscrossed the Midwest soliciting delegates for Tilden. He funded a bureau that bought space in newspapers around the country for puff pieces about Tilden. Another bureau paid by Tilden broadcast hundreds of thousands of pro-Tilden tracts across the nation.

If lavish expenditure and meticulous planning could secure the prize, Tilden would win it. As one letter writer to the *Cincinnati Enquirer,* a Liberal Republican sheet, put it, "No movement to make a candidate for the Presidency without regard to public opinion was ever better organized than that to put up Samuel J. Tilden at St. Louis. He has directed it himself from the beginning, with the aid of a select circle of strikers in his employ and plenty of money to grease the wheels of the machine. He treats the nomination as a matter of business, to be made successful by management, as patent medicine is by liberal advertising."[2]

If Tilden had many assets, each of the other contenders for the Democratic laurels had serious liabilities. At the St. Louis national convention, Pennsylvanians, always jealous of New Yorkers, would nominate General Winfield Scott Hancock, probably the most able division and corps commander in the Union army during the war, as their favorite son. Considerable sentiment for Hancock also existed among southern Democrats, who remembered his leniency toward them as commander of the Texas-Louisiana military district created by the Military Reconstruction Act of 1867. In 1880 Hancock became Democrats' standard-bearer. In 1876, however, most eastern Democrats considered Hancock a bit "flaky," largely because of what they deemed to be heresies on the money question in the state platforms adopted by Pennsylvania Democrats in 1875 and 1876.

Delaware's Thomas Bayard, clearly one of the two ablest Democrats in the Senate, was sound on specie resumption so far as northeastern Democrats were concerned. New York banker August Belmont, who had served as the Democrats' national chairman from 1856 to 1868, strongly preferred Bayard to Tilden, whom he despised for personal reasons. Bayard was also quite clearly the first choice of most southern Democratic politicians. Yet that preference, as Bayard himself and many others recognized, was the rub. Any candidate favored by ex-Confederates would inevitably fuel Republicans' thus far invincible bloody-shirt campaigns against the Democracy. Because Tilden seemed likely to carry New York, Bayard, to Belmont's dismay, was willing to stand aside for him.

Ohio Senator Allen G. Thurman also had supporters, but for two reasons it was unclear at the start of the year whether he could win his own state's endorsement. First, even though he had witheringly criticized Sherman's specie resumption bill when the Senate debated it, he seemed less committed to greenbackism and destruction of the national banking system than the majority of Ohio Democrats were. Second, his

Governor Samuel J. Tilden of New York. (Courtesy of Photography Collection, Miriam and Ira D. Wallach Division of Arts, Prints and Photographs, New York Public Library, Astor, Lenox and Tilden Foundations.)

uncle, ex-Governor William Allen, also sought the presidential nomination. Thus the state convention that selected Ohio's delegates to St. Louis promised to be a real donnybrook.

That showdown occurred in Cincinnati on May 17. By a vote of 366 to 308, Ohio Democrats adopted a platform that named Allen as the state's favorite son and "request[ed]" its delegates to St. Louis to support him. That platform, which the majority of the convention's platform committee had in fact opposed, also demanded "the immediate and unconditional repeal of the Republican resumption law; the defeat of all schemes for resumption which involve either contraction of the currency, perpetuation of bank issues, or increase of the interest-burden of the debt; the gradual but early substitution of legal-tenders for national bank notes; [and] the issue by the General Government alone of all the circulating medium, whether paper or metallic." Here was greenbackism in full flower. Here, also, were a platform and a candidate that no eastern Democrat, other than perhaps a Pennsylvanian, could possibly accept.[3] The headline of a Democratic newspaper in Baltimore wonderfully captured easterners' scorn for Ohio Democrats' action: "Ohio's Rag-baby Madmen; Bill Allen for the Presidency; Inflation in Its Worst Form; The Idiotic Platform of a Lot of Lunatics; Senator Thurman Slaughtered."[4]

Thurman would get a few votes at St. Louis, but the Cincinnati convention effectively demolished his chances. Rutherford Hayes, for one, was astonished by the Democrats' action. "Judge T. is decidedly the ablest and best man of his party in Ohio, and has rendered it the most service," he wrote to one correspondent. "Yet the 'howling idiots' (Democratic managers) put Allen over him!" "Our Democratic friends have blundered as usual," he informed Alphonzo Taft two days later. "We can count with confidence on their doing it at the smallest opportunity."[5] "Ohio has killed Thurman & done Allen no good" among Kentucky's Democrats, wrote former Kentucky Congressman James Beck. Thurman's elimination, indeed, only enhanced the probability that Kentucky Democrats would support Tilden at St. Louis. They preferred Bayard, but Tilden seemed to have the best chance of winning. "*We must win*," stressed Beck, "& no personal feeling for anybody shall influence me. I am going to St. Louis to work (on the outside) for the most available man."[6]

If Thurman's humiliation at Cincinnati turned some Democrats who were still on the fence toward Tilden, it also meant that western soft-money men at the convention would be divided. Most of those worthies spurned the antique Allen. Their man was Indiana Governor Thomas Hendricks. Hendricks had served two terms in the House of Representatives in the early 1850s, and between 1863 and 1869 he had represented Indiana in the Senate, where he was a sharp critic of Republican policies. To boot, midwestern Democrats considered Indiana's electoral votes indispensable to any projected majority the Democrats might amass in 1876, especially after Hayes's victory in Ohio in 1875. Hendricks's supporters never let Democrats forget that fact. Yet on April 19, the same Indiana Democratic convention that committed the state's delegates as a unit to Hendricks also opposed any "contraction of the volume of our paper currency," insisted that greenbacks be substituted for national banknotes, and demanded that the Specie Resumption Act "should at once be repealed without any condition whatever."[7] Hendricks worked even harder than Tilden to round up western delegates, but that platform rendered him poisonous to most eastern Democrats.

Though all of Tilden's competitors for the nomination had weaknesses, Tilden, despite his strengths, faced at least four formidable obstacles. One was the eagerness of western Democrats in the House of Representatives to force a repeal of the Specie Resumption Act even before the national convention met. Such a move would define the party's monetary policy no matter what the national platform said and, easterners feared, destroy the party's chances in their states no matter who the nominee was. Visiting Washington to confer with Bayard in mid-February, an appalled Belmont wrote home that "the Democrats in Congress are more disorganized on the Currency question than ever before, & I fear the crazy demagogues of the West will carry the day."[8] "The House, the Democratic part of the House, will do no sensible or right thing on the subject of the currency," echoed Speaker Kerr six weeks later. "The voluntary and wicked offense of most of the Democrats is that they view the great national question of the currency through the popular fancies and heresies that prevail in their respective localities and districts never extending their thoughts to embrace the whole country."[9] Tilden's friends on the House Banking and Currency Committee could only try to stall repeal as long as they could, but it was nip and tuck all the way, as many worried letters to Tilden and his advisers that spring make clear.

Second, although hard-money Democrats from the West Coast strongly favored Tilden, he faced considerable opposition in the Midwest. This animus went beyond loathing for Tilden's well-known hard-money principles, since some midwestern Democrats, such as Speaker Kerr of Indiana, themselves favored a speedy resumption of specie payments. The farmers who powered the Granger movement and other midwestern antimonopoly men had long sought the regulation of railroad rates and had declared open war against lawyers who did the railroads' bidding. Therefore, they hardly took kindly to a Wall Street attorney who had amassed a fortune financing, combining, and thereby strengthening the very railroad corporations they crusaded against. Even beyond that stigma, Tilden was a New Yorker through and through. New York candidates had dragged Democratic presidential tickets down to defeat in 1864, 1868, and 1872, westerners ranted, and they had had enough. "You are utterly wrong in your judgment about the strength of Mr. Tilden," Kerr warned Manton Marble, owner and editor of the *New York World* and an enthusiastic Tilden booster, on March 31. "The elements of his weakness are numerous," Kerr explained. "Some of them are personal; others arise out of his relationship to politics in New York and others out of the important fact that he is the candidate of New York. I have admonished you many times that the West does not intend this year to take a New York man."[10]

Tilden's "relationship to politics in New York" constituted an even more formidable obstacle to his nomination. Tilden's role in bringing down Boss Tweed had offended the braves of Tammany Hall. Nevertheless, they had rallied behind him in 1874 to prevent incumbent Republican Governor John A. Dix from winning a second term. But in 1875 Tilden, obsessively solicitous of his reputation among Liberal Republicans, had insisted that a Liberal lead the Democratic state ticket and coldly refused to do anything to help the Tammany men on it. This rebuff caused "Honest" John Kelly, the new sachem of Tammany Hall, to declare open war on Tilden. Had Kelly known that a stacked blue-ribbon commission appointed by Tilden in 1875 to examine suffrage rights in New York City would recommend a revision of the city's charter in 1877 to restrict the vote in municipal elections exclusively to propertied taxpayers, he would have been angrier still. Had that referendum passed (it did not), unpropertied Irish Catholic immigrants, the backbone of Tammany's renewed hold on New York City's municipal government, would have been disfranchised. Tilden intended that result. The lifelong Democrat was no democrat. He was a wealthy elitist, just like his fellow members of the silk-stocking Manhattan Club. But so were many of the Liberal Republicans whose support he so coveted.

In any event, Tilden's failure to support Tammany candidates in 1875 sufficed for Kelly. Early in 1876 he announced that Tammany men would never vote for Tilden as a presidential candidate and would not mobilize New York City voters for him should he get the nomination. Instead, they would support Hendricks. Thus, Kelly and other Tammany Democrats loudly insisted—and the news spread across the country like wildfire—that Tilden could not carry New York in November against any likely Republican nominee. "Is Mr. John Kelly opposing Gov. Tilden?" a worried Nebraska Democrat wrote to Marble as early as March 20. "Is it possible that State can favor Gov. Hendricks?"[11]

Tammany's warriors would later carry their war against Tilden to the St. Louis convention itself. There, Tammany men paraded the streets with placards announcing that Tilden could never carry New York and would lead Democrats to another defeat if nominated. Thus dissident New York Democrats subverted the strongest argument in favor of Tilden's nomination. "Tilden's domestic foes are laboring earnestly to prove to the West & South that he is the weakest candidate for New York," groaned one Tilden man.[12]

Tilden's apparent vulnerability in New York worsened in May when Marble, Tilden's ablest and most influential newspaper proponent, finalized a deal that had secretly been in the works for months to sell the *New York World* to a Philadelphia consortium headed by Tom Scott, president of the Pennsylvania Railroad (and deeply implicated in Blaine's railroad troubles). The consortium installed William H. Hurlbert, who had once worked for Marble and whom Bayard had dismissed as an "airy fairy," as its new editor.[13] Hurlbert instantly silenced the *World*'s pro-Tilden drumbeat and indicated sympathy for the anti-Tilden dissidents. "The importance of carrying New York is fully appreciated," that state's Democratic Senator Francis Kernan warned Tilden's secretary in mid-May. "Hence the importance of correcting any impression that Gov Tilden is not sure to carry it."[14]

News of Tilden's supposed weakness in New York heightened the fourth roadblock between him and the nomination—Democrats' traditional rule requiring a two-thirds rather than a simple majority at the national convention to win the prize. Maine's Democrats recognized the problem. When they endorsed Tilden for the nomination at a state convention on June 13, they also called for a junking of the two-thirds rule at St. Louis. This proposal had no prayer of adoption. The two-thirds rule constituted the best hope of derailing Tilden's lavishly funded express.

Where, after all, was Tilden to get the necessary votes? Ohio and Indiana Democrats had committed to other men, and many other westerners were hostile. "The insanity that prevails there, and to a great extent in the South on the currency question is an impossible barrier in his way," Kerr had written to Marble on March 31. Tilden's friends boasted that only he could carry New Jersey, but with regard to the nomination, New Jersey's Democratic Senator Theodore Randolph wrote to Marble from Washington on April 7 that "Tilden has no great strength with us." Instead, New Jersey's delegates to St. Louis intended to offer former Governor Joel Parker as a favorite son. Democratic insiders from Pennsylvania reported to Tilden and Marble that Philadelphia Congressman Samuel J. Randall, a strong opponent of Scott's seemingly unbreakable lock on the state legislature, might back the reformer Tilden. Randall, however, controlled only eight votes in the Pennsylvania delegation; Senator William Wallace, who would lead the delegation to St. Louis, strongly preferred Hendricks. Pennsylvanians eventually nominated Hancock primarily to avert an open rupture between Randall and Wallace.

This information meant that Tilden's best chance of mustering the necessary two-thirds majority would be in the South. Every Democrat counted on carrying every former slave state, with the possible exception of South Carolina, in November.[15] Tilden nonetheless had exceptionally few personal contacts among southern Democrats. Nor did he know what they expected of their candidate.

Working with Henry Watterson, editor of the *Louisville Journal-Courier,* and former California Senator William M. Gwin, who had once represented Mississippi in Congress, the methodical Tilden set out to establish the necessary contacts and learn what southerners wanted. Watterson urged Tilden to reassure southerners about his commitment to states' rights, but their top priority was clear. Most southern Democrats, contrary to Kerr's belief, cared not a fig about greenbacks, specie resumption, or reform. Their priority, aside from toppling the remaining state Republican regimes in Florida, Louisiana, and South Carolina, was to select a Democrat who could win the presidency and thus halt federal support for blacks' voting rights. In only one ex-Confederate state did Democrats say a word about money or reform prior to the national convention; that state was Tennessee, and most of its Democrats were greenbackers who favored Hendricks.

Hence, southern Democrats expressed alarm at the reports that internal divisions in New York could prevent Tilden from carrying that state.

On May 29, for example, a New Orleans Democrat who only a week earlier had promised to work on Louisiana and other southern delegates for Tilden, wrote to Marble in alarm. Since his earlier letter, "the Ohio madness has developed with absolute frenzy, the division in New York has grown to the proportion of intestine war, and the 'World' has passed into Hurlbert's hands & can no longer be reckoned as one of T's supporters." Consequently, "We feel here that Tilden's chances have been seriously impaired, as the South will follow the man with the strongest backing; if the breach widens at home Tilden's hopes will be swallowed up in it." Southerners would then back Bayard, who would lose. "Of course," he added dejectedly, "if a blunder is possible the Democrats will make it."[16]

Tilden's friends, therefore, made sure that virtually every influential southern Democrat who visited New York City that spring was introduced to Tilden at his Gramercy Park home. Tilden's allies and agents also strove to reassure southerners that he—and only he—could carry New York for the Democrats. Tilden, in short, spent so much money advertising his invincibility because he had to. And to a great extent, those efforts succeeded. Most southern state conventions sent uninstructed delegations to St. Louis. As southerners privately informed Tilden, they feared that any public endorsement of him would ignite a backlash against him in the North. But they accepted the logic iterated and reiterated by Tilden's propaganda. Three northeastern states provided the key to Democratic victory, and neither Hendricks nor Allen had a prayer of carrying them. If Bayard was a certain loser, many southerners would have preferred Hancock to Tilden. But when they learned in St. Louis that Pennsylvanians were the only northerners willing to back Hancock and that even their support for him was suspect, they gravitated toward Tilden.

John Kelly and other Tammany men arrived in St. Louis days before the convention opened on June 27 to try desperately—and unavailingly—to slow that movement. They lured southern delegates to their hotel suites and attempted to persuade them to shun Tilden and back Hendricks instead. Yet newspaper correspondents reported from St. Louis that the anti-Tilden men seemed hopelessly disorganized compared with the smooth operation Tilden had on the ground. On several occasions before the convention opened, western Hendricks men begged Kelly to challenge New York's unit rule just as Pennsylvania Republicans had at Cincinnati, hoping to avert Tilden's nomination.

According to Kelly, twenty-two of New York's seventy delegates opposed Tilden, but they could not vote for anyone else so long as the unit rule held and the delegation's majority determined who got New York's votes. Surprisingly, however, Kelly adamantly refused to challenge the unit rule. He insisted that he was honor bound to obey the instructions of the state convention. Not even the circulation of an open letter opposing Tilden's nomination that was signed by scores of prominent New York Democrats, including August Belmont and most of the state's judges, could slow the Tilden express. By the night of June 26, his nomination appeared certain, despite the two-thirds rule.

Aside from that rule, the Democratic national convention differed from its Republican counterpart in several other respects. Like the Republicans, the Democrats awarded each state two delegates for each electoral vote it possessed; however, the Democrats allowed no delegates from territories (with the exception of Colorado, whose admission to statehood was pending) to vote or to serve on committees. The convention's total vote was therefore 738, making 492 the magic two-thirds majority. By the morning of June 27, observers believed that Tilden would get more than 400 votes on the first ballot.

That morning quickly became blisteringly hot, hardly a surprise in St. Louis in late June. Men fainted in droves as they waited in line to buy tickets to the convention hall's spectators' galley. Aside from delaying the convention's announced starting time, the stifling heat did little to diminish Tildenites' control of it. Days before the convention opened, the Democratic National Committee had selected Henry Watterson, Tilden's loyal Kentucky ally, to serve as temporary president of the convention. Just like the Republicans, the Democrats' first order of business was to select the various committees, almost all of which Tilden men dominated. By far the most important of these was the platform committee, for like the Republicans, the Democrats decided to adopt a platform prior to balloting for the presidential nominee. Tilden's confident friends fully supported this order of convention business.

Most delegates, and certainly most newspaper reporters, anticipated a battle royal over the platform, since Democrats disagreed so sharply over the money question, the Catholic school question (many ferociously opposed a constitutional amendment on the grounds that it would interfere with states' control over education), and civil service reform. Appointed by three o'clock in the afternoon of the convention's first day, the fractious platform committee met without agreement until midnight.

Resuming deliberations the next morning, it was not ready to report until 2:15 in the afternoon of the twenty-eighth.

The Democrats (like the Republicans) allowed each state's delegation to choose its representative for the platform committee in advance of the convention's opening, and the names were simply announced on the afternoon of June 27. Leading the western soft-money men were former Congressman Daniel Voorhees of Indiana and General Thomas Ewing Jr. of Ohio. Son of Ohio's most prominent antebellum Whig politician and brother-in-law of General William Tecumseh Sherman (who had been raised in the Ewing household), Ewing had joined the Democratic Party after the war, as did a remarkable number of former Whigs in the North as well as the South. More important, Ewing had become the most forceful and able exponent of greenbackism in the Ohio Democratic Party. As a campaign orator, he had led Governor William Allen's unsuccessful reelection bid in 1875, captained his forces at the May 1876 Cincinnati Democratic convention, and dictated the state platform that eastern Democrats found so appalling.

Against this relentless bruiser, hard-money men on the platform committee needed a champion who could be just as resolute. They naturally turned to New York for such leadership. Most New York delegates wanted Manton Marble to serve as their man on the committee. However, the delegation's chairman, Lieutenant Governor William Dorsheimer, insisted that he personally represent New York. Marble deferred to him, a decision that he later told Tilden was a grave mistake. It was a mistake because Marble, at Tilden's behest and with his frequent input, had written out a national platform in advance of the convention—one that they deemed safe for eastern Democrats. At St. Louis, the platform committee had to consider resolutions offered from the floor before it met. Nonetheless, the central issue was whether the committee would accept the platform Tilden wanted.

Studded with brilliant rhetorical flourishes, Marble's platform was far more coherent, comprehensive, and compelling than the document the Republicans had cobbled together at Cincinnati. At the request of West Coast Democrats, he incorporated much tougher anti-Chinese language than the Republicans had adopted. He also took steps to neutralize the expected anti-Catholic campaign by Republicans. At the request of Francis W. Bird of Massachusetts, onetime leader of that state's Radical Republican wing, a Liberal Republican bolter in 1872, and now an ardent Tilden man, he arraigned Republicans' corruption in fulsome detail. What gave this masterpiece its power, however, was its iteration and reiteration of the need for "reform." Almost every plank, indeed, began, "Reform is necessary. . . ."

We "do hereby declare the Administration of the Federal Government to be in urgent need of immediate reform," rang the platform's first sentence. Democrats accepted the amendments of the Constitution "as a final settlement of the controversies that engendered civil war" and insisted on the "total separation of Church and State." Still, reform was necessary to save Americans "from a corrupt centralism which, after inflicting upon the States the rapacity of carpet-bag tyrannies, has honey-combed the offices of the Federal Government itself with incapacity, waste, and fraud; infected States and municipalities with the contagion of misrule; and locked the prosperity of an industrious people in the paralysis of hard times. Reform is necessary to establish a sound currency, restore the public credit, and maintain the national honor."[17] And so it went.

The platform blasted Republicans for exploiting anti-Catholic prejudice with their call for a constitutional amendment on schools; for reviving "sectional hate" with their bloody-shirt campaigns; for failing to restore specie payments; for extravagance and high taxes that had taken from the people, since the end of the war, "thirteen times the whole amount of legal tender notes and squandered four times this amount without accumulating any reserve for their redemption"; for giving extravagant land subsidies to railroads rather than saving federal land for actual settlers; for their protective tariff, "a masterpiece of injustice, inequality, and false pretense"; and for a foreign policy that "exposed our brethren of the West Coast" to Chinese prostitutes and competition from coolie labor. These wrongs all demanded reform, as did the corruption and peculations of the Grant administration, which the platform listed in lavish detail. "All these abuses, wrongs, and crimes, the product of sixteen years' ascendancy of the Republican party," summarized Marble's powerful document, "create the necessity for reform confessed by Republicans themselves; but their reformers [i.e., Bristow] are voted down in convention and displaced from the cabinet [Bristow resigned the day after the Cincinnati convention ended]." Hence, "reform can only be had by a peaceful civic revolution. We demand a change of Administration, a change of parties, that we may have a change of measures and men."

All Democrats at the St. Louis convention applauded this language. None of it explains the long ordeal that occupied the platform committee, although its West Coast members insisted on sharpening Marble's language about Chinese immigration. Rather, the sticking point, as expected, was the plank on money. Marble and Tilden had hoped to avoid any explicit reference to the Specie Resumption Act and especially to its repeal. Various versions of the proposed platform can be found in the Manton Marble Papers at the Library of Congress, but the precise language of the money plank Marble carried to St. Louis and the platform committee's secret deliberations on it can only be inferred from the convention's debate and subsequent correspondence. That plank denounced "the financial imbecility and immorality" of Republicans for failing in the eleven years since the end of the war to resume specie payments or to make any preparations to do so. Instead, it averred, Republicans had "obstructed resumption by wasting our resources and exhausting all our surplus income, and while annually professing to intend a speedy return to specie payments, [have] annually enacted fresh hindrances thereto." Marble apparently wanted the platform's next sentence to read as follows: "We demand a judicious system of preparation by public economies, by official retrenchments, and by wise finance" that would enable speedy resumption.

For Ewing and the other soft-money men, this language was intolerable. It left the impression that specie resumption was the Democrats' sole goal. Thus, they insisted on adding a sentence bluntly demanding immediate and complete repeal of the Specie Resumption Act. Hard-money men could not stomach that, but Dorsheimer, to Marble's disgust, agreed to a sentence that stated: "We denounce the Resumption clause of the Act of 1875, and we hereby demand its repeal." This phrasing hardly satisfied the westerners, but by a vote of 18 to 16, the committee adopted it and prepared to present the platform to the convention late in the morning of June 28. When Marble was informed of this decision, however, he insisted that a "revision committee" rework the platform before its presentation. Attending its meeting, but not an official member of the platform committee, he inserted four words in the platform. Following the "hindrances" language he had written, the platform now read: "As such a hindrance, we denounce the Resumption clause of the Act of 1875, and we here demand its repeal."[18] That insertion was intended, much to the dismay of Ewing, to imply that resumption was still Democrats' top priority. Still, the platform committee adopted the revised platform by a vote of 29 to 9 and reported it to the convention floor in the afternoon of June 28.

Though not a tough negotiator, William Dorsheimer was a tall and distinguished-looking man. Hence the chairman of the platform committee, a Virginian, asked him to read the committee's handiwork to the gathered delegates. As soon as Dorsheimer finished, Ewing was on his feet with a minority platform offered by himself and other members of the platform committee from Indiana, Pennsylvania, Kansas, Tennessee, West Virginia, Iowa, and Missouri. This would remove the sentence about the resumption *clause* Marble had amended and substitute the following: "The law for the resumption of specie payments on the 1st of January 1879, having been enacted by the Republican Party, without deliberation in Congress or discussion before the people, and being both ineffective to secure its objects and highly injurious to the business of the country, ought to be forthwith repealed." In short, Ewing and his cohorts insisted that the entire law, not just the clause fixing a date for resumption, be repealed.

Ewing's speech defending this proposed substitution launched the convention's most contentious debate. The majority's platform, complained Ewing, implied that Democrats objected only to the date set in Sherman's law—indeed, that Democrats sought resumption *earlier* than January 1, 1879. He wanted no such thing. More important, that language left "the rest of the act to stand unobjected to, and by implication, approving it." It "commits us to issuing gold bonds to take up the costless fractional currency. It commits us to the reduction of the legal-tender money by having bank paper take its place, thus increasing the power of an already dangerous monopoly—a monopoly that is thoroughly hated by the mass of the Democracy of the country. It commits us to the perpetuation of the national banking system," a policy "to which the Democracy—my friends of the West I am sure—are almost unanimously opposed."

At this point, easterners were shouting that Ewing had exceeded his allotted time, while westerners were calling for him to carry on. Here, Dorsheimer, who had, in Marble's opinion, unconscionably and unnecessarily allowed mention of the Specie Resumption Act in the platform when he had the votes on the committee to squelch it, redeemed himself. As a concession to the westerners, both he and New York Senator Francis Kernan urged the convention to give Ewing more time. Before Ewing could resume, however, Dorsheimer, who still had the floor, delivered the convention's most decisive speech. "I propose here to make a straight issue between soft and hard money," Dorsheimer announced.

"If you want soft money give your votes to the resolution offered by the most distinguished soft-money advocate in the United States. But if you want to leave the hard-money men some chance to carry their States, then stand by the report of the committee, which was a compromise so great that a protest has been signed by every one of the Eastern Democratic States, and to which I have put my own signature." That compromise offered easterners "some hope, but if you declare, in the language of the gentleman from Ohio, General Ewing, for a repeal forthwith, then abandon all your hopes." New York, Connecticut, and New Jersey would be lost.[19]

Before the vote on Ewing's minority platform, Voorhees replied for the West. He was tired of hearing New Yorkers moan about what was necessary to carry their state. Did not the states for which he spoke—West Virginia, Ohio, Indiana, Missouri, Tennessee, Iowa, and Kansas—"have a right to be heard on this subject . . . are they not to be considered? Do they amount to nothing?" Whatever they amounted to, they lacked the votes to carry Ewing's proposed revision. It went down to defeat, 219 to 550. Then the entire platform was adopted by a vote of 651 to 83, and a motion to reconsider that vote was shouted down. "Dorsheimer did magnificently today," Marble telegraphed Tilden that night.[20] From Tilden's perspective, he had indeed.

After the platform fight, the nominations of and balloting for the presidential candidates seemed anticlimactic. The nominating speeches for Bayard, Hendricks, Joel Parker of New Jersey, Allen, and Hancock were strikingly short. Kernan's speech for Tilden was longer and attempted to convince delegates from all regions that they needed a man who had already achieved reform in elective office. The issue on which the 1876 election would be determined, Kernan insisted, was "administrative reform." "You warm-hearted men from the South who have been . . . wronged as no people ever have," he asked rhetorically, do you not need reform under which you "shall be allowed to manage your own affairs, and shall be freed from plundering adventurers, who are eating up the substance of your people and taking from you all real republican government?" Destitute farmers and unemployed laborers in the West, just as in the East, also required "reform." The man most likely to win the votes of those who needed it, because he had already demonstrated as New York's governor that he could achieve it, hymned Kernan to wild cheers, was Tilden.

After Kernan sat down and before the convention's secretary could continue the alphabetical roll of states to elicit other nominations, a remarkable event occurred. In brazen violation of the convention's rules, which stipulated that only seconders of a nomination could gain the rostrum after a main nominating speech, Tammany's John Kelly, who had for a full week trashed Tilden's chances of winning, boldly strode to the rostrum and began speaking. The stunned presiding officer, former Illinois Congressman John McClernand, apparently believing that Kelly had flip-flopped and was seconding Kernan's nomination of Tilden, allowed him to speak. But Kelly had experienced no last-minute conversion. New York's restrictive unit rule prevented him and other anti-Tilden men from voting their beliefs, he complained. He intended to express them now. Democrats must win this election, he insisted, or the Democratic Party would be finished forever. New York candidates had dragged Democrats down to defeat in 1864, 1868, and 1872 and would do so again in 1876 if Tilden were nominated. The election's outcome, even in New York, depended on Democrats' ability to carry the October state elections in Indiana and Ohio, where, though he did not say so, Democrats worshipped soft money. With Tilden at the head of the national ticket, Democrats would lose both Ohio and Indiana and thus the national election. With Hendricks, whom Kelly urged delegates to nominate, they could carry both states in October and November and win the White House, even without New York. What a case for this Irish Democratic leader of Tammany Hall to make!

It did no good, as the first ballot quickly showed. Tilden ran far ahead, with 403½ votes. Every delegation gave him some support, except for those from Colorado, Delaware, Indiana, Kansas, New Jersey, Ohio, and Pennsylvania. Arkansas, California, Connecticut, Florida, Kentucky, Maine, Massachusetts, Minnesota, Mississippi, Nebraska, New Hampshire, New York, Oregon, Rhode Island, South Carolina, and Vermont supported him unanimously. Virginia gave him 17 of its 25 votes. Hendricks ran a distant second with 133½ votes. He received all the votes from Colorado, Indiana, Kansas, and Tennessee and the majority of those from Illinois, along with a scattering of support from Alabama, Iowa, Maryland, Michigan, Missouri, Nevada, and North Carolina. With Pennsylvania's unanimous support and a scattering of votes from the South, Hancock ran third with 77, while Allen amassed a mere 56. Only New Jersey stuck by Parker, while Bayard garnered only 31 votes.

The convention moved immediately to a second vote. Alabama, Colorado, Delaware, Louisiana, and Missouri shifted all their votes to Tilden. After Missouri gave its 30 votes to Tilden, only New Jersey, which adhered to Parker; Pennsylvania, which clung to Hancock; Tennessee, which stood by Hendricks; and Ohio and West Virginia, which voted again for Allen, resisted the pro-Tilden landslide. Tilden needed 492 votes for a two-thirds majority. On the second ballot he garnered 508. The convention then made his nomination unanimous.

Exhausted by the long day's tumultuous events, the convention postponed nomination of a vice presidential candidate until the following morning. Everyone recognized that the defeated soft-money men required a bone. That night the telegraph lines between St. Louis and Indianapolis hummed. Prior to the convention, Hendricks had said that he would never accept second place on the ticket. But he was the man Democrats now wanted to balance the ticket in order to mobilize soft-money Democrats behind it. Telegrams to Hendricks on the night of the twenty-eighth and the early morning of the twenty-ninth begged him to accept. "We stood by you from first to last, and now ask you to stand by us," Tennesseans pleaded. "For God's sake, accept!" read another message.[21]

The following morning only Hendricks was formally nominated, and on a perfunctory ballot he received 730 votes, with eight Ohioans who presumably thought Allen deserved the honor abstaining. Warnings by two Indiana delegates that Hendricks might refuse to accept the nomination went unheeded. On at least three occasions on June 29, Hendricks told reporters in Indianapolis that he was leaning against acceptance but would wait to confer with Indiana's delegation before making a final decision.

Only two other incidents on the convention's final morning require mention. First, after Hendricks's nomination, Kelly again took the floor and announced that despite what he and other Tammany men had been saying for the past five months, they would work as hard as they could for Tilden's election. Second, Democrats chose the members of the party's national campaign committee, by a vote of individual state delegations, before they adjourned. Congressman Abram Hewitt was New York's choice. Because he was a Tilden confidant, and because the national committee would be headquartered in New York City, Hewitt became its chairman.

Democrats thus left St. Louis with a potential national ticket and a national platform meant to straddle the party's serious internal rift over the money issue. Yet three immediate reactions to their actions there revealed the flaws of that attempt. Charles Francis Adams Jr. of

Massachusetts, a well-known Liberal Republican, had attended the Fifth Avenue Hotel conference on May 15 and announced that he preferred Tilden to Bristow as a presidential candidate. Yet as soon as he saw the Democratic ticket, he wrote to Tilden and said that he could never vote for him if Hendricks were his running mate. Democrats simply must not renege on the pledge in the Specie Resumption Act, a worried New Yorker wrote to Tilden on July 3. "To say (as the platform does) that the resumption clause is itself an obstacle to resumption, and to propose its naked repeal, is (as it seems to me) to talk nonsense, and what is worse, very dishonorable and disgraceful nonsense." Tilden, he urged, must rectify this in his letter of acceptance, especially because "Mr. Hendricks exults in the expression, as being equivalent to an abandonment of any policy looking toward resumption by the government."[22]

Yet if Liberal Republicans and hard-money Democrats expressed consternation at the concessions to soft-money men on the ticket and in the platform, inflationists were even more furious. They threatened to bolt to a separate Greenback ticket that had been nominated by a sparsely attended convention in Indianapolis on May 17, the same day that the Ohio Democratic state convention met. For president, the Greenbackers had chosen New York City's aged millionaire philanthropist Peter Cooper, founder of the famous Cooper Union and, coincidentally, Abram Hewitt's father-in-law. As Cooper's running mate, they picked California Senator Newton Booth. Motivated primarily by genuine sympathy for the unemployed, Cooper reluctantly accepted the nomination on the condition that neither the Republican nor the Democratic platforms endorsed Greenback demands that unbacked legal tender notes be made the country's exclusive currency, which, of course, neither did. In contrast, Booth, who was an antimonopoly man, not a greenbacker, instantly and indignantly rejected his nomination. His action forced Greenbackers to schedule another convention in Philadelphia in early July, where they would select Ohio's Samuel F. Cary to replace Booth on the third-party ticket.

The impending Philadelphia meeting of Greenbackers, as well as Pennsylvania Democrats' previous commitment to greenback nostrums, explains why one soft-money Democrat, outraged by Tilden's selection at St. Louis, vented his exasperation in a Philadelphia newspaper. On July 1, Blanton Duncan of Louisville, Kentucky, wrote a letter to the editor of the *Philadelphia Press* arguing that the hard-money platforms adopted by Republicans and Democrats had infuriated those suffering the most from the ongoing depression. Those platforms, he exclaimed, would create at least a million votes for the Greenback ticket. "The double-faced [Democratic] platform and ticket of the New York politicians need only exposure to be repudiated by honest men. 'We are coming father Abraham, millions strong.' Our motto will be 'relief,' and not Tilden reform."[23]

That this self-appointed champion of the destitute sharply differentiated between a campaign aimed at reform and one aimed at economic relief is of utmost importance. In his obsessive quest for Liberal Republican support in the midst of a depression, Tilden may have bet on the wrong horse. Yet even Liberals, as noted, were disgusted by what Democrats had done in St. Louis. Like the Republicans after their Cincinnati convention, the Democrats still had much hard work to do to mount an effective and coherent campaign.

THE CAMPAIGN

After their national conventions, both Republicans and Democrats sought to mobilize as many of their traditional supporters as possible with appeals to party loyalty; incitement of racial, religious, and sectional prejudices; and hurrah techniques. It is doubtful that those voters paid much, if any, attention to newspaper editorials, party platforms, or campaign literature.[1] Rather, the leadership of both parties aimed their printed material at a different group—educated and politically informed Liberal Republicans and Independents, men who scorned the reflexive partisan devotion of the great majority of the electorate. Indeed, after the conventions, the competition between Democrats and Republicans for Liberal support intensified. As a result, just as in 1875, a marked congruence characterized what the two parties said and did.

Democratic and Republican newspapers, for example, proudly announced when one Liberal Republican or another endorsed their respective candidates as though they had bagged trophies. In late June and July, however, politicians believed that the acceptance letters Hayes and Tilden had to draft provided the key to this competition. Both men received conflicting advice about what to say. Both openly sought to court Liberal Republicans. Both had to clear hurdles to do so.

The process of writing and releasing letters resembled a tennis game. Just as Tilden and Marble had waited to see the Republicans' national platform before making the final revisions to the Democratic platform they sent to St. Louis, so Hayes waited to see the Democratic platform before he wrote his letter. Swamped with solicited and unsolicited advice from Carl Schurz, George William Curtis, and many others, Hayes released his letter on Saturday, July 8. It appeared in newspapers around the country on Monday, July 10. Tilden awaited Hayes's letter before he wrote his own, but he was also forced to engage in a delicate minuet with Hendricks so that the two men's acceptance letters did not contradict each other. As a result, to the growing exasperation of Democrats, Tilden and Hendricks did not release their letters until August 4.

Almost from the moment of Hayes's nomination, advice poured into Columbus about what the governor should say. What is most obvious from this flood of letters is how absolutely crucial these correspondents considered Hayes's acceptance letter. Both before and especially after the Democratic convention, they variously identified Hayes's letter as "the Gettysburg of this campaign," "the pivot on which the result of the canvass will turn," and "now of supreme importance."[2] "That very much, perhaps everything, depends on your letter of acceptance, need not be said," asserted a Connecticut Republican on July 1.[3] "Never in American history," hyperbolized Carl Schurz from St. Louis on July 5, "was there a letter of acceptance of such exceeding importance, and for which the people looked with so much anxious interest."[4] Talk about pressure! As early as June 22, one advice giver joked, "I dare say you are getting more advice per square inch now than you can withstand without a first-class safety valve."[5]

Two things primarily generated that pressure. Savvy Republicans instantly recognized the strength of the Democratic ticket. Hendricks gave Democrats a leg up in Indiana, and Tilden would have great appeal among Liberal Republicans and other Independents in the East. "We have before us a strong, dangerous enemy!" William H. Smith warned Hayes from Chicago.[6] "The St. Louis nominations are very strong, and they show that the Democratic party has recovered its wits," George William Curtis concurred from New York. "In New York, Mr. Tilden is strong as a party manager, as a hard money man, and above all as a ring masher and reformer. This last consideration commends him most warmly to the great Independent vote."[7]

Most Republicans, however, worried far more about the clear inferiority of their own platform to the gem that Tilden and Marble had composed for the Democrats. "Our platform is certainly thin and weak, & is so thought here by our own people," one Republican groused from Washington even before the Democrats met.[8] "I shall be glad if your letter of acceptance rises higher than the platform," Edward L. Pierce wrote from Massachusetts. "I served on the Committee but was not satisfied with the result."[9]

Rectifying the deficiencies of the Republican platform in light of the strengths of the Democratic one constituted Hayes's chief task. Yet Hayes quickly learned that Republicans disagreed about what those deficiencies were. Californians wanted him to take a tougher stance against Chinese immigration. Others complained that, unlike the Democrats, the Republicans had made no overt appeal to Germans in their platform. Others faulted the omission of any call for a retrenchment of governmental expenditures and a reduction of tax rates and urged Hayes to make that call himself. Still others, including John Sherman, cited the importance of exploiting anti-Catholic sentiment and urged Hayes to affirm his commitment to a constitutional amendment on the schools question, especially since the Democratic platform appeared to oppose one by pronouncing public education exclusively a state affair. Several correspondents, in a message later echoed by editorials in the *New York Times,* planted a seed that would shape much of what Hayes subsequently did. Hayes, they argued, should go out of his way to conciliate white southerners, especially former Whigs. These southerners ached to break away from the Democrats, they said, and only the color line that had been drawn in the South kept them in the Democratic Party. If Hayes could indicate his distaste for that color line and, just as important, for a politics drawn along sectional lines by a bloody-shirt campaign, he might engender a political realignment in the South.

By far the most frequent advice Hayes received, however, especially from eastern Republicans and Liberal Republicans such as Schurz, was the need to stress his personal dedication to civil service reform and honest government, his determination to punish crooked officeholders ruthlessly, and his unflinching commitment to hard money and specie resumption. "In their platform and their candidate," warned a Bostonian, "the democrats have given the best assurance in their power that they seriously mean reform. They will force that issue in spite of any attempt to make the campaign on war issues," and Hayes must meet that attack.[10] Reform was the only issue this year, echoed a New Yorker. "The Bloody shirt [would] not be a safe flag to follow" because it would alienate Liberal Republicans.[11]

Curtis, the editor of *Harper's Weekly* and a prominent proponent of civil service reform who had strong ties to Liberals in New York, perhaps said it best. Because of Tilden's nomination, reform, not finances or southern policy, would be the central issue of the campaign. "Your letter is of vital importance," he wrote. Hayes must issue "a bold unequivocal statement that the present system of appointment to subordinate offices and positions under Government tends directly to monstrous extravagance and official carelessness and is a direct temptation to dishonesty, and that it should be radically reformed." If Hayes followed that statement with a pledge to serve only a single term, since "the re-eligibility of the President is a constant and perilous temptation to an exercise of the appointing power," he could neutralize Tilden's appeal to Liberals. The Republicans, Curtis continued, faced a real struggle. "The universal prostration of industry and stagnation of business, with the disgust at Belknapery, Babcockery and Schenckery, and the absence of any overpowering vital issue like slavery, the war, and reconstruction, have produced a deep desire for change." Republicans must convince "discontented people . . . that Republican success is more likely to give them what they want than Democratic. And the proof of all this will be sought in the plain, clear, unmistakable words of the candidate."[12]

From the moment he learned of his nomination, Hayes had in fact understood the importance of appealing to Liberals by addressing civil service reform in his acceptance letter. Even before the Democrats met, Hayes informed one lieutenant that "I am now thinking of emphatic talk for Civil Service reform."[13] In contrast, Hayes initially hesitated to even mention the money question, as his views on specie resumption were already well known. Besides, if Democrats took the hard-money ground, resumption would not be an issue in the campaign. The Democratic plank calling for repeal of the resumption clause and a flood of letters decrying the evasiveness of the Republicans' monetary plank changed Hayes's mind. "Gen. Hawley did us signal injury" on the financial question, complained one of Hayes's closest Ohio advisers. "It would be a fatal mistake," therefore, if Hayes did not reaffirm his commitment to resumption in his letter.[14] Because of the Democratic platform, wrote another adviser, you must "reassert your opposition to the repeal of the act for resumption of specie payments in 1879. . . . The public sentiment in favor of hard-money in the East and I think over the country at large is overwhelming, and you cannot be too emphatic in regard to it." Republicans deplored "the timidity of the Republican platform on this head, whereas the Democrats and their candidate as represented by W. Dorsheimer were outspoken and almost defiant in their tone at St. Louis."[15]

Yet quite unlike civil service reform and the school question, Hayes was bombarded with conflicting advice on money from Indiana Republicans. They agreed, wrote one from Indianapolis, "that the *very least* said [about the money issue in Hayes's letter] the better for us. There is an all pervading demand for the repeal of the date fixed for resumption and any attempt to endorse the measure as it now stands would defeat us in this state *beyond any question*." "Say as few words as possible in amplification of currency resolution," pleaded another Indianan.[16] Hayes, in sum, would have to walk a very fine line, and ultimately he relied heavily on language that Schurz sent him on July 5.

Despite the immense pressure, Hayes delivered a first-rate letter—clear, forceful, and relatively short at eight paragraphs. Only a constitutional amendment, he wrote, could place public schools "beyond all danger of sectarian control or interference. The Republican party is pledged to secure such an amendment."[17] As for the currency question, "I regard all the laws of the United States relating to the payment of the public indebtedness, the legal-tender notes included, as constituting a pledge and the moral obligation of the Government, which must, in good faith, be kept." The uncertainty of businessmen that had caused the current depression "can be ended in but one way—the resumption of specie payment. . . . If elected, I shall approve every appropriate measure to accomplish the desired end, and shall oppose any step backward." Thus, although Hayes implied that repeal of the Specie Resumption Act would be such a step backward, he refused to endorse that law forthrightly.

The spoils system and especially congressmen's control over executive appointments, Hayes maintained, had destroyed the ideal of independent government service envisioned by the founders. Because congressmen and senators now allotted federal offices in their districts and states, "the offices in these cases have become not merely rewards for party service, but rewards for services to party leaders. This system destroys the independence of the separate departments of the Government. It tends directly to extravagance and official incapacity. It is a temptation to dishonesty." By impairing the executive's capacity for oversight of appointees' performance, "it obstructs the prompt removal and sure punishment of the unworthy." Thus, "in every way it degrades the civil service and the character of the Government." Hence the current patronage system must "be abolished. The reform should be thorough, radical, and complete." The founders "neither expected nor desired from the public servant any partisan service"; rather, they intended that civil servants should be secure in their tenure except for malfeasance or incapacity. "If elected, I shall conduct the administration of the Government upon these principles, and all the constitutional powers vested in the Executive will be employed to establish this reform." Then came the ten-strike. Because incumbent presidents could not resist abusing patronage to promote their own reelection, wrote Hayes, I now state "my inflexible purpose, if elected, not to be a candidate for" a second term.

Hayes devoted the last part of his letter to the South. The "first necessity" for complete southern recovery from the war, Hayes maintained, was "an intelligent and honest administration of the government, which shall protect all classes of citizens in their political and private rights. What the South most needs is peace; and peace depends upon the supremacy of the law." All southerners' constitutional rights must be honored. If so, the "always unfortunate" and potentially "disastrous" division of parties along racial and sectional lines could be ended. What is more, the federal government could then "promote . . . the efforts of the people of those states to obtain for themselves the blessings of honest and capable local government." What Hayes clearly implied here—in a bid to southern former Whigs, as the *New York Times* correctly surmised— was opposition to corrupt carpetbagger regimes and restoration of white home rule. "If elected," Hayes concluded in this preview of his policy toward the South, I "shall labor for this end. Let me assure my" southern countrymen that my administration "will be one which will regard and cherish their truest interests—the interests of the white and of the colored people, both and equally—and which will put forth its best efforts in behalf of a civil policy which will wipe out forever the distinction between North and South in our common country."

Hayes undoubtedly meant this. He would say much the same thing in his inaugural address nine months later. Yet within six weeks of the release of this letter, he was privately urging Republican speakers to wave the bloody shirt because "our main issue must be *it is not safe to allow the rebellion to come into power.*"[18] The publication of Hayes's letter ended his public role in the campaign. Presidential candidates did not personally campaign at that time; others did the work. Hayes, however, closely watched events and frequently offered private advice to the Republicans who carried the burden of getting him elected. Repeatedly, he privately wrote to Republican campaigners such as James Garfield, James G. Blaine, Oliver Morton, and Carl Schurz that "the true issue in the minds of the Masses is simply, shall the late rebels have the government?"[19]

William Wheeler's acceptance letter appeared in papers on July 20. It differed slightly from Hayes's effort. Unlike Hayes, Wheeler explicitly said that the 1875 Specie Resumption Act must be honored, not repealed. Unlike Hayes, Wheeler specifically called for a retrenchment of federal expenditures and the abolition of unnecessary federal offices. Unlike Hayes, Wheeler candidly admitted "the imperfections and short-comings" of the Republican Party even while praising "the honest purpose of its masses to retrieve all errors and to summarily punish all offenders against the laws of the country." Republicans, he concluded, appealed "to the intelligence and conscience of all who desire good government, good will, good money, and universal prosperity" for their "continued support."[20] Even August Belmont thought Wheeler had delivered an able letter that would help the Republicans. Nonetheless, public attention was understandably focused on Hayes's statement.

Reaction to Hayes's letter was mixed. Regulars such as Conkling, Morton, and Illinois' John Logan scoffed at the language about civil service reform. When Hayes also learned that Grant considered the one-term pledge an implied rebuke aimed at him, Hayes hastily assured Grant that he had meant nothing of the kind. Most Republicans and Liberal Republicans, in contrast, very much liked the letter. On July 20 Ethan Allen, chairman of the Liberal Republican National Committee, issued a public letter canceling a national nominating convention previously called to meet in Philadelphia on July 26.[21] Hayes's single-term pledge and commitment to civil service reform, he said, meant that all Liberals could and should support Hayes. Schurz now publicly endorsed Hayes, and he would work to convince Germans and other Liberals to back him. Nonetheless, Schurz worried for the remainder of the campaign that Hayes's initial letter did not suffice and that Hayes must say more to reassure the Liberals.

Schurz had two main concerns. First, the support of Hayes by Morton and Conkling men at Cincinnati, for the purpose of stopping Blaine's nomination, allowed Democrats to argue plausibly that Hayes was obligated to these notorious spoilsmen. Whatever his professions, Democrats charged, Hayes would be a prisoner of "Grantism" if elected. Only a change of parties, not just of Republican presidents, they repeatedly declared, could achieve the civil service reform sought by Liberals. Second, Schurz worried increasingly about assessments on federal office-holders' salaries to raise funds for the Republican campaign, a practice that flagrantly violated the promises of Hayes's acceptance letter.

Carl Schurz. The nation's most prominent Liberal Republican, Schurz showered Hayes with advice after his nomination and campaigned hard for him. (Courtesy of the Library of Congress. LC-USZ62–15582.)

That concern, in turn, was occasioned by the leadership of the Republican National Committee. Like the Democrats, state Republican delegations to the national convention had selected their members of the national committee, but the election of its officers was deferred to a meeting of the committee in Philadelphia on July 8. The function of the Republican committee, like that of its Democratic counterpart, was to coordinate speakers' tours among the different states, prepare and distribute campaign literature, and, most important, raise and allot money. Fund-raising was the main reason both parties located their committee headquarters in New York City, although Republicans would divide their executive committee between New York and a western headquarters in Chicago. Composed of members from every state and, for Republicans, federal territories, national committees were far too large and unwieldy to manage a campaign. Smaller executive committees had that responsibility, and the national chairman chose those committees.

From the moment of Hayes's nomination, Edward F. Noyes, Ohio's committee member, worried that the chairman and executive committee might be hostile to Hayes's interests. Roscoe Conkling was hoping to replace Republicans' longtime national chairman Edwin D. Morgan, a prodigious fund-raiser, with Alonzo B. Cornell, chairman of the New York Republican state committee. Noyes also knew that New Hampshire's William E. Chandler, secretary of the national committee for the previous eight years, was Blaine's choice for chairman and that Chandler was busy gathering proxies from southern and western states that were unlikely to send men to Philadelphia. Thus Noyes set out to gather proxies of his own and eventually had Ohioans representing Louisiana, Arkansas, and Nevada at Philadelphia. He also pressed Hayes to get Chandler to remain on as secretary, but Chandler refused Hayes's request.

Noyes initially preferred Cornell for the chairmanship. But when Morgan warned Hayes that Cornell would be a disaster, since he could raise no money from New York businessmen, who dismissed him as a partisan hack, Noyes decided to seek the chairmanship himself at Philadelphia. The meeting itself was surprisingly well attended, with only Kansas, West Virginia, and Arizona Territory lacking representation. Republican rules mandated that a majority of the entire committee, not just those in attendance and voting, choose the national chairman. Hence it took 25 of 49 votes for election. New Hampshire's Chandler had dropped out of the running. On the first ballot, Noyes got 11 votes and Cornell 10. The front-runner was Michigan's Zachariah Chandler, with 22 votes. On the second ballot, Chandler received 26 votes, but he deferred appointing an executive committee until a later date.

The choice of Chandler was a mistake, if not an unmitigated disaster. By itself, it almost neutralized everything Hayes had done to reach out to Liberals. As secretary of the interior in Grant's administration, Chandler provided proof that Republicans could never escape "Grantism." But his job in Washington also meant that Chandler would be an absentee national chairman and that its executive committee and secretary would have to do most of the work. For that latter post, the meeting chose the little-known R. C. McCormick (coincidentally, Allen G. Thurman's son-in-law), Arizona Territory's member of the committee who never made it to Philadelphia. During the campaign, McCormick was frequently at odds with Chandler and repeatedly threatened to quit.

Zach Chandler's Washington job also impaired his ability to solicit money personally from businessmen in New York and Boston, the traditional foci of Republican fund-raising, although both parties found their usual moneymen strapped for cash because of the depression. Chandler, in any event, had his own ideas about an alternative source for the "sinews of war." Of what use was control of the national executive branch, Chandler believed, if Republicans could not assess the salaries of those thousands of federal jobholders? Almost as soon as he was elected, Chandler, without seeking permission from the committee, geared up a thorough and ruthless operation to extract 2 percent of the annual salaries of clerks and others in federal departments. Every payday for the remainder of the campaign, his agents forced hapless federal workers to fork over the 2 percent of their salaries. These were the "assessments" that so appalled Schurz and other Liberals.

As early as July 24, Hayes assured Schurz, "I think this assessment business will not be pushed by our committee." Technically, Hayes was correct. Chandler's minions, not the national committee, relentlessly harassed federal employees to pony up. "I hate assessments," Hayes sighed in a letter to William H. Smith on August 10, as evidence of Chandler's doings mounted. By September, eastern newspapers were printing stories of the assessments. "If assessments are made as charged," an exasperated Hayes wrote to McCormick on September 8, "it is a plain departure from correct principles and ought not to be allowed. I trust the committee will have nothing to do with it."[22]

For all his private assurances and protests, however, Hayes repeatedly refused to heed Schurz's pleas that he issue more public statements, in the form of letters or speeches, reaffirming his opposition to partisan exploitation of the federal workforce. Why? One can only speculate. A gentleman and a scholar (as Noyes had called him at Cincinnati), Hayes may have deemed further public statements unseemly and improper personal electioneering. More likely, he thought no further reassurances were necessary to bring Liberal Republicans back to the Republican column. As early as mid-July, fear that ex-Confederates would take control of the federal government should Tilden win seemed enough to do the trick. Here, two pieces of evidence suffice to explain Hayes's confidence.

On July 6 the *New York Times* republished a letter that John D. Defrees had written to the *Indianapolis News*. Now a resident of Washington, D.C., Defrees had once been the leading Whig and Republican newspaper editor in Indiana before becoming a leader of the Liberal Republican movement there in 1872. Announcing his support for Hayes and Wheeler, Defrees asserted that there was only one issue in 1876: "Shall the control of the Government be handed over to those who attempted its destruction or be retained by those who hazarded life and fortune for its preservation. . . . When thus presented no union man need be told his duty." Then Defrees added another reason why Indianans should not support the Democrats, one clearly aimed at hard-handed, anti-railroad farmers: "The St. Louis convention selected a very nice, prim, little, withered-up, fidgety old bachelor, about one-hundred and twenty-pounds avoirdupois, who never had a genuine impulse for man nor any affection for woman, the very prince of 'Wall Street speculators and coupon clippers' as a true representative of the Democratic party!"[23] In other words, how could real men vote for such an effete featherweight?

Then, on July 8 and 9, a shoot-out between black state militia members and armed whites occurred in Hamburg, South Carolina. The whites came from surrounding Edgefield County and nearby Augusta, Georgia. Accounts of this fracas differ, but between five and ten blacks had been shot dead, most of them unarmed after they had already surrendered. News of the Hamburg "massacre" proved the tipping point for Thomas Wentworth Higginson of Massachusetts. Higginson had commanded a regiment of black troops in the Civil War, joined the Liberal Republican movement in 1872, and attended the Fifth Avenue Hotel meeting in May 1876. The Hamburg massacre, he wrote in a letter to the editor of the *New York Times* in mid-July, dictated that Liberal Republicans must support Hayes. "Of what use are all our [Liberals'] efforts to lay aside the issues of the war," asked Higginson, "if they are to be kept alive by our white fellow-citizens of the South? The spirit that sends armed men [from Georgia] across the South Carolina border today may just as easily send them across the Pennsylvania border next year, if it secures the aid of a Democratic national administration."[24] It is little wonder that Hayes assured Congressman James A. Garfield in early August that *"the danger of giving the rebels the government,* is the topic that people are most interested in."[25] In this letter, Hayes also mentioned the Catholic school question, Tilden, and his one-term pledge as key issues. A Liberal backlash against Chandler's ham-handed assessment program did not make his list.

Schurz was not the only civil service reformer who was worried that Hayes and his Ohio Republican allies were not doing enough to reassure Liberal Republicans on the reform issue. By the fall, New Yorker Curtis was badgering Hayes with complaints that Ohio Republicans had downplayed reform both before and after that state's October election, whose outcome Democrats and Republicans alike deemed crucial. Hayes assured Curtis that all Ohio Republicans supported reform, but they cared much more about southern Democrats' threat to retake control of the national government and the Catholic threat to public schools. It was those issues, not reform, averred Hayes, that would bring them to the polls.

Even crusty Republican regulars such as Indiana's Oliver Morton, who privately expressed contempt for goody-goody reformers like Schurz, could help blunt Democrats' edge in the competition for Liberals by publicly skewering the Democrats' self-announced credentials as reformers. Although the crippled Morton needed two canes to hobble around and could give speeches only while seated, he was a master of bloody-shirt oratory. Once Congress finally adjourned in August, Morton returned to Indianapolis and there delivered the following blast. The Democratic Party, he told his adoring Republican audience on August 11, consists of "hungry cormorants, long-deterred expectants, gangrened instigators of rebellion, the Northern sympathizers who trod the narrow isthmus between open treason and resistance to the Government fighting for its life, the slave drivers who have lost their occupation, and the innumerable caravan of dead-beats and adventurers." Anyone who believed that this crowd favored reform, Morton deadpanned, "must indeed be the most hopeless of idiots."[26]

Democrats had always anticipated a Republican bloody-shirt campaign. To defuse it, both northern and southern Democratic state platforms since the early 1870s had pronounced the sectional issues associated with the Civil War to be permanently settled. For the same reason, their St. Louis national platform condemned Republicans' attempts to reignite "sectional hate" as a desperate effort to divert public attention from their own corrupt record and the paramount need for "reform." Accordingly, Democrats deplored the news about Hamburg, and northern Democrats in Congress implored their southern colleagues to publicly denounce the killings. Some southerners, desperate for a Democratic victory, simply hoped that the other shoe would not drop before November. "There is no doubt of Tilden's election unless Jeff Davis writes a letter from Liverpool or Ben Hill should make a speech in defense of Andersonville," wrote an Alabamian.[27]

Nonetheless, in the days and weeks following Tilden's nomination, his closest allies worried most—and with good reason—about the awkward straddle on the money question adopted in St. Louis. Correspondents, including Liberals such as Charles Francis Adams Jr., warned Tilden that this two-faced stance alienated eastern Liberal Republicans, whom Tilden had courted so avidly since 1874. "I am afloat," Yale's William Graham Sumner wrote to Marble on July 10. "I w[oul]d vote for Tilden if it were not for Hendricks."[28]

Hendricks compounded the problem when he briefly addressed an Indianapolis crowd on the night of June 29. Precisely what Hendricks said is unclear, but the Republican *New York Times* quoted him as asserting that "the platform adopted at St. Louis declared that the resumption clause of the act adopted in 1875 shall be repealed, and the repeal of that clause carries with it every feature of the law which is bringing about the contraction so hurtful to the interests of the country."[29] This language could be and was interpreted in various ways. All of them outraged hard-money men, because Hendricks had pointedly ignored the remainder of the plank that committed the Democrats to specie resumption. Some believed that Hendricks meant that if the January 1, 1879, date for resumption were repealed, resumption would never be achieved because there would be no further attempt to reduce the greenbacks in circulation. Others believed that he meant exactly what Thomas Ewing Jr. had argued at St. Louis should be the Democrats' platform: a pledge to repeal the entire third section of the Specie Resumption Act, not simply the January 1, 1879, deadline.

"If you could do anything to induce Governor Hendricks of Indiana *not* to accept his nomination, you would do a good thing for the Democracy," one appalled Democrat wrote to Tilden in mid-July. "With him you will have a big load to carry. . . . In short, he spoils your chances in the East and is of no advantage to you in the West."[30] Other alarmed Democrats recognized the impossibility of dumping Hendricks from the ticket. They instead begged Tilden and Abram Hewitt, the Democrats' national chairman, to rectify the damage Hendricks had done, make sure that Tilden's and Hendricks's acceptance letters "give the same interpretation of our platform purposes," and stop Hendricks from "giving a strained construction of the platform on the currency resumption."[31] "If Tilden & Hendricks cannot agree upon harmonious treatment of the currency question in the acceptance letters," August Belmont groaned in late July, "we may as well give up at once."[32]

Tilden "well understood that I shall have to make up all deficiencies which anybody else speaking for the party shall create" and recognized that he must coordinate the language in his letter with that of Hendricks.[33] For the latter purpose, he invited Hendricks to meet him in Saratoga, New York, on July 15. Before heading east, however, Hendricks aggravated their breach by telegraphing an Indiana congressman that House Democrats must repeal the resumption clause of the 1875 act immediately to comply with the platform's mandate. On his return from Saratoga he repeated that insistence to Democrats in Cleveland. Hard-money Democrats were appalled. They realized they had little hope of substituting a new measure pointing toward resumption if the resumption clause were repealed. "We are doing so well where the Convention left us that it is tempting fortune and fate for the House to tamper with the situation," a deeply concerned Tilden wrote to Hewitt, a member of the House Banking and Currency Committee, on July 15 after his first meeting with Hendricks. "At any rate, *our friends had better not commit themselves to details of a new proposition until after the letters of acceptance are out.*" Rather than spotlighting their internal divisions over money, said Tilden, "we should exalt the reform issue on which we are united, and on which our antagonists can not resist us or defend themselves until it absorbs the whole public attention."[34] Just as Hewitt and other hard-money Democrats had stalled to prevent western Democratic congressmen from pushing for repeal until after the Democratic convention adopted a platform, they now stalled to await Tilden's long-delayed letter.

One view of the Democratic national ticket: The "Grand National
Democratic Banner," printed by Currier and Ives, stresses the reform issue
on which Tilden and Hendricks agreed. (Courtesy of the Library of Congress.
LC-USZ62–14981.)

THE BETTING REFORM CAMPAIGN "PUT UP OR SHUT UP."

"REFORM IS NECESSARY IN BETTING.
"REFORM IS NECESSARY IN GAMBLERS.
REFORM IS NECESSARY IN SHAM REFORMERS
"REFORM IS NECESSARY IN HUMBUG.
REFORM IS NECESSARY IN POLITICAL TRICKSTERS.
"REFORM IS NECESSARY IN RED TAPE.
REFORM IS NECESSARY IN THE RAG BABY.

July 22, 1876

Another view of the Democratic national ticket: Thomas Nast's devilish cartoon from July 22, 1876, titled "The Democratic (Deformed) Tiger 'Fixed,'" highlights the ticket's two-faced stance on the money issue. (From Morton Keller, The Art and Politics of Thomas Nast *[New York: Oxford University Press, 1968].)*

Tilden received plenty of advice on topics other than the need to off-set Hendricks, who repeatedly wrote to Tilden that instant repeal of the resumption clause would assure Democratic triumphs in both Ohio and Indiana. One New Jersey man, for example, begged Tilden to stress the suffering of the unemployed, a topic Hayes had skirted. "The mass of the laboring classes will rejoice at an encouraging word from you on these points. It is the great prostration of business and the poverty of the people that will be one of the principle [sic] causes of electing you."[35] Like Hayes, Tilden also received advice from westerners warning that any explicit commitment to resumption would drive western voters to the Greenback ticket. A New Yorker advised just the opposite. Hayes's acceptance letter, he sneered, showed that he had no more intelligence "than a child" and thus had left Tilden "a clear field." Since Hayes had relied exclusively on "barren promises" about resumption, Tilden should list the concrete measures necessary to achieve it. "Let the people see that you are not, as your rival certainly is, a mere puppet in the hands of others. Speak, speak as if ex cathedra, for your position now . . . will cause anything you say, that appears to come from conscious power to handle the subject, to sink deep in the public mind."[36]

Tilden did speak, or at least write—and at considerable length. After a second meeting with Hendricks at Saratoga on July 28, where the two men compared notes, and a third on August 4, Tilden and Hendricks re-leased their letters simultaneously from that posh resort. A 5,000-word dissertation, Tilden's lengthy opus mixed ingenious analysis and adroit argument with sheer poppycock. Tilden began with the economic situa-tion and what might mend it. Excessive taxation by the government, or "consumption," as he called it, since the end of the Civil War had caused the depression that "is depriving labor of its employment, and carrying want into so many homes."[37] By Tilden's calculations, federal taxes had amounted to $4.5 billion since 1865, and those of state and local govern-ments $3 billion more. This drain of money and potential investment capital from the private economic sector was the cause of the depression, and, Tilden boasted, he had presciently warned of this inevitable result as early as 1865. Had Republican governments recycled that money in ways that promoted general prosperity, the impact would not have been so severe. Instead, Republicans had wasted it on bloated public payrolls, government-funded boondoggles, and sheer theft. Therefore, the way to revive the economy was to retrench governmental expenditures, slash taxes, and allow the people to keep their own money.

Modern economic historians have demonstrated that Tilden's analysis was flatly wrong. For fifteen years after the Civil War, annual federal revenues did exceed ordinary expenses by a considerable amount. But the government used that surplus to buy back war bonds, a fact that Sherman, among other Republicans, touted in his 1876 campaign speeches. Thus Washington pumped hundreds of millions of dollars back into the private economic sector, and much of that money served as investment capital in manufacturing enterprises. Whatever caused the depression, it was not a money shortage produced by excessive taxation. Nor would slashing taxes end it.

A secondary cause of the current hard times, according to Tilden, was "the systematic and insupportable misgovernment imposed on the South." Worthless bonds were overissued, destroying public credit. "Oppressive" taxes confiscated property and "destroyed its market value," thus undercutting "the prosperity of the whole country." Other than an obligatory pledge to protect the rights of all citizens if elected, this was all Tilden said about "the Southern Question," in sharp contrast to Hayes's fuller discussion.

Tilden's prescriptions for the money question made more sense. Democrats' national platform, he averred, "demanded . . . a resumption of specie payments on the legal-tender notes of the United States." Resumption also required that national banks be able to redeem their notes in gold. To do that, Tilden astutely argued, the federal government should sell for gold the U.S. bonds each national bank had been required to deposit in exchange for the national banknotes it issued. The gold would then be distributed to the banks so that they could resume specie payment on national banknotes "without contracting their loans to their customers, or calling on any private debtor for payment." Government interest payments would remain the same; they would simply go to the new bondholders rather than to the national banks. Here, Tilden made a brilliant, if only implicit, appeal to western Democrats who hated national bankers and feared an increase in interest payments on bonds under the terms of the Specie Resumption Act.

Nor, according to Tilden, would resuming specie payments for greenbacks require any contraction of their circulation. If the government slashed frivolous expenditures, accumulated the resulting savings, and sold bonds abroad for gold, it would soon have enough to bring most greenbacks to par with gold. To absorb the remainder, the government could sell interest-bearing bonds purchasable in greenbacks.

The best time for resumption, Tilden added, was the earliest time it could be done with "a certainty and ease that will inspire confidence and encourage the reviving of business." Setting an arbitrary date was foolish. Without adequate preparations, "a legislative command fixing a day" was a "sham," "a snare and a delusion." Since January 1875, when the Specie Resumption Act was passed, the Republican administration had made no such preparations. "It cannot be doubted that the substitution of 'a system of preparation' without the promise of a day, for the worthless promise of a day without 'a system of preparation,' would be the gain of the substance of resumption in exchange for its shadow."

Tilden ended his letter with a discussion of civil service reform but added little to what the platform had already said about Republican malfeasance and the need to appoint honest men. He did, however, aim a zinger at Hayes's one-term pledge. To discourage "delusive expectations," he felt compelled to express his "conviction that no reform of the civil service in this country will be complete and permanent until its Chief Magistrate is constitutionally disqualified from re-election; experience having repeatedly exposed the futility of self-imposed restrictions by candidates or incumbents."

Eastern hard-money Democrats and some Liberal Republicans loudly cheered Tilden's letter and promised their support. Among Liberal Republicans, for example, the entire Adams clan in Massachusetts and Yale's William Graham Sumner came on board. Charles Francis Adams Jr. would publish a series of articles urging other Liberals to support Tilden. Those same men had long regarded Thomas Hendricks as a loose cannon, yet his letter, in part because of its brevity compared with Tilden's tome, was in many ways a more effective campaign document—keeping in mind that only a small fraction of the potential electorate bothered to read these things.

The letter also showed that in their consultations Tilden had convinced Hendricks that he must reassure Liberal Republicans on the money question. Hendricks reaffirmed his position that the Democratic platform committed the party and its representatives in Congress to immediate repeal of the date fixed for resumption in the Republicans' Specie Resumption Act. But he insisted that "no one desires a return to specie payments more earnestly than I do" and that he regarded "an inflation of the currency" as inimical to the restoration of prosperity as "artificial measures for the contraction of the currency."[38] He did not understand repeal of the resumption clause "to be a backward step in our return to specie payments but the recovery of a false step." Democrats' determination to achieve that repeal because it was a "hindrance" to resumption had "been distinctly declared" at St. Louis. Resumption, he argued, could be achieved without "producing an artificial scarcity of currency or disturbing public or commercial credit." And Democrats would achieve it in a short time by pursuing "wiser financial policies" that relied on the retrenchment of governmental expenditures and the promotion of prosperity.

Of course, Hayes and Wheeler too had promised to promote prosperity while acknowledging hard times, but what is striking is that none of the four men, nor either national platform, said a word about immediate *relief* for the destitute. Instead of increased public expenditures and governmental job programs for the unemployed, which Democrats had used during James Buchanan's administration to combat the relatively mild depression after the panic of 1857, they spoke of slashing governmental expenditures, firing federal employees, and reducing taxes on the propertied. The need to court Liberal Republicans obviously explains this tack, but it hardly promised help to unemployed men who could barely feed their families.

As the "ins" during a severe depression, Republicans had already incurred the electorate's wrath, and Hayes, for one, considered "Hard Times" the Republicans' "deadliest foe."[39] With regard to Ohio's important October election, Hayes told ex-Congressman John A. Bingham that "the result is much in doubt, simply because the times are so hard, and the cry for change is so popular. If the money pressure was less severe and the demand for labor better, there would hardly be a contest."[40] A few days before the November election, Hayes wrote in his diary, "The hard times, if we are beaten, may be assigned as the great and sufficient cause."[41]

Nonetheless, Democrats continued to stress administrative "reform" rather than presenting any concrete proposals for immediate economic relief that might help the destitute. At least one experienced Democratic leader considered this tack a mistake that might hand the Republicans victory. On October 25, Horatio Seymour, the Democratic presidential candidate in 1868, flatly warned Tilden that he was going to lose the votes of suffering Irish Catholic laborers in towns and cities. "The word 'reform' is not popular with working men. To them it means less money spent and less work."[42] Democrats' failure to offer a credible and distinctive program for ending hard times, in short, probably contributed to Republicans' remarkable comeback in the elections of 1876.

Like Tilden, Hendricks announced his commitment to civil service reform in his letter. Like Tilden as well, he included the obligatory promise that Democrats, if elected, would protect the constitutional rights of black and white citizens alike. Yet Hendricks, quite unlike Tilden, devoted most of his adroit discussion of the South to a blistering attack on Republicans' waving of the bloody shirt. "I regard the man who would arouse and foster sectional antagonisms among his countrymen as a dangerous enemy to his country," Hendricks declared. "The strife between sections and between races will cease as soon as a power for evil [i.e., control of the federal government] is taken away from a party that makes political gain out of scenes of violence and bloodshed."

Finally, Hendricks addressed a question that Tilden had utterly ignored in his own letter—Republican fear-mongering about Catholics' purported assault on public schools. "The man or party that would involve our schools in political or sectarian controversy is an enemy to the schools," averred Hendricks. Without mentioning Republicans' call for a constitutional amendment on the matter, he disparaged its necessity. "The common schools are safer under the protecting care of all the people than under the control of any party or sect. They must neither be sectarian nor partisan, and there must be neither division nor misappropriation of the funds for their support."

On the very day that Tilden and Hendricks released their letters, in fact, House Democrats finally got around to acting on the constitutional amendment Blaine had presented in mid-December. On August 4 Democrats reported Blaine's proposed sixteenth amendment from the House Judiciary Committee, which had unanimously agreed to it, with one minor and one significant addition. The key section of Blaine's amendment, which Democrats kept, read: "and no money raised by taxation in any State for the support of public schools, or derived from any public fund therefore, nor any public lands devoted thereto, shall ever be under the control of any religious sect [the committee inserted 'or denomination' here]; nor shall any money so raised or land so devoted be divided between religious sects or denominations." But then the committee's Democratic majority added the following language: "This article shall not vest, enlarge, or diminish legislative power in the Congress."[43] This language clearly reflected the state's rights sensibilities of Democrats who abhorred as heinous centralization the language of the Thirteenth, Fourteenth, and Fifteenth Amendments explicitly granting power to Congress to enforce them with "appropriate legislation." Republicans immediately protested that the sentence rendered the amendment a nullity, for Congress would have no power to stop state and local officials from flouting it. Nonetheless, Democrats had the votes in the House, and they forced a vote the next day. This proposed sixteenth amendment garnered the necessary two-thirds majority by a vote of 180 to 7, with 98 men, including almost all Republicans, abstaining.

Hayes observed this proceeding with great interest from Columbus. Virtually from the moment of his nomination, he had urged Ohio Republicans in Congress such as Garfield and Sherman to give speeches demanding passage of Blaine's amendment that could be used as campaign documents against the Democrats. On August 4 he again pressed Garfield for a speech pillorying the Democrats' attempt to bury Blaine's amendment in committee. After reading reports of the August 4 proceedings, Hayes asked Garfield, "Is it not an effort to get rid of an issue without accomplishing what the public sentiment demands? It seems to me you should amend it. Strike out the clause that gives Congress *no* legislative power, and insert the usual clause giving Congress power to enforce it by appropriate legislation."[44]

On August 7, the very day the Senate took up the amendment passed by the House, Hayes wrote to Sherman that "the House has made a serious mistake" in adopting it. Here he pointed out other flaws in the proposal—flaws that, although Hayes did not say so, also existed in the amendment Blaine had originally proposed. "Schools are aided in New York and other places by appropriations from public funds, which are plainly sectarian in character. Those funds . . . may be from taxation for general purposes. The thing to be prohibited is not merely a *division of school funds* but the application of *any public* money to the sectarian schools." Hayes then urged that Republicans amend the House version in the Senate, adding the usual language about Congress's enforcement powers, and return it to the House. "If the House refuses to concur, it will make an issue which will destroy all chances of Democratic success in the fall."[45]

Upon receiving Hayes's letter, Sherman gave it to New Jersey Senator Frederick Frelinghuysen, who had already noted the same loopholes. After flaying the powerlessness of the federal government to enforce the ban on public aid to Catholic schools, Frelinghuysen noted that "a more serious objection" was that the proposed amendment applied only to divisions of public school funds. "There is not a word in the amendment that prohibits public money from being appropriated to theological seminaries, to reformatories, to monasteries, to nunneries, to houses of the Good Shepherd, and many kindred purposes." In some states Catholics had been taxed to support Protestant institutions, and in others Protestants taxed to fund Catholic institutions. This must be stopped. Besides, he added, since the amendment referred only to public school funds, it did not prohibit the use of other taxes to aid sectarian schools. Thus Frelinghuysen proposed an alternative amendment for the Senate's consideration, as did other Republicans. Indiana's gruff Morton summed up the Republican objections: the House version had so many holes "that you can drive an omnibus through it."[46]

The Republican-dominated Senate Judiciary Committee reported a new amendment on which the Senate voted on August 17, over strident Democratic protests. It prohibited the appropriation and use of any public property, revenue, or bonds for "the support of any school, educational or other institution under the control of any religious or anti-religious sect, organization, or denomination" or of any institution where religious creeds were taught. Furthermore, it prohibited the teaching of any religious creeds in schools or institutions that received public funding, with one important exception that was certain to infuriate Catholics. "This article shall not be construed to prohibit the reading of the Bible in any school or institution."[47] This Republican version also granted authority to Congress to enforce it with appropriate legislation.

Republicans lacked a two-thirds majority in the Senate, and the amendment failed by a vote of 28 to 16. Every Republican vote was in the affirmative, and all the negative votes were by Democrats. Nonetheless, 27 senators did not vote because they were absent, paired, or abstaining. Thus House Democrats would not have a chance to reject the Senate amendment and hand Republicans the election, as Hayes had hoped. Still, he took the outcome philosophically. To him, the presentation of a Republican alternative sufficed, whether or not it passed. "As to the school issue, the Dems are so afraid of it that they will perhaps do anything to get it out of the way," he wrote to Garfield five days before the Senate voted. "The question is now in good shape just as it stands. The Senate Committee has reported *our* amendment, and the House gave the Democratic amendment. Let the people choose. It is not important to pass it through the Senate at this Session. Let it be debated, and considered by the Country."[48]

Well into the fall, Hayes considered "the School or Catholic question" to be a winner for Republicans.[49] Hayes probably erred in this assessment. By passing an amendment in the House that was virtually identical to Blaine's original proposal, which lacked any language whatsoever about congressional enforcement, Democrats had gone far toward neutralizing the issue. Contrary to Hayes's analysis, voters might not see much difference between the House and Senate versions.

While Congress was debating different versions of the Blaine Amendment, House Democrats finally moved to repeal the resumption clause—that is, the January 1, 1879, date for resumption—of the Specie Resumption Act. The beleaguered Abram Hewitt, trying to juggle his dual roles as national committee chairman and Tilden's man on the House Banking and Currency Committee, had struggled for weeks to stop impetuous western Democrats from attempting repeal in the hope that the acceptance letters of his party's candidates would deter any action before Congress adjourned. The letters, of course, did no such thing. Tilden implicitly condoned repeal, and Hendricks once again explicitly demanded it. Thus Hewitt's last defense crumbled. Democrats brought a repeal bill to the floor on August 5, the very day newspapers published the Democratic candidates' letters. Hewitt sought to substitute a bill to appoint a committee to study the most effective ways to prepare for resumption and report its findings in December, but his motion failed by 12 votes. The House then passed the repeal measure by a vote of 106 to 86. Hewitt wrote to Tilden on August 6 that "all the hard money men" voted against repeal, and if the 101 House members absent from the vote had been present, it would have lost. In fact, 25 Democrats, 19 of them from the East, opposed repeal. Still, Democrats bore the responsibility. Republicans split 9 to 61 against repeal; Democrats split 97 to 25 in favor.

The weary Hewitt greeted this result as philosophically as Hayes had accepted the congressional stalemate on the constitutional amendment. "There was no hard feeling & no bitterness remains," he exulted to Tilden. "The hard money men have made their record & the soft money men have got the repeal, and no longer any excuse for not carrying their states." The matter "is in the best possible shape. The party is committed to specie payment by the platform & your admirable letter, and by Hendricks' mushy acquiescence." To boot, after the vote on repeal, Democrats had immediately passed a resolution establishing a commission to study resumption, "so that we can say that we have made provision for investigation and elaboration of a practical scheme for resumption. On the whole I now think that the matter has been managed as well as the difficulties of the situation would admit."[50]

As all Democrats, including Hendricks, had recognized all along, the House action was sheer posturing, since the Republican Senate would never consider, let alone approve, repeal legislation. Nor did anyone believe that the Democrats stood within reach of taking the Senate. Hence a stalemate had developed on the vexing money question. Both parties promised specie resumption as soon as practically possible. Now, neither spoke about a draconian contraction of the currency supply. Western Democrats' demand for abolition of the national banking system and substitution of greenbacks for national banknotes had been ignored. For voters who insisted on that outcome, the separate Greenback Party seemed the only option, and both Democratic and Republican leaders in Ohio and Indiana feared defections to that ticket. Otherwise, voters were confronted with two major parties that had approached congruence on the money question. During the last two or three months of the campaign, it became less and less salient.

By late August, indeed, the parties had also approached congruence on the civil service reform and Catholic school issues. In the competition for Liberal Republican support, Democrats clearly had an edge on the reform issue. Their cry that a new party, not just a new Republican president, was needed to clean out the Augean stables in Washington had force. Zach Chandler, William E. Chandler, James G. Blaine, Simon and Don Cameron, Oliver Morton, and other well-known spoilsmen working for Hayes's election gave that cry additional force. Yet the Democrats also had a vulnerability, one that Tilden and his campaign team were well aware of—their southern wing. Southern Democrats, including South Carolina gubernatorial candidate Wade Hampton, assured Tilden that they would do all they could not to embarrass his chances in the North, but the northern Republican press pounced on every story of ex-Confederates intimidating, murdering, and maiming blacks in the South to prevent them from voting. "CONDITION OF THE SOUTH: THE MISSISSIPPI PLAN IN SOUTH CAROLINA," screamed a headline in the *New York Times* on October 10. The *Times* and other Republican papers also reported stories about the forceful suppression of the black vote in Alabama, Georgia, Mississippi, and Louisiana. In one issue, the *Times* listed the name of every Union army veteran fired from his position by the Democratic House of Representatives and every Confederate veteran hired to replace them. The bloody shirt, as Hayes recognized, was Republicans' strongest weapon. It could offset Democrats' appeal to Liberals on the reform issue, and it could rouse Union army veterans and other Republican regulars who had stood by Grant in 1872.

By September, if not earlier, the two candidates had reached a stalemate of sorts on campaign issues. On some, they had neutralized each other; on others, the balance in terms of influencing voters tipped in opposite directions, at least in the North, where both parties focused their attention. To break that stalemate, both turned to smearing the rival candidate, perfecting organizations that could turn out the vote (a task that required gobs of money, whether used legally or illegally), and above all, winning the state elections taking place before the presidential showdown on November 7. Rightly or wrongly, both Republican and Democratic leaders believed that those state results, especially in Ohio, Indiana, and West Virginia, could generate the momentum to determine November's outcome.

With a few notable exceptions, attempts to smear the other party's standard-bearer sought primarily to deter Liberal Republicans, rather than rank-and-file supporters, from supporting him. The Fifth Avenue Hotel meeting in May had pronounced personal honesty the chief criterion for any presidential candidate. In his public letter canceling the proposed Liberal Republican national convention in Philadelphia and endorsing Hayes and Wheeler, Ethan Allen also declared that "the great distinction" of the Republican nominees "is that they are thoroughly honest as well as capable." Thus each party challenged the honesty of the other's candidate, as well as his credibility as a reformer.

Attacking the corruption, peculation, and dishonesty of Republican officeholders was the mainstay of the Democratic campaign from the start. Democratic speakers and newspaper editors asked for and received from the Democratic National Committee detailed lists of every Republican scandal that had been unearthed. Attaching this mud to the upright Hayes personally, however, proved difficult. Nonetheless, Democrats tried. Some spread utterly spurious stories that, on two occasions during the war, Hayes had pocketed money enlisted men had given him to send to their families. Outraged, Hayes gathered testimony from officers who had served with him in West Virginia to explode those charges, but it proved to be unnecessary because very few people believed the smears. In retaliation for Republican charges about Tilden's record as a taxpayer during the war, some enterprising Democrats discovered that Hayes had filed no income tax returns for 1868 and 1869, his first term as Ohio's governor. This exposure deeply embarrassed Hayes. "If no returns were made in the two years 1868 and 1869," he groused to his diary, "it was because no returns were called for," since his income was so low in those years.[51]

By far, the most potentially damaging charge Democrats leveled against Hayes sought to deter Germans, not just Liberal Republicans, from voting for him. Hayes, they cried, was a Know-Nothing bigot whom no foreigner dared support. The basis of this allegation was a letter that Hayes's secretary, Alfred E. Lee, had written in July (without Hayes's knowledge) to a nativist organization known as the American Alliance, thanking it for endorsing Hayes's candidacy. Somehow Democrats found this letter, and in early October every Democratic newspaper in the country printed a facsimile of it. That exposure sent Republicans in Wisconsin and Chicago into a tizzy because of its likely impact on Germans. Hayes assured Schurz, William H. Smith, and others that the charge was false and that Germans in Cincinnati would attest to that fact. "It is perfectly well-known [in Ohio] that I do not favor the exclusion of foreigners from the ballot or from office, and that I *do oppose* Catholic interference and all sectarian interference with political affairs, and especially with the schools," he wrote to R. C. McCormick on October 14. "This last point is influential, particularly with non-Catholic foreigners. It has not, I suspect, been sufficiently urged in the canvass."[52] "The Know Nothing charges are more than met," he assured Smith six days later, "by charging Democrats with their Catholic alliance. It is felt by our Protestants and free thinkers [among Germans] to be both important and true. Tilden's Gray Nuns Act with suitable headlines and comments is a complete reply."[53] Here Hayes referred to Tilden's signing into law in 1875 a Democratic measure allowing Roman Catholic nuns to teach in New York's public schools, a law that the new Republican majority in the state legislature immediately repealed in 1876. If Democrats were going to stigmatize Hayes personally as an anti-immigrant bigot, Hayes wanted Republicans to tar Tilden personally as a lackey of the Catholic Church, even though Tilden had in fact signed the repeal of the Gray Nuns Act. Unlike many other Republicans who were downplaying the religious issue by October, as his lament to McCormick makes clear, Hayes continued to believe that anti-Catholicism was a potent Republican weapon until the end of the campaign.[54]

Democrats' few attempts to smear Hayes paled beside the savage personal attacks Republicans launched against Tilden. Long before his nomination and throughout the subsequent campaign, the *New York Times* labeled Tilden a sham reformer. Tilden, it cried, had cooperated with Boss Tweed until the *Times* had exposed him. As of the summer of 1876, his much-touted commission investigating New York's canal ring had netted only a single conviction. Republican laws passed in 1874, not Tilden's oversight in 1875, had reduced state expenditures, contrary to Tilden's boasts that he had done it. More important, the *Times* as well as other Republican newspapers and campaign speakers charged that Tilden had illegally appropriated railroad bonds for his personal profit. Those papers gleefully pointed to a lawsuit by the St. Louis, Alton, and Terre Haute Railroad charging that Tilden had stolen $775,000 worth of stocks and bonds. Tilden's business career, Sherman charged in one campaign speech, had been spent in "the wrecking of corporations."[55] "Had Mr. Tilden been content to rank with the Fisks and Goulds and Scotts of the Democratic Party, the story of the railroad wrecks, and the devices by which he enriched himself at the expense of confiding shareholders and bondholders, would have possessed no special interest," concurred one *New York Times* editorial. But that record disqualified Tilden for the presidency.[56]

Although neither Republicans nor Democrats had offered any prospect of immediate relief to unemployed and desperate workers, the former used their attacks on Tilden's business career to expose the hypocrisy of his alleged sympathy for the suffering poor. According to the *Times,* which clearly influenced scores of other Republican newspapers as well as Republican campaign speakers, Tilden was a greedy financier who took over companies, bled their assets dry for his own profit, and then left their employees to deal with the wreckage. One accusation charged that Tilden owned a mine in Michigan and had illegally paid its workers in company store scrip, rather than real money, defrauding the government of tax revenue in the bargain. After gaining control of an iron mill in the small town of Brady's Bend, Pennsylvania, echoed another exposé, he had coldheartedly closed it down, thus consigning virtually the entire town to economic misery.

By far the most lethal charge that Republicans leveled at Tilden, however, involved the federal income tax Congress had levied in 1862. According to the *Times* and scores of other Republican newspapers, Tilden had grossly underreported his income in 1862 and 1863 to reduce his tax liability. In the fall the *Times* alleged that Tilden had made between $5 million and $10 million during the war years but had declared no more than $170,000 as taxable income. For 1862, Tilden had declared a highly suspect $7,000 of income. Thus, Republicans charged, he was guilty of defrauding the government and perjuring himself in signed statements. He was, in short, a cheat and a liar.

"The 'Bloody Shirt' Reformed." Thomas Nast presents a wonderfully sardonic visual image of the Republicans' campaign against Tilden. This cartoon from August 11, 1876, alludes to July's Hamburg massacre, suggesting that for southern Democrats, "reform" meant the slaughter of innocent blacks. (From Morton Keller, The Art and Politics of Thomas Nast [New York: Oxford University Press, 1968].)

"'The Solid South'—Gaunt and Hungry," from October 21, 1876, refers to Republican charges that Tilden's victory, under a bogus banner of reform, would allow ex-Confederates to loot the federal treasury through federal compensation for their wartime losses. (From Morton Keller, The Art and Politics of Thomas Nast [New York: Oxford University Press, 1968].)

Tilden's wartime record constituted another Republican line of attack, and these charges were obviously aimed at Union army veterans and other loyal northerners, as well as at Liberals. The litany moved from his advocacy of compromise with secessionists before the firing on Fort Sumter to his refusal to attend a mass Union rally to his supposed authorship of the Democrats' peace plank in 1864. What this record meant, Republican speakers such as Morton and Sherman charged, was that, if elected, Tilden might honor the demands of southern Democratic congressmen that *Confederates* receive monetary compensation from the federal government for property losses suffered during the war and for the federal export tax on cotton that southerners had been forced to pay between 1864 and 1868. By early October Republicans dropped the subjunctive voice. Now they wildly charged that Tilden would certainly honor such Confederate claims if elected. Here was the culmination of the Republicans' bloody-shirt campaign against Tilden.

Tilden relied on surrogates such as Manton Marble, Abram Hewitt, and New York Judge James Sinnott to rebut most of these accusations. For the explosive income tax charge, for example, Tilden and Hewitt got Sinnott, who had been Tilden's law clerk during the war, to go over Tilden's accounts and issue a public letter denying the accusations, in response to a postdated public letter from Hewitt requesting that he address the matter. In October Charles Francis Adams Jr. wrote an article in the highbrow *North American Review* denouncing Republicans' attacks as mere "campaign rubbish." In reply, Republicans hooted that Sinnott's supposedly careful accounting was balderdash, while a *Times* editorial pilloried Adams's essay as "a priggish, pretentious article, inaccurate in many of its references to recent history, disingenuous and sophistical in its reasoning, and blind to almost everything against the purpose to which it is written."[57]

In late October Tilden issued a public letter to Hewitt (actually written by Marble) denying that he would ever honor any Confederate claims against the federal government. Pennsylvania's William Bigler, a one-time governor and U.S. senator, immediately told Tilden that "it will aid the good cause immensely." "Your letter on Southern Claims should be printed in blue ink on a large poster and posted up everywhere," gushed another Democrat. "The letter is the crowning glory of a successful campaign." Southerners, too, approved of the masterful letter, a Virginian wrote to Tilden. "This letter knocks the last prop, from under the false fabric of campaign, [Republicans] have inaugurated."[58] Even a Liberal

Republican editor who was supporting Hayes believed that Tilden's letter "destroys the republican campaign and will elect him."[59]

Democrats, moreover, were not entirely on the defensive on the "southern question." As noted earlier, in 1875 Republicans had drawn a sharp distinction between the necessity of preventing ex-Confederates from seizing control of the national government—a winning issue, from their perspective—and continued federal intervention in the South to protect black voters and prop up Republican state regimes—a certain political loser, in their opinion. Thus Republican congressmen had killed Grant's request for authority to intervene in Louisiana and Arkansas and to suspend habeas corpus in parts of the South. And members of Grant's cabinet, in part to propitiate nervous Ohio Republicans, had turned down Mississippi Governor Adelbert Ames's request for federal military help. In addition, some northern Republican state platforms that year had openly condemned federal intervention in the South as an outrage. Actual enforcement of Reconstruction in the South was the last thing most northern Republicans wanted on their campaign agenda in 1876.

With regard to this matter, however, one northern Republican mattered more than all the others—the incumbent president who had foresworn a third term. Grant was appalled by whites' bulldozing tactics in Louisiana, Mississippi, and South Carolina. In a message to the Senate on July 31, he condemned "the late disgraceful and brutal slaughter of unoffending men at the town of Hamburg, South Carolina" and "the murders and massacres of innocent men for opinion's sake or on account of color" in Louisiana and Mississippi.[60] He asked for no new congressional authorization, but on his instructions in August, Secretary of War Don Cameron ordered William Tecumseh Sherman, the commanding general of the army, to hold all troops not on duty in the West ready for insertion in the South to protect blacks' voting rights. In September Attorney General Alphonzo Taft issued similar instructions to all U.S. marshals, with an explicit reminder that they could deputize as many men as necessary to protect the polls. Democrats immediately denounced these steps as evidence that Republicans intended to carry the election by force rather than allowing an honest vote. Events came to a head in South Carolina in October.

On October 7 South Carolina's incumbent Republican Governor Daniel H. Chamberlain, who was running for reelection against Democrat Wade Hampton, issued a proclamation ordering the Democratic rifle clubs that had been disrupting Republican campaign rallies and murdering blacks for months to disperse and surrender their arms to state authorities. If they did not do so within three days, he warned, he would call on Washington to send federal troops to put them down. The Democratic state committee immediately issued a public protest stating that Chamberlain had no right to do this since these law-abiding rifle clubs had committed no crimes. In reply, Chamberlain insisted "that the lawlessness, terrorism, and violence to which I have referred far exceed in extent and atrocity any statements yet made public. . . . My only offense," he added, "is too great caution in obtaining evidence, and too great delay in exercising my utmost powers to protect our citizens."[61]

When the rifle clubs refused to hand in their arms and disperse, Chamberlain made good on his threat and asked Grant for aid. On October 17, one week before Tilden's "southern claims" letter appeared and three weeks before election day, Grant issued a proclamation announcing his intention to send in troops if the rifle clubs did not disperse within three days. This was precisely the action that, for more than a year, Republicans had feared would turn not just southern but also northern voters against them. Some prominent Liberal Republicans who had been supporting Hayes made a last-minute switch to Tilden. Gleeful Democrats believed that the combination of Tilden's letter and Grant's proclamation sealed Tilden's victory. "The changes induced by the Proclamation & Mr. Tilden's letter of yesterday are so numerous," gushed one Pennsylvanian, "that we actually begin to think we may carry the state in spite of the frauds of Philadelphia."[62]

Only what happened at the polls on election day, however, would determine the accuracy of such boasts and the impact of the stances each party had chosen. Yet the election's outcome reflected far more than a referendum on the appeals made in national platforms, acceptance letters, newspaper editorials, and campaign speeches. It depended more fundamentally on the ability of state and local organizations to bring their party's supporters to the polls and on the ability of the parties' national committees to facilitate that effort through their allotment of funds, speakers, and campaign materials. If the preliminary state and congressional elections held in some states prior to November—elections that both parties considered decisive—are an accurate indication, both national committees left much to be desired.

THE ELECTIONS OF 1876

Many elections, not just a single nationwide referendum on the parties' presidential candidates, took place in 1876. Loosely coordinated state and local committees in thirty-seven states, not hierarchical national organizations, bore the brunt of getting men to the polls. In addition, key states had gubernatorial contests scheduled for November 7, when the balloting for presidential electors would occur. These included North Carolina and all three Deep South states where Republicans still controlled the state government—Florida, Louisiana, and South Carolina—but also important northern states such as Illinois, Massachusetts, and New York. How voters responded to those state races could influence the presidential results. Reaction to the parties' congressional candidates, most of whom would also be chosen on November 7, could influence the presidential tally as well.

That most congressmen would be chosen on the day of the presidential contest marked a significant change in the nation's electoral calendar. Until the 1870s, different states held state and congressional elections in different months of both odd- and even-numbered years, beginning with the spring contests in New England, through the summer, and into the fall. In 1872 Congress passed a law to standardize congressional elections. Starting in 1876 all elections for members of the House of Representatives were to be held on the Tuesday after the first Monday in November of even-numbered years. In 1875, however, Congress had revised that law to exempt states that would be forced to amend their state constitutions to reschedule state and congressional elections for November. In 1876 this revision meant that in addition to Alabama's gubernatorial election in August, the Republican strongholds of Vermont and Maine would select governors and congressmen in September, as would Georgia on October 4. The new state of Colorado, along with Indiana, Ohio, and West Virginia, would elect state officials and congressmen on October 10, four weeks before the balloting for president.

Political insiders watched these early elections intently for clues about the outcome of the presidential contest. No one expected Republicans to carry Alabama or Georgia, but Republican newspapers cited the reduction of the party's gubernatorial vote from earlier elections as evidence of Democrats' determination to suppress the black vote across the South in November. Nor were Republican victories in the gubernatorial and congressional races in Vermont and Maine a surprise. Nonetheless, the substantially larger margins of victory achieved in both states compared with 1874 and 1875 occasioned joy among Republicans that their once-disillusioned supporters were coming back to the polls. In 1874, when Republicans carried two of Vermont's three House seats, for example, the three Republicans' collective vote had been 24,437. In 1876, when Republicans carried all three seats, the collective vote was 40,908—a jump of over 65 percent. Republicans carried all five of Maine's congressional seats in both elections, yet their total vote in 1874 had been 53,248, compared with 73,815 in 1876—an increase of almost 40 percent. Similarly, whereas Republicans' majority in Maine's 1875 gubernatorial election had been less than 4,000 votes, in 1876 their margin climbed to 15,000.

In October, Democrats captured West Virginia's governorship and its three House seats, as all but the most unrealistically optimistic Republicans had expected. Colorado's results, in contrast, were a surprise, for no one outside that new state had enough reliable information to predict the results with any accuracy. Thus when Republicans captured the state's lone House seat, the governorship, and healthy majorities in both houses of the state legislature, eastern Republicans exulted. Because Colorado's state legislature, rather than its minuscule electorate, would choose its presidential electors, the October results assured Hayes three electoral votes. Whether Colorado's results foreshadowed the November vote in the three states farther west was unclear. By the summer, however, savvy California Democrats worried that their state and local organizations were badly fractured by infighting. In addition, when the hero of California's Independent People's Party, Senator Newton Booth, rejected the Greenback Party's vice presidential nomination and returned to California to campaign strenuously for Hayes and Wheeler, Republicans' chances of carrying the largest West Coast state improved.

Throughout 1876, however, Republicans and Democrats considered the October races in Indiana and Ohio the most important early contests because of their size. Indiana had fifteen electoral votes, and Democrats had carried eight of its thirteen House seats in 1874. Those offices as well as the governorship were at stake in October. Secretary of state was the leading statewide office contested in Ohio, but its twenty House seats, thirteen of which had been captured by Democrats in 1874, were deemed an exceptionally important prize by both parties. Ohio and Indiana were also two of the few states in the country where the independent Greenback Party might play a significant role in the outcome of the October and November elections. Hayes and Hendricks, both sitting governors of their respective states, had been nominated in part to help their parties carry those states in October. To ensure victory, however, Republican and Democratic politicos from both states sought aid from their respective national committees almost as soon as those committees were organized. The justification for these pleas was that October's results in Indiana and Ohio would determine who won the White House in November.

Such outside aid could take three forms. National committees could dispatch and pay the travel expenses of popular out-of-state speakers such as stem-winder Robert Ingersoll, whose nomination speech for Blaine had thrilled the Republican national convention. They could pay the printing and mailing costs for campaign documents and canvassing booklets. Most important, they could send cash to help defray the costs of state and congressional campaigns, although Republicans and Democrats both charged that the enemy would deploy such funds to buy votes. Indeed, when Hayes told his diary on November 1 that "hard times" would be the reason if he lost, he explained that desperation would cause unemployed men to sell their votes to Democrats who were in the market for them.

In any event, the Democratic National Committee clearly outperformed its Republican counterpart in the first two of these responsibilities. Managed by Colonel William Pelton (Tilden's nephew) until Hewitt could return to New York after Congress adjourned in August, the Democratic National Committee did a splendid job of routing speakers to key states and preparing and distributing campaign materials. Its employees were functionally departmentalized. By September, a literary bureau had distributed more than 5 million campaign documents shaped like pocket-sized railroad schedules. Hewitt also prepared and broadly distributed *The Campaign Textbook,* a 750-page catalog containing purported evidence for every charge of Republican corruption the Democratic campaigners could possibly level. A separate bureau of correspondence also drafted and distributed editorials, many of them written by the hardworking Manton Marble, to Democratic newspapers around the country.

Hewitt, ambitiously if unsuccessfully, also tried to extend the organizational techniques Tilden had perfected in New York to other states. The national committee sent thousands of blank canvassing books to state committees for distribution to local and precinct committees. In these books, party workers were to record the names and political leanings of every potential voter in the nation so that the Democrats could bring out every Democratic voter on election day. The success of this scheme, of course, depended on the skill and initiative of local Democratic leaders, many of whom were not up to the task. Republicans, or at least the Republican National Committee, made no such attempt. Even so, in many states, Democratic and Republican workers generated astounding levels of voter turnout. In eight states it would surpass 90 percent of the eligible electorate, and the nationwide participation rate soared to 81.8 percent, compared with 71.3 percent in 1872.

Not all Democrats applauded their national committee's efforts. Thomas Ewing Jr., himself a victorious congressional candidate that year, told Tilden that Democrats could sweep Ohio's October elections with the aid of Greenbackers, who ran no separate candidates for state office or in most congressional districts. Yet, he bitterly complained, the national committee had written Ohio off prematurely and had utterly refused to help Democrats there. Similarly, Wade Hampton, the Democratic gubernatorial candidate in South Carolina, told Marble in the fall that the national committee had repeatedly failed to respond to requests from South Carolina Democrats for aid and advice about how they could best avoid hampering Tilden's chances in the North. Louisiana Democrats echoed those complaints about the national committee's cold shoulder. Indeed, with one minor exception, both parties' national committees studiously ignored the South. Nonetheless, Democrats seemed more satisfied with the actions of their national committee than did Republicans.

Republicans, especially those in Indiana, privately and publicly complained that their national committee refused requests for speakers. The committee, in fact, flatly denied that it had any responsibility for scheduling such appearances. When state and local activists sought fresh campaign documents from the national committee, it forwarded those requests to a separate Republican congressional campaign committee in Washington that sent dated and overly long reprints of Republican speeches in the House and Senate. An Indianapolis correspondent fumed, in a *New York Times* article published on August 15, about "the most perilous indifference in that [Republican] National Committee. They know as well as Tilden knows that Indiana is the crucial state at the present stage of this struggle. They know as well as Tilden that he is sending money almost by the carload into the State" in order "to buy votes outright."[1]

Money, indeed, was the crucial consideration for both parties' state and local committees. Both national committees found it hard to raise funds. Each spent a little less than $300,000 (approximately $6 million in current dollars) on the entire campaign, a trifling amount by modern standards. Those funds had to cover salaries for each committee's staff as well as printing, mailing, and travel expenses. The remaining balance was all they had to meet the many requests for monetary aid. Contrary to Republican charges, Tilden, who had lavished his own money freely to secure the Democratic nomination, proved to be tightfisted during the general campaign. Much of the money Democrats raised, in fact, came from large donations by Hewitt and his brother-in-law Edward Cooper, the campaign's treasurer and son of the fabulously wealthy Peter Cooper, the Greenback presidential candidate. Both men also borrowed heavily from banks on their personal accounts to meet Democratic needs. Tilden himself dispersed about $115,000, most of it raised by his friends, during the campaign. Shortly before the October contests, even August Belmont, no Tilden fan, sent a servant to Tilden's Gramercy Park mansion with ten thousand-dollar bills for use in Indiana and Ohio. "I should have wished to send more," Belmont explained, "but I have been fearfully hit since 1873, & am catching it still every day by the continued depreciation of my property."[2] Altogether, Democrats poured $60,000 into Indiana before its October election. What money the national committee had left after paying for printing and speakers' costs was concentrated exclusively in New York, Connecticut, and New Jersey.

Indiana Republicans therefore had good reason to complain about the apparent niggardliness of their national committee. That cold shoulder is surprising. At its first meeting on July 8, the committee had identified Indiana's October contest as the key to the entire election. There, Republicans faced a formidable and popular Democratic gubernatorial candidate in James D. "Blue Jeans" Williams. After the Republicans' original candidate withdrew, they recruited their own strongest man, future President Benjamin Harrison, to compete against him. The real problem, however, was the strength of Greenback sentiment in the state. That third party ran its own gubernatorial candidate as well as independent candidates in most congressional districts. At least four-fifths of the Greenback Party's supporters, groaned Republican leaders, were normal Republicans. Unless they got outside money to fund a propaganda campaign to bring these defectors back to the party fold, defeat in October and thus in November was certain.

Indiana Republicans' estimates of how much money it would take reached fantastic dimensions. In a conversation with Hayes on his way to Indiana after the adjournment of Congress, Oliver Morton asserted that $100,000 was required. Another told the national committee that only $800,000 would suffice. Zach Chandler, for one, wanted to waste no money on Indiana whatsoever. Thus, the *New York Times* report from Indianapolis quoted earlier was part of a well-coordinated campaign to extort money from the national committee in New York. On August 1 General Judson Kirkpatrick published an open letter to Hayes prescribing how to meet the Greenback threat. "A bloody-shirt campaign, with money, and Indiana is safe; a financial campaign, and no money, and we are beaten." Yet "the National Committee has done nothing for Indiana. Alone they are fighting their battles and bravely, but unless the National Committee wakes up and does its duty to you, to the party, and to the country, defeat is certain in October."[3]

Hayes, who claimed that he was too "land-poor" to contribute any money himself to the Republican campaign, worried deeply about Indiana.[4] On August 15 he pleaded in vain to the sullen Roscoe Conkling (who gave only a single speech in his hometown during the entire campaign) to speak in Indiana and Ohio. "I am satisfied that the State Election in Indiana is of the greatest importance," Hayes wrote to James Root, Illinois' member of the national committee, a week later. "Without dwelling on the topic I now write to urge liberal—I mean exceptional liberal appropriations to Indiana of material aid. Too much cannot in my judgment be done."[5] Root persuaded the Chicago branch of the national committee to send $7,000 to Indiana. Under enormous public pressure, Chandler also relented. He agreed to provide Indiana with $40,000 in four installments between late August and October 10.

Both parties also lavished nonmonetary aid on the crucial Hoosier State. Throughout September and early October, rumors circulated in the Republican press that Democrats were sending gangs of thugs and repeat voters from Philadelphia, Baltimore, and neighboring Kentucky to carry the Indiana election by fraud. Aside from outside speakers such as Blaine, Schurz, and Ingersoll, Republicans had other weapons to off-set that threat. Because of Indiana's perceived importance, as early as July, leaders of the Grand Army of the Republic, including Ohio Republican Congressman James A. Garfield, had called for a grand encampment of Union army veterans to meet outside Indianapolis in late September and early October. According to later newspaper accounts, those veterans sent any Democratic thugs they encountered in Indianapolis packing. They did nothing, however, to stop Kentucky Democrats from infiltrating southern Indiana on October 10.

That gathering of army veterans outside Indianapolis also provided the occasion for Ingersoll to deliver the Republicans' most vivid bloody-shirt address of the campaign. Almost every Republican newspaper in the North reprinted this incendiary harangue. "I am opposed to the Democratic party, and I will tell you why," thundered Ingersoll. "Every state that seceded from the United States was a Democratic State. . . . Every man that tried to destroy this nation was a Democrat. Every enemy this great republic has had for twenty years was a Democrat. Every man that shot Union soldiers was a Democrat." And so it went. Confederates who starved Union prisoners of war were all Democrats. Slaveholders, Ingersoll wildly charged, were all Democrats. So were Lincoln's assassin and the men who cheered his foul deed. "Soldiers," he concluded, "every scar you have got on your heroic bodies was given to you by a Democrat. Every scar, every arm that is lacking, every limb that is gone, every scar is a souvenir of a Democrat."[6] It is little wonder that most Union army veterans voted Republican in November.

In Indiana and elsewhere, Republicans also had the national administration on their side, an important if easily overlooked resource. According to an 1871 federal law, federal judges in all cities with populations over 20,000, which included Indianapolis, could appoint supervisors to challenge fraudulent voters and deputy U.S. marshals to protect polling places. Election judges appointed by both parties bore the responsibility of tallying votes once the ballot boxes were opened, but the appointed supervisors could make sure they counted accurately. Because virtually all federal judges in 1876 were Republican, Republicans had an army of federally appointed and paid officers to police the polls and limit Democratic fraud—at least in large cities and selected districts in the South. According to one of the closest students of this election, in 1876 Grant's administration spent approximately $291,000 for 11,501 deputy marshals and 4,863 election supervisors throughout the country. Fully $80,000 of that amount was expended on the Democratic fiefdom of New York City, but the point is that Republicans had access to financial resources over and above the meager amount raised and spent by the national committee.

Nonetheless, by September, Hayes had grown increasingly pessimistic about the Indiana race. Just as in Ohio, he wrote to numerous correspondents, reliably Republican farmers and Union army veterans had left Indiana to move farther west. They had been replaced by intransigently Democratic Catholic immigrants. If as many Republicans defected to the Greenback state ticket as predicted, defeat seemed sure. Thus, on September 9 Hayes urged William H. Smith, president of the Western Associated Press, to prepare Republicans around the nation for defeat in Indiana. It was now "a Democratic state. Emigration of Republicans West and the greenback heresy have made it so." Still, defeat there would not be the end of the world. *"October will not decide the election unless both Ohio and Indiana go the same way.* This is the truth. We ought to see that it is so understood everywhere."[7]

Hayes told others that Republicans would carry Ohio, but privately, he was increasingly worried about the outcome there. Democrats had mounted an impressively vigorous campaign even without outside funding. And because William Allen's soft-money wing of the Democracy had written the state platform and chosen the state ticket, Greenbackers nominated no state ticket and few congressional tickets of their own. Thus, Hayes feared that soft-money Democrats who would vote for Cooper in November or abstain because they hated Tilden, and perhaps some deluded Republicans, would go Democratic in October. Even worse, although Hayes was delighted with the quality of the congressional candidates the Ohio Republicans had recruited, he considered the head of the Republican statewide ticket, though an honest soldier, "a load—a heavy load—to carry" because he had been "mixed up with the temperance crusade which was so hateful to all Germans and many others."[8] Indeed, in August Hayes had forcefully instructed William Dean

Howells, who was writing his official campaign biography, to omit any reference to the fact that Hayes had joined the Sons of Temperance as a young man. The "wet" vote was simply too important to antagonize.

On October 10 Democrats won the Indiana gubernatorial election by some 5,000 votes out of the 444,000 cast. Although the original Greenback candidate for governor had withdrawn only days before the election on the grounds that his candidacy was unfairly helping Democrats at Republicans' expense, his replacement still won more than 13,000 votes. If as many as four-fifths of those votes had come from Republican defectors, as Indiana Republicans had repeatedly warned, Greenbackers had cost Benjamin Harrison the election. Democrats also ran up a statewide plurality of more than 7,000 votes in the simultaneous congressional elections. Nonetheless, Republicans won nine of the state's thirteen House seats, compared with only five in 1874. Indiana, in short, seemed likely to go for Tilden and Hendricks in November. But the outcome appeared sufficiently doubtful that the Republicans' hard-pressed national executive committee in New York sent an additional $10,000 to Indiana during the four weeks prior to November 7.

Despite Hayes's fears, Republicans won Ohio's statewide seats by some 6,900 votes, a larger margin than Hayes himself had amassed in 1875. In addition, Republicans won twelve of the state's twenty House seats, a gain of five seats since the 1874 debacle. Together, Indiana and Ohio gave Republicans nine additional congressmen. Explaining Ohio's result to R. C. McCormick, the national committee's secretary, Hayes said that reliably Republican counties in rural areas "have given their full high-tide majorities. The cities, like Springfield, where business and manufacturing prospers, have done well. Our losses are in cities and towns where the hard times pinch." Non-Catholic Germans and other immigrants, he boasted, "have stood by us except the trading classes in Cincinnati, who feared a loss of Southern trade. . . . We shall double our majority here in Ohio without effort."[9] Ohio Democrats agreed with Hayes about the pattern of the vote, but they refused to give up on the November election. After begging Hewitt to send an experienced organizer from New York to work on the rural areas in Ohio, one Democrat told Tilden that "had the same attention been paid to the country that was given to the cities, Ohio would have been carried in October. It can yet be carried."[10] Perhaps for that reason, Zach Chandler, who had haughtily refused to spend any of the Republican National Committee's funds on Ohio prior to the October election, sent it a piddling $5,000 during the four weeks before the November balloting.

After the October contests, Hayes wrote to many Republicans that, as he had always expected, the outcome of the election now depended on New York and a few southern states: North and South Carolina, Florida, and Louisiana. During the campaign's remaining weeks, indeed, New York was the particular target of Republican charges that Tilden, if elected, would agree to federal reimbursement of Confederates' wartime losses. At the last minute, moreover, Republicans tried to panic New York City's financial community with a wild charge that, should Tilden win, Englishmen would refuse to purchase American bonds. That purported embargo would utterly frustrate attempts at specie resumption. First in a newspaper article and then in a speech at the Democrats' exclusive Manhattan Club, August Belmont skillfully eviscerated that canard, even though Republicans mocked Belmont's argument as sheer sophistry. By the end of October, most Democrats were confident of victory. Republicans, in turn, were reduced to hoping that their gubernatorial candidates—as well as the election supervisors appointed to prevent fraudulent voting in Democratic cities, and especially in New York—could help Hayes carry key states.

This hope was not as far-fetched as it might seem. In 1844 extraordinarily popular Democratic gubernatorial candidates had helped James K. Polk eke out a narrow victory over the Whig candidate Henry Clay. Four years later, Whigs turned the tables; strong gubernatorial candidates in New York and Pennsylvania had helped Zachary Taylor carry those two mega-states and win the White House. Thus, both Democrats and Republicans in 1876 considered the quality of their gubernatorial candidates critical in terms of mobilizing support for presidential electors in different states. The Republican National Committee, for example, sent money to only one southern state that year. That was North Carolina, where the Republican gubernatorial candidate, the popular Thomas Settle, appeared to have an excellent chance of defeating his Democratic rival, wartime governor Zebulon Vance. Settle, in fact, ran slightly better than Hayes in November; nonetheless, he too lost the state.

Both parties, however, focused primarily on the North. Once Illinois Republicans nominated the formidable Shelby Cullom for governor, Democrats endorsed the previously nominated Greenback gubernatorial candidate, sensing that such an alliance provided their only hope of victory. As noted earlier, Tilden desperately sought support from Liberal Republicans in Connecticut, New Jersey, and New York, the three northeastern states that he and other Democrats considered indispensable for a Democratic victory. Primarily to influence Liberals in those states, he helped engineer the Democratic nomination of Charles Francis Adams for governor in Massachusetts. Although Democrats had carried the statehouse in 1874, few people believed that Adams could actually do so again in 1876, and he did little more than issue a few public letters praising Tilden. Besides, Massachusetts Republicans had scored an equally significant coup among Bay State Liberals—Nathaniel P. Banks. Banks, the first Republican Speaker of the House of Representatives and then a three-term Republican governor in the late 1850s, had had a checkered military career as a Union officer during the Civil War. After the war, however, he reentered Massachusetts politics and won three congressional elections by crushing majorities between 1866 and 1870. In 1872 Banks bolted to the Liberal Republicans and lost to a Republican regular in a redrawn congressional district. In 1874, when he ran as an Independent, he routed his Republican opponent. In 1876 this Union army veteran campaigned in his own district—and many others—as a straight-out Republican and won yet again.

Though few Democrats expected to carry the Bay State for Adams and Tilden, all calculations of a Democratic majority in the electoral college hinged on capturing New York's thirty-five electoral votes. For that reason, and because they feared a solid Democratic South, Republicans were determined to deprive Tilden of New York. Both parties therefore considered the selection of strong gubernatorial candidates to be critical, yet both parties in New York were deeply divided over those choices. The machine Republicans loyal to the disappointed Conkling insisted that Alonzo Cornell, himself a failed candidate for national chairman, be the nominee. Reform elements pushed for William Evarts, who had served as one of Andrew Johnson's defense attorneys during his Senate impeachment trial and then as attorney general during the last months of Johnson's administration (he would later serve as Hayes's secretary of state). Evarts was anathema to the machine men. To avoid a nasty brawl, the Republican state convention somewhat surprisingly gave the nod to a man that Cornell hated—Edwin D. Morgan, the former governor, U.S. senator, and national party chairman. Morgan, by all odds, was the strongest man Republicans could run, and Hayes was immensely pleased with the choice because it might help his chances in New York.

New York Democrats were also split. Manton Marble, the former editor who served the Democrats so loyally during the campaign, hungered for the nomination and believed, with good reason, that Tilden should support him. Courting Liberal Republicans remained Tilden's top priority, however. He insisted that Democrats nominate Lieutenant Governor William Dorsheimer, himself a onetime Liberal. Tammany Hall Democrats, who had grudgingly acquiesced in Tilden's presidential nomination only after frantically trying to prevent it, refused to accept Dorsheimer or any other Liberal that Tilden might anoint. Yet the Tammany men's choice, Clarkson Potter, was unacceptable to Tilden. A fatal rupture thus threatened the Democratic state convention, so to save face, Tilden's forces surprisingly named former Governor Horatio Seymour as a compromise choice, with Dorsheimer again the candidate for lieutenant governor. Seymour's nomination carried the convention by storm, and the Democrats immediately adjourned without waiting to see whether Seymour would accept the honor. Having publicly pledged on several occasions after his defeat in the 1868 presidential election never to seek office again, Seymour intransigently declined. A hastily reassembled convention then chose the unexciting Lucius Robinson, the incumbent state controller, who refused to campaign personally because the duties of his current office were too pressing. To the extent that the gubernatorial race would affect the outcome in New York, Republicans had an apparent edge.

In contrast, Democrats had a clear advantage in the state races to be decided on November 7 in the three Deep South states still controlled by Republicans. Louisiana's controversial incumbent Republican Governor William Pitt Kellogg, who had remained in power only through the repeated interventions of federal troops, dared not seek reelection. Instead, Republicans nominated Stephen Packard, the U.S. marshal who headed the notoriously corrupt customhouse ring in New Orleans. Against him, Democrats ran Francis T. Nicholls, a socially prominent lawyer who had lost an arm and a leg in Confederate military service during the war.

In Florida, the only state of the three where blacks did not constitute a majority of the registered electorate, Republicans renominated incumbent carpetbag Governor Marcellus Stearns. Stearns was the bitter enemy of Republican Senator Simon Conover, who briefly ran as an Independent to prevent Stearns's reelection. That Republican split gave the edge to Democrat George F. Drew, a former Whig and opponent of secession who might appeal to moderate whites.

In South Carolina, incumbent Republican Governor Daniel H. Chamberlain was seeking reelection. He had pleased white taxpayers and alienated many black Republicans by slashing expenditures and state tax rates after his election in 1874. For a while, therefore, grateful Democrats considered letting Chamberlain run unopposed. Instead, they nominated Civil War hero Wade Hampton, perhaps the best known and most popular white man in the state. Hampton, not Tilden, was expected to generate a huge increase in white turnout.

In these three states, as well as elsewhere in the South, the basic Democratic message was the same: white supremacy required ousting Republicans from control of state governments or preventing them from retaking it where Democrats were already in the saddle. According to this logic, any white man who voted Republican betrayed his race and his region. As already noted, in the Deep South states, including Florida, Democrats used armed rifle clubs to disrupt Republican meetings and threats or actual violence to deter blacks from voting. In both Louisiana and South Carolina, however, Democrats also sought to persuade blacks to support their candidates, either by promising fair treatment should Democrats win or by threatening economic reprisals, such as eviction from lands they sharecropped, if blacks voted Republican. Democrats were brazenly candid about their tactics. "All will admit that it is the colored vote of Louisiana that has ruined the State," began an editorial in the Democratic *New Orleans Picayune*. Those blacks owed their livelihoods to white employers, the editor believed, and they should be sacked and reduced to starvation if they continued to vote Republican. Those white employers must aggressively warn blacks of the consequences. "The test of negro fidelity will be: *if you vote for Packard you are the enemy of your employers and of Louisiana;* if you vote for Nicholls you are the friends of your employers and of the State."[11] Ex-Confederate General Martin Gary of South Carolina was even blunter in an October speech. "South Carolina is a white man's State, and in spite of nigger majorities the Democrats are going to rule it."[12]

Little statistical evidence exists that a significant number of blacks actually voted Democratic in the South, although Democratic poll watchers in the three Republican states and elsewhere undoubtedly stuffed ballot boxes with fraudulent Democratic tickets purportedly cast by registered blacks who were too frightened to vote at all. Instead, what characterized the election in former slave states was an astonishing increase in the number of whites casting Democratic ballots in the presidential, gubernatorial, and congressional races. Table 4 in appendix A illustrates both the increasing solidarity of blacks behind Republicans, despite the violence perpetrated against them, and the enormous increase in white turnout for Democrats.

On November 7, 1876, some 2 million more men cast presidential ballots than had done so four years earlier. Hundreds of thousands of Republicans and even more Democrats had sat out the 1872 election. Their return to the polls accounts for much of this increase. Nonetheless, it is obvious that both parties also mobilized new supporters. As noted earlier, the turnout rate of eligible voters soared from 71.3 percent in 1872 to 81.8 percent in 1876. This is the highest rate of voter participation ever achieved in an American presidential election. As shown in table 2, slightly less than 1.5 million, or three-fourths, of these additional voters backed electors pledged to Samuel J. Tilden. About 600,000 of those votes, or two-fifths of the Democratic increase, came from the fifteen former slave states. Almost all of that number came from angry whites determined to secure what they called "home rule." In contrast, between 1872 and 1876, Republicans added fewer than 18,000 votes to their column in those fifteen states, and in the seven Deep South states that originally formed the Confederacy, Republican turnout actually declined between 1872 and 1876. Of vast importance, as will soon be made clear, Republicans and Democrats from Florida, Louisiana, and South Carolina (where Republicans still controlled the state governmental machinery), reported different results. Based on the Democratic totals, Tilden amassed 4,300,590 votes nationally, compared with the 2,863,614 votes cast for Horace Greeley and Charles O'Conor combined in 1872. Whereas Grant had gotten 3,597,132 votes in 1872, Hayes, according to Democrats, won 4,036,298 in 1876; Peter Cooper, the Greenbacker, garnered 81,747; and a separate Prohibitionist candidate attracted a mere 9,522 supporters. Thus Grant's 750,000 popular-vote plurality over Greeley had been converted in 1876 to a 264,000 popular-vote plurality for Tilden over Hayes. Had northern Republicans failed to add significantly more voters to their column than Democrats did between the off-year congressional elections of 1874–1875 and the 1876 election, that Democratic plurality would have been much greater still.

The distribution of popular votes among the states, not the size of the nationwide plurality, was what counted, of course, and those votes (excluding the Prohibitionist votes in 1872 and 1876) are recorded in table 5. Table 6, in turn, lists the turnout rates by state in 1872 and 1876, as well as the size of the Democratic and Republican margin of victory over the other and the victorious party's percentage of the total vote in each state.

The official returns submitted by the various states to Congress on which these tables are based were not known until at least a month after the November 7 election. Still, they vividly illustrate the impact of three factors on voters in 1876: the depression that began in late 1873 and continued to cause immense hardship in 1876, the substitution of a lifelong Democrat for a lifelong tormentor of Democrats at the head of the Democratic national ticket, and the racial polarization of southern politics that emerged only after the 1872 elections. That all three of these developments clearly benefited Democrats testifies again to the importance of the increase in the northern Republican vote between 1874–1875 and 1876. Yet these tables tell us more than just that.

One thing they reveal is the stark sectional polarization of the vote. Republicans carried seventeen of twenty-one northern and western states—eighteen of twenty-two, if Colorado is included. The change in the South was far more dramatic. In 1872 Grant narrowly won Delaware and West Virginia and eight of eleven former Confederate states. In 1876 Democrats carried every former slave state and West Virginia (which was carved from a former slave state), often by overwhelming margins. Granted, Republicans and Democrats from Florida, Louisiana, and South Carolina vehemently disputed the presidential results from those three states, and in each, the winning margins in both the presidential and the gubernatorial races proved to be exceptionally close. Yet the congressional results reported in tables 1 and 3 point indisputably to the establishment of a solidly Democratic South in 1876, a pattern that would affect American politics well into the twentieth century. In 1872 Republicans won forty-three of seventy-three (58.9 percent) House seats from the ex-Confederate states. In 1874–1875 that number had plunged to only fourteen of seventy-three, or less than 20 percent of the total. In 1876 Republicans won only eight of the seventy-three, whereas in the North and West they doubled the number of seats won by Democrats.

The lopsided Republican and Democratic margins in several northern and southern states also attest to the resectionalization of American politics that first became apparent in the 1850s but was then camouflaged by Republicans' competitiveness in the South between 1867 and 1872. Democrats won four northern states in 1876, just as they had won three in 1868. Those four states provided Tilden with sixty-five crucial electoral votes, but in none did Democrats garner as much as 53 percent of the vote. In contrast, Republicans in Massachusetts, Rhode Island, Vermont, Iowa, Kansas, Nebraska, and Minnesota ran, on average, an astonishing 22 percentage points ahead of their Democratic foes. The Democratic tilt in some southern states was even more mind-boggling. Democrats reaped 72 percent of the vote in Georgia, 70 percent in Texas, 68 percent in Mississippi, 61.5 percent in Kentucky, and 60 percent in Alabama; only in Kansas and Vermont did northern Republicans approach those margins.

The figures also reveal that the huge surge in voter turnout between 1872 and 1876 was unequally distributed in terms of both its size and its impact on the election's outcome. In some northern and at least three southern states, the result was breathtaking. For the first time ever, more than a million citizens voted in New York State on the same day. In Pennsylvania it was three-quarters of a million, and over half a million men trooped to the polls in Ohio and Illinois. Rates of voter turnout may be an even better measure of voter interest in this election than absolute numbers. According to the estimates of voter participation presented in table 6, almost 90 percent of eligible voters cast ballots in New York, but that rate—which seems astonishing in comparison to today's abysmally low figures—was topped by Ohio, Vermont, Florida, Indiana, North Carolina, and especially Iowa and South Carolina, where few if any eligible voters avoided the polls. In fact, the number of votes recorded in South Carolina exceeded that state's entire adult male population—a clear indicator of fraud.

Nonetheless, these figures attest to the extraordinary success of Republican, Democratic, and third-party men in getting their voters to the polls—at least in most states. Yet surely this stupendous turnout also reflected authentic voter interest in the outcome. Shortly after Hayes's nomination, George W. Curtis had told him that the 1876 election lacked compelling issues compared with earlier contests. Curtis was simply wrong. Modern research has shown that, without question, some incalculable fraction of the electorate, especially in cities, lacked any issue orientation. Yet only what was at stake in the election's outcome can account for the astonishing surge in the number of voters who went to the polls. For northern Republicans, preventing former Confederates from seizing power in Washington and smiting Catholics were compelling issues. For hundreds of thousands of Democrats, punishing Republicans for the depression, for their undeniable corruption, and, among southern whites, for their hateful Reconstruction regimes constituted an even more compelling incentive to go to the polls and throw those rascals out. What distinguished the 1876 presidential election, in short, was not simply its infamous disputed electoral votes. Proportionately more Americans cared about the outcome of this contest than was true of any other presidential election in American history.

That said, the number of additional voters and their impact on the election's outcome varied considerably from state to state and region to region. In only four of the thirty-seven states recording popular votes did Republicans outgain Democrats between 1872 and 1876. Yet those four states—Iowa, Kansas, Minnesota, and Nebraska—were Republican bastions that hardly needed the additional votes. In all four, Republicans could have won in 1876 simply by mobilizing the same number of votes received in 1872. Elsewhere, Democrats outpaced, and often far outpaced, Republicans in additional votes recorded in 1876 versus 1872. In Virginia, for example, the Democratic gain was more than twenty times that of Republicans, and in North Carolina, Maryland, Kentucky, Maine, and Pennsylvania it quintupled Republicans' increase. The Democratic vote in South Carolina quadrupled between 1872 and 1876 because of a tremendous surge in white turnout. In some states, surely, these outsized Democratic gains accounted for the capture of electoral votes. The disparity in the two parties' gains between 1872 and 1876 was especially crucial in the four northern states Tilden carried, but in all of them, the Democratic breakthrough had begun in 1874. Among the additional voters who appeared between 1872 and 1876, for example, Democrats outpolled Republicans by 7,500 votes in Connecticut, 27,000 votes in Indiana, 27,000 votes in New Jersey, and a mind-boggling 85,000 votes in New York. In all those states, as table 6 reveals, those gains dwarfed Democrats' ultimate margin of victory.

The Democratic achievement in New York City and Brooklyn, which together gave Tilden and the rest of the Democratic ticket a 71,000-vote plurality that overwhelmed Republicans' upstate majorities, was especially impressive. Republicans immediately charged fraud, but if so, the Democrats had overcome significant hurdles to effect it. State law limited the registration of new voters to a single week in late October. That left enough time for the Republican-appointed chief election supervisors to check the addresses given by each new registrant against an amazingly complete list they had generated of who lived in virtually every dwelling in the city. Thus the Republican supervisors at each polling place on November 7 had lists of illegal voters. Beyond that, polls were open only between 6 AM and 4 PM, which prevented laborers from voting after their workday ended. Beyond even that, voters had to deposit seven separate ballots for president, governor, congressman, members of the state legislature, and so forth in seven separate ballot boxes, and ballots placed in the wrong box would not be counted. If Democrats brought as many illiterate and ineligible voters to the polls as Republicans charged, they had done an exceptional job of coaching them how to vote correctly.

In New York and other states, the skewed geographical distribution of the parties' votes had important consequences. In 1874 Republicans had carried only fifteen of New York's thirty-three House seats; in 1876 they won seventeen, despite Tilden's victory. Similar geographical skews occurred elsewhere. For example, in staunchly Democratic Missouri, where Tilden got almost 58 percent of the vote and the Democrats' gain was almost double that of the Republicans between 1872 and 1876, Republicans picked up four House seats they had lost in 1874.

Nonetheless, the disparity in vote changes and their practical impact among states, rather than within them, most demand attention. The absolute drop in the Republican vote between 1872 and 1876 in Arkansas, Texas, Alabama, and Mississippi attests to Democrats' ruthless determination to prevent blacks from voting, although some of that decrease may have represented the defection of so-called scalawag whites to Democrats once they drew the color line. But the decimation of the Republicans' black vote, guaranteeing almost certain Democratic victories in November, best accounts for the drop in turnout rates between 1872 and 1876 in Alabama, Arkansas, and Texas, as well as the relatively low rate of 63.5 percent in Georgia, that so differentiated these southern states from the rest of the country. (Turnout rates in Rhode Island, which had the nation's strictest suffrage requirements, had always been low.)

If Democrats massively outgained Republicans in most states between 1872 and 1877, much of that gain in fact had no impact on who won the election. Democrats amassed a total gain of 230,697 votes in five southern states they would have won in 1876 simply by matching their votes in 1872: Georgia, Kentucky, Missouri, Tennessee, and Texas. More important, fully 653,338 additional Democratic votes recorded in 1876 were cast in northern states that Republicans still won. This sum includes a truly astounding gain of 154,163 in Pennsylvania, as well as increases of 77,698 in Ohio and 70,605 in Illinois. When one considers that only 1,100 additional Democratic votes in either Oregon or Nevada or 2,000 in California would have given the state and thus the election to Tilden, the frustrating futility of Democrats' herculean effort to get out the vote elsewhere becomes stark.

Take closely contested Ohio, for example. Hayes had badly exaggerated the ease with which Republicans could carry it in November. Soft-money Democrats did not defect to Cooper or abstain in droves, as he had predicted. Tilden ran 12,000 votes ahead of Democrats in October, and Hayes defeated him by only some 7,500 votes. "State pride," one furious Ohio Democrat wrote to Tilden on November 8, contributed to that slim edge, but in fact, Hayes would have been beaten had this Democrat's earlier pleas for help from the national committee been heeded. "Immense sums of money were spent by the Republicans between the October and November elections," he bitterly complained. "The expenses of men were paid to the Philadelphia [Centennial] Exposition to keep them from the polls, others were hired to hunt two or three days for game, others were sent away to perform some kind of work etc. etc., and direct bribery was used wherever it would work."[13]

Even though the Democratic increase in the North between 1872 and 1876 did not yield electoral votes for Tilden, it brought the two major parties to a competitive equilibrium in the North's most populous states that would last for twenty years, until the realignment of the 1890s. Political scientists and historians have long noted that the 1876 election inaugurated a two-decade-long era of closely contested elections between the major parties. That only one electoral vote separated them in 1876, and that the congressional elections that year reduced the Democratic edge in the House of Representatives from seventy to only nine seats, supports this observation.[14] The popular vote in the North in 1876 explains it. Returning Republican voters who had abstained or defected in 1872 and 1874, Democratic abstainers in 1872, plus legions of new recruits made most northern states far more competitive than they had been four years earlier. Aside from Iowa and Massachusetts, the most heavily Republican states that year were all lightly populated. Elsewhere, the story was different. In Illinois a 54,000-vote Republican edge over Democrats in 1872 was reduced to less than 20,000. In Indiana a 21,000-vote Republican margin was converted to a 5,500-vote Democratic edge. In Ohio the Republican edge dropped from 46,000 votes in 1872 to 7,500 in 1876, in Michigan it sank from 57,000 to 25,000, and in Pennsylvania it plummeted from 137,000 votes to 22,000. Across the

North, Democrats had become much more competitive, just as in the South, Republicans were markedly less competitive. However counter-intuitive the observation may appear, in 1876 the two-party system of Democrats and Republicans simultaneously became more unbalanced sectionally and more balanced competitively.

Table 7 illuminates the changes between 1872 and 1876 by aggregating the absolute votes cast in the states from different regions and then computing the differentials in the percentages won by Democrats and Republicans. In 1872 Republican New England and the plains and western states of Kansas, Nebraska, Nevada, Oregon, and California were by far the least competitive regions of the country whereas the border states, upper South, and lower South remained closely competitive. By 1876 the heavily Democratic Deep South, despite the close elections in three of its states, had become by far the least competitive region in the country, while the most heavily populated regions of the North were now closely competitive.

Table 5 also allows an assessment of the Greenback vote's impact on the election. For months, both Republicans and Democrats had reported that white southerners cared nothing about the money and reform issues. Those reports proved accurate. Peter Cooper did not receive a single vote in ten of the eleven former Confederate states. Democrats there did a remarkable job of holding their troops in line. In the North, with the exception of Pennsylvania, Cooper's vote was concentrated in the Midwest. Only in Indiana did it affect the outcome of the race, for there, Cooper's 17,000 votes tripled the Democratic edge over Republicans. If the great majority of Indiana's Greenbackers were dissident Republicans, as the state's Republicans had long warned, they cost Hayes 15 electoral votes. Those would have brought his total to 181, only 4 short of victory, in the northern states alone. In Pennsylvania, Ohio, Michigan, Illinois, and Iowa, in contrast, most Greenback votes were probably cast by renegade Democrats who were unhappy with Tilden's commitment to specie resumption and his apparent acceptance of the hated national banking system. In Illinois, at least, this guess can be tested, for there, Democrats had endorsed the Greenback candidate for governor. On the same day that Illinois voters gave Hayes a 19,000-vote margin over Tilden, they elected the Republican Shelby Cullom governor with only a 6,800-vote majority. Cullom actually received 1,000 more votes than Hayes, while his Democratic-Greenback opponent outdrew Tilden by 14,000 votes, more than enough to account for Cooper's entire vote in Illinois.

The official returns took weeks to tabulate, but by the night of November 7 and the early morning of November 8, telegraphed reports to the two parties' national headquarters in New York City seemed to indicate a Tilden landslide. Even then it was clear that he had carried Connecticut, Indiana, New Jersey, and New York, with their 65 electoral votes. The size of the Democratic margins first reported from southern states was simply astounding. By early Tuesday evening, a Pennsylvania Democrat telegraphed Manton Marble from outside Philadelphia (where reports from the South apparently arrived earlier than in Manhattan) that Tilden had already locked up 184 electoral votes, with California, Oregon, Florida, Wisconsin, Louisiana, and South Carolina yet to be heard from. Another telegraph wired at 8 PM claimed Florida for Tilden by at least 10,000 votes and Louisiana by the same margin, if not more. Early in the morning of November 8, George Smith, the Pennsylvania Democrat on whom Marble relied for information, wired that his latest dispatches now gave Tilden a 1,700-vote lead in Florida and a margin of 3,000 in South Carolina. To joyous Democrats, in short, Tilden seemed headed for more than 200 electoral votes, a comfortable surplus over the 185 necessary to win. Some Democratic newspapers in New York City thus prepared headlines for their morning editions announcing that Tilden was the next president.

Even before midnight, a deep gloom had enveloped Republican headquarters at New York's Fifth Avenue Hotel. Crowds of the party faithful, eager for news, had long since dispersed in disappointment, going home or to a favorite bar to seek solace in strong drink. A despondent Zach Chandler, certain of Hayes's defeat, had retired to his room with a whiskey bottle for comfort. When Daniel Sickles, a former Republican congressman and envoy to Spain for most of Grant's presidency, visited the headquarters near midnight, he found only a single clerk still on the premises. Convinced that Tilden would win, he had gone to the theater that night. Now he was curious to see the results coming in. They indicated that Tilden had probably locked up 184 electoral votes and Hayes only 166. But he also found reports that Chandler had neglected to read. They suggested that only a small fraction of Florida's results were in and that South Carolina and Louisiana were close, with the heaviest black districts yet to report. Among those three states, where Republicans controlled the returning boards that would officially determine who had carried them, there were 19 electoral votes, precisely the number needed to give Hayes the 185 necessary to win. Sickles immediately recognized this possibility and drafted a telegram to be sent to the Republican governors of South Carolina and Louisiana, a former Republican senator from Florida, and the Republican state chairman in Oregon, where the reported results were still so close that no one could tell which party had carried it. The message consisted of two brief lines. "With your state sure for Hayes, he is elected. Hold your states."[15] Sickles wanted to send these telegrams out over the signature of Zach Chandler, who by then was snoring upstairs in a drunken stupor. The committee clerk strongly demurred. By serendipity, Chester A. Arthur, customs collector in New York and a member of Conkling's machine, appeared. He endorsed Sickles's plan and then went home while Sickles awaited replies to his urgent messages. By dawn of November 8 he had received favorable replies from South Carolina and Oregon, but no word from Florida or Louisiana, so the weary Sickles went home.

Half an hour later, national committee member William E. Chandler, who had voted in New Hampshire before returning by train to New York, appeared at Republican headquarters, followed shortly by John C. Reid, managing editor of the Republican *New York Times*. The latter carried dispatches that Florida and Oregon had gone Republican. At Reid's urging, the editorial board of the *Times* had refused to concede defeat, and now he and Chandler, after learning what Sickles had done, sniffed victory. They raced upstairs to awaken the hung-over Zach Chandler, who told William Chandler to do whatever he thought necessary. William Chandler then sent his own telegrams to Florida, Louisiana, South Carolina, Oregon, and Nevada announcing that Hayes would win if they could hold their states for him.

"A Doubtful Election" read the headline of the editorial in the early-morning edition of the *Times* on November 8. Admitting that it was still too soon to be sure of the results, it credited Tilden with 184 electoral votes and Hayes with 181, including those from Oregon, Louisiana, and South Carolina. "That leaves Florida alone still in doubt," bluffed the editors. "If the Republicans have carried that State, as they claim, they will have 185 votes—a majority of one."[16]

Hours after this hopeful editorial hit the streets, a somewhat recovered Zach Chandler finally appeared to confer with the other Republican leaders who had gathered in the rooms rented by the Republican National Committee. Then he issued a terse, amazingly brazen statement to the press: "Hayes has 185 votes and is elected." Meanwhile, William Chandler had telegraphed Hayes in Columbus: "One majority is as good as twenty if we hold it but we are more liable to be cheated out of it."[17] Hayes had gone to bed on Tuesday night convinced that he had lost, but, as he later told his diary, he and his wife had quickly accepted this result and fallen asleep. Now the uncertainty about the results from Florida, Louisiana, and South Carolina offered a possible reprieve from that defeat. It would not be Hayes, however, but the regular Republicans who had only grudgingly accepted his nomination, as well as the Republican still in the White House, who would work frantically over the next four weeks to make Zach Chandler's brash statement a reality.

THE DISPUTED RESULTS

The bold declarations by Zach Chandler and the *New York Times* on the morning of November 8 provoked disbelief, consternation, and—among the most quick-witted Republican and Democratic politicos—frantic activity to either prove or deny those assertions. Rutherford Hayes, for one, remained convinced for almost a week that he had lost the election. "The Democrats have carried the country and elected Tilden," he told reporters that very afternoon, "as it now seems necessary for the Republicans to carry all the States now set down as doubtful to secure even a majority of one."[1] As late as Sunday morning, November 12, he told his diary that "the figures indicate that Florida has been carried by the Democrats. No doubt both fraud and violence intervened to produce the result. But the same is true in many Southern States." Later in the same diary entry, Hayes expressed a belief that became firmer with each passing day: "A fair election in the South would undoubtedly have given us a large majority of the electoral votes, and a decided preponderance of the popular vote." Yet later that same day he received a telegram from William Dennison (Ohio's wartime governor) in Washington "which seems to open it all up again." "You are undoubtedly elected next President of the U.S.," wrote Dennison. "Desperate attempts are being made to defeat you in Louisiana, South Carolina & Florida but they will not succeed."[2]

Though Hayes at first discounted the assertions that he would win, Tilden initially expressed confidence that he had done so. In contrast, Manton Marble was unnerved by the Republican claims. How, he wondered, could Republican reports from the three southern states differ so dramatically from the information he had received on the morning of November 8? Even on November 9 his man outside Philadelphia assured him that the Democrats had a 1,700-vote majority in Florida and had carried South Carolina by 3,000 votes. No longer sure that this information was accurate, Marble told his contact to head south to double-check returns while Marble went to the man's home in Bryn Mawr, Pennsylvania, where telegraphic connections with the South were faster than in New York. "Send me your latest returns," he telegraphed George Smith from that locale on November 10.[3]

What most unnerved Democrats about the Republican pronouncements, however, was not the superior accuracy of Republican information from the South but rather Republicans' apparent intention to use their control over the returning boards in Florida, Louisiana, and South Carolina to count Hayes in no matter who had actually won the popular vote. "If Louisiana can help them to defeat you," August Belmont wrote to Tilden on November 9, "their Returning board will count you out—they are determined to win *at all hazards.*"[4] Announcing that he and two other Kentucky Democrats were leaving for New Orleans that very night, Louisville's Henry Watterson telegraphed Tilden on November 9 that "our friends in Louisiana need moral support and personal advisement. Have Bayard[,] Thurman[,] Barnum[,] Randall[,] McDonald[,] Dorsheimer[,] Kernan and others go to New Orleans at once. A strong Demonstration will defeat designs of Returning Board."[5] That same day Abram Hewitt sent a telegram to a number of prominent Democrats, telling them to head to New Orleans to oversee the vote count. The following day, Friday, November 10, Hewitt's telegram appeared in the press, alerting Republicans to Democratic plans.

A few Republicans acted even before they learned of Hewitt's telegram. As soon as Zach Chandler announced that Hayes had won on the morning of November 8, William Chandler made plans to go to Florida. He left New York that afternoon, stopping in Washington overnight. Worried Democrats in the capital told Tilden that Chandler's goal was to intercept and doctor returns from the outlying districts of Florida before they reached Tallahassee. Meanwhile, Zach Chandler received telegrams from the incumbent Republican governors of Florida and Louisiana, begging that federal troops be sent to protect their governments, including the returning boards, from armed Democratic mobs. Chandler forwarded those telegrams to Grant, along with his own pleas

Congressman Abram S. Hewitt. A wealthy iron and steel manufacturer, Hewitt chaired the Democratic National Committee in 1876. He worked heroically to salvage Tilden's election, but many Democrats later blamed him for sabotaging Tilden's chances by agreeing to the creation of the Federal Electoral Commission of 1877. Later, in 1886, Hewitt won a famous three-way election for the mayoralty of New York City that pitted him against the youthful Theodore Roosevelt and the Single-Taxer Henry George. (Courtesy of the Library of Congress. LC-DIG-cwpbh-0375.)

that the president help mobilize Republican "statesmen" to go to New Orleans to counter the Democratic effort.

Grant proved to be the most important Republican actor by far in the week after the election. On November 9 he went to Philadelphia for the next day's closing ceremonies of the Centennial Exhibition, and he worked the telegraph wires from that city. On November 10 he sent two telegrams to William Tecumseh Sherman, the army's commanding general, which he then had published in the press. These ordered Sherman to send more troops to New Orleans and Tallahassee, even though it meant weakening the force then in Columbia, South Carolina. The officers in charge, Grant told Sherman in the first telegram, should "be vigilant with the force at their Command to preserve peace & good order and to see that the proper & legal boards of Canvassers are unmolested in the performance of their duties." Any evidence of fraudulent vote counting "on either side," he added, "should be reported and denounced at once. No man worthy of the office of President would be willing to hold it if 'counted in' or placed there by any fraud."[6] In the second telegram he added that the job of the troops in Louisiana was to ensure "a peaceful count of the ballots actually cast," a phrase that would later embarrass Republicans. "The presence of citizens from other States, I understand, is requested in Louisiana to see that the Board of Canvassers make a fair count of the vote actually cast. It is to be hoped that representative and fair men of both parties will go."[7] The following day he telegraphed General Philip Sheridan from Washington and asked him to go to New Orleans, where there was great "apprehension of violence" during "the Canvassing of the vote of the state of La." "The Military have nothing to do with counting the vote," Grant explained. "Its province is to keep the peace and to protect the legal Canvassing board in the performance of its duties. The gentlemen of both political parties who will be there will observe the conduct of the Canvassers."[8]

Public reaction to these orders split along partisan lines. Predictably, Republicans praised Grant. Just as predictably, Democrats were less pleased. Hewitt told a reporter from the Republican *New York Times* that Grant's action was unjustified and unconstitutional. "Here we are with Tilden certainly elected by a majority of 18 votes in the college," fumed a New Orleans Democrat to Marble on November 11, "& S.C. Fla. & La. filled with troops to swindle the people out of their hard won victory."[9] "Well organized plan supported by troops to cheat us in count of vote," Watterson wired Tilden from the same city two days later.[10]

Grant did more than dispatch federal soldiers to protect Republican canvassing boards. On July 10 and 11 he also sought to recruit a team of Republican "visiting statesmen" to counter the Democrats that Hewitt was sending to Louisiana. In Philadelphia he signed up longtime Republican Congressman William D. Kelley and, by telegraph, approached Congressman James A. Garfield; Senator John Sherman; U.S. District Judge Stanley Matthews, Hayes's old college chum; and ex-Governor Edward F. Noyes from Ohio. Grant also contacted Senator John Logan of Illinois; Benjamin Harrison, the Republicans' recent gubernatorial candidate in Indiana; J. Courtland Parker, a renowned lawyer from New Jersey; William M. Evarts, Edward L. Stoughton and ex-Governor John A. Dix of New York; Matthew Quay, Pennsylvania's secretary of state; and Iowa Congressman John A. Kasson. Not all these men answered Grant's call, but ultimately, some twenty-five prominent northern Republicans appeared in New Orleans.

A similar number of Democrats arrived there. If anything, the team the Democrats sent to New Orleans to aid Watterson and the Kentuckians was even more distinguished than that of the Republicans. What was most striking—and certainly what immediately caught Hayes's eye—about this group was how many of them were former Republicans who had joined the Liberal Republican bolt in 1872 and then supported Tilden in 1876. These former Republicans included John M. Palmer and Lyman Trumbull, former governor and former U.S. senator, respectively, from Illinois; James R. Doolittle, former Republican senator from Wisconsin; George W. Julian, former Free-Soil and Republican congressman from Indiana; Andrew Curtin, Pennsylvania's Republican governor during the war; and Professor William Graham Sumner of Yale. Other Democrats included Samuel J. Randall of Philadelphia, whom the Democrats would choose as Speaker of the House to replace the late Michael Kerr, and William Bigler, the former governor and U.S. senator from Pennsylvania. "Hewitt's men are many of them ex-Republicans, and of course bitterly prejudiced against their late associates," Hayes groused to Carl Schurz in an unsuccessful effort to get him to go to New Orleans on November 13. "The Democrats made a mistake in sending so many ex-Republicans," he wrote to Sherman, one of the Republican statesmen, on November 27. "New converts are proverbially bitter and unfair to those they have recently left."[11]

When Florida's Governor Marcellus Stearns telegraphed Grant on November 13 that Hewitt was sending Democratic observers to Tallahassee,

Grant tried to recruit Republicans to go there too. On the whole, the cast of characters sent to Florida was less distinguished than those the Democrats and Republicans dispatched to Louisiana. By far the shrewdest among the Democrats was New York's Manton Marble, who would work frantically with Florida Democrats to save Tilden's election well into February 1877. Connecticut Senator William Eaton; Missouri's James Broadhead, whom Grant had appointed a special U.S. attorney to help prosecute the Whiskey Ring; and L. O. Saltonstall of Boston added heft to the Democratic delegation. Initially, William E. Chandler was the chief Republican, but within a week he would be joined by Kasson of Iowa, Noyes of Ohio, and General Lew Wallace of Indiana, all of whom had originally gone to New Orleans.

For a month after the presidential election of 2000, tens of millions of Americans were mesmerized by the dispute over which candidate had carried Florida and, with it, the election. Armies of Democratic and Republican lawyers descended on the state, as did hundreds of newspaper and television reporters. Each party sought favorable rulings from different judges. Night after night on the news, Americans watched election officials from different Florida counties struggling with hanging chads. Tension mounted as the date for the meeting of the electoral college in early December neared.[12]

Although there was no television or radio in 1876 to give live reports, that year, Americans confronted not simply a single undecided state but a three-ring circus with two important sideshows. The latter, discussed later, involved the possible constitutional ineligibility of a Republican elector in both Oregon and Vermont. The circus involved disputed votes in South Carolina, Florida, and Louisiana. Both parties claimed to have carried all three states, and hordes of newspaper reporters from across the country descended on them. Circumstances differed in the three, but there were some eerie similarities to the 2000 dispute over Florida. One was the pressure to have electors chosen before the federally mandated meeting of the electoral college on Wednesday, December 6. This pressure grew especially severe in Florida and Louisiana, because outlying counties and parishes with no telegraphs or railroads proved exceedingly slow in getting their returns in. Just as in 2000, moreover, Republicans and Democrats enlisted as many lawyers as they could. When Chandler discovered, to his dismay, that only two Republican lawyers practiced in the entire state of Florida, he called on the administration in Washington to send government investigators as reinforcements. The chief function of these men, as well as of the visiting statesmen themselves, was to secure affidavits and prepare briefs that could be submitted to the state returning boards either challenging or defending the returns from individual election districts. But in Florida and South Carolina, just as in Florida in 2000, courts also played a crucial role in attempting to shape the outcome. Most important, just as in Florida in 2000, Republicans controlled the executive branch and thus the returning boards in all three states.

Two other similarities bear mention. First, despite Democrats' early and wildly optimistic reports, the vote in all three states was extraordinarily close—especially in South Carolina and Florida. Second, just as Democrats protested in 2000 that thousands of Florida's blacks had been denied access to the polls, it was clear in all three southern states in 1876 that thousands of black Republicans had been prevented from voting. "I believe that with a fair election in the South, our electoral vote would reach two hundred and that we should have a large popular majority," Hayes wrote to Schurz on November 13.[13] Hayes was unquestionably right. Had blacks been allowed to vote freely, Hayes easily would have carried all three states in dispute, Mississippi, and perhaps Alabama as well. Democrats at the time and later pro-Democratic historians who cried that the election had been stolen by Republicans, that it was "the fraud of the century,"[14] conveniently ignored the clear evidence of the force, intimidation, and fraud used by Democrats to keep blacks from the polls.

Nonetheless, fraud certainly characterized the election in all three states, and both parties were guilty of it. There was a reason, after all, why the number of votes cast in South Carolina exceeded the number of potential voters. Alone among the three states, South Carolina had no registration law. Some whites and probably some blacks voted more than once at different polling stations. Hundreds, if not thousands, of Georgians crossed the Savannah River to vote in South Carolina before returning home to vote in Georgia. The returns from Edgefield County, where whites forcibly stopped hundreds of blacks from voting, were little short of miraculous. South Carolina had conducted a census of the state's population in 1875, yet Edgefield reported 2,000 more votes than the county's entire adult male population, with a Democratic majority of over 3,000 in a county that Republicans had carried in every election since 1868.

Some of the parish returns in Louisiana proved just as inventive. The three parishes of Ouachita, East Baton Rouge, and West Baton Rouge had 2,103 whites and 5,330 blacks on the official lists of registered voters. Even Democrats admitted that Republicans had carried the three by 2,900 votes in 1872 and 2,600 votes in 1874; in 1876, however, Democrats claimed a combined majority of more than 3,000 votes in those three parishes. The returns from West and East Feliciana parishes, located east of the Mississippi River along the boundary between Louisiana and Mississippi, seemed especially outrageous to Republicans. The registration lists for the former in 1876 showed 406 whites and 2,218 blacks, yet the reported vote was 485 for Tilden and 20 for Hayes. In East Feliciana, registered blacks outnumbered registered whites 2,127 to 1,004 in 1876, yet the returns showed not a single vote for Hayes and 1,743 for Tilden. These parishes, Republicans protested, had been "bulldozed," a term derived from the practice of giving blacks a dose of the bullwhip if they threatened to vote Republican. Not so, retorted Democrats. Blacks had voluntarily refused to vote or else had cast votes for the Democratic ticket to express their disgust with the sleazy state Republican administration. Republican cries of bulldozing were simply excuses to have the Republican returning board throw out legitimate Democratic votes, they claimed. Besides, Democrats asserted, Republicans had used a fraudulent trick to remove thousands of Democrats in New Orleans from the registration lists shortly before the election to depress the statewide Democratic vote.

In Florida, as in Louisiana, many local officials were for sale to the highest bidder. In fact, Republican William Chandler had brought $10,000 in cash with him to Tallahassee. An appalled Lew Wallace watched the Florida returning board interrogate county election commissioners about the returns they submitted. "It is terrible to see the extent to which all classes go in their determination to win," Wallace told his wife. "Nothing is so common as the resort to perjury, unless it is violence—in short, I do not know whom to believe. . . . Money and intimidation can obtain the oath of white men as well as black to any required statement. A ton of affidavits could be carted into the state-house to-morrow, and not a word of truth in them."[15] Similarly, Republican lawyer Francis Barlow of New York, who had gone to Florida at Grant's request, publicly charged that several hundred votes cast for Republicans in one Florida county were totally fictitious. The race was so tight in Florida that if those votes were disallowed, Florida would go to Tilden, and Democrat George Drew would win the governorship.

Fraud and chicanery abounded in all three states, and even before a single state canvassing board met, both Democrats and Republicans shouted that if their party did not win the three states it would be because of fraud and corruption. When a train sent from Tallahassee to gather votes from Florida's westernmost counties derailed on November 8, for example, Republican Governor Marcellus Stearns, who was fighting desperately to hold on to his office, sent a telegram to national committee headquarters in New York alleging that the train had been "Ku-Kluxed" to prevent Republican votes from being counted. "This shows that Florida is believed to be for Hayes on an honest count."[16] Similarly, Democratic Senator Joseph Randolph of New Jersey, traveling to New Orleans at Hewitt's request, stopped in Greensboro, North Carolina, and announced that the returns from Louisiana gave Democrats a majority of 7,569 votes "and that any other report by the Returning Board would be a fraud, and would be denounced as such; that Florida had gone Democratic, and that a certificate of election given to a Republican would necessarily be a fraud."[17] In short, both sides attempted to pressure returning boards before they met, and the Democratic cry about a stolen election appeared days before a single vote had officially been counted.

Understanding what happened in the three states requires a relatively detailed examination of events in each. Before undertaking that examination, however, it is important to clarify the stakes involved and the national atmosphere at the time. Tilden had 184 electoral votes and needed only one more from some state to reach the magic total of 185. But that was not the only way he could win. If any grounds could be found to convince Congress to refuse to count some electoral votes, as had happened in 1864, 1868, and 1872, it was possible that no one might obtain the necessary majority. In that case, the House of Representatives would pick the president, and it was certain to choose Tilden. For that scenario to work, however, Democrats had to prevent Hayes from getting all 19 contested electoral votes from the South or pick off 1 vote from the states he had apparently won. The only way Hayes could win, in short, was to reach 185 electoral votes and then rely on Republicans in Congress to prevent Democrats from throwing any of them out. Before a single southern state reached a decision, therefore, Republicans and Democrats were publicly jousting over whether the Republican president of the U.S. Senate had sole authority to count the electoral votes sent to Congress.

Meanwhile, Democrats from around the country were threatening to use armed force to make sure Tilden was inaugurated in March. Reminding Marble that he had predicted even before the Democrats' national convention that Republicans would use fraud to steal Louisiana's electoral vote, one New Orleans Democrat fumed, "To me it seems that if the spirit of liberty still survives the issue is Tilden or Civil War. Will the northern democracy fight?"[18] The Tilden papers are filled with telegrams from both northern and southern Democrats promising to raise armed vigilantes on Tilden's behalf once he gave the word. Some Democrats even spoke of appointing a Democratic Civil War general such as George B. McClellan or Winfield Scott Hancock to command this Democratic army. To his great credit, Tilden rejected these offers of armed aid and repeatedly called on his supporters to remain calm and peaceful. This pacific stance infuriated some southern Democrats. One angrily wrote to Tilden from Tallahassee on November 28, "The entire democracy of the south feel more than ever that they are leaning on a bag of mush when they look for aid and comfort from the north."[19]

Some Republicans pooh-poohed this talk of armed insurrection. Others immediately likened these threats to southern Democrats' treasonous secession in response to Lincoln's election in 1860 and blustered about welcoming another armed showdown. Others took the threat more seriously. Newspapers therefore buzzed in late November when Grant increased the size of the military force assigned to Washington. The nation, in short, watched what was going on in the three disputed states with great interest and deep apprehension.

So too, of course, did Hayes and Tilden, both of whom had official duties to attend to during the final months of their respective gubernatorial terms. Virtually every diary entry by Hayes for November and early December alluded to the disputes. His confidence waxed and waned as different newspaper reports came in daily. Hayes insisted that the Ohio Republicans in Louisiana do nothing underhanded to influence the result. "We are not to allow our friends to defeat one outrage and fraud by another," he instructed Senator Sherman on November 27. "There must be nothing crooked on our part."[20] On December 5 Hayes conferred in Columbus with Sherman, Garfield, and other Ohioans who had returned from New Orleans. Assured that nothing untoward had happened in New Orleans, he wrote to Schurz the following day, "I have no doubt that we are justly and legally entitled to the Presidency."[21] As will shortly become clear, if Hayes actually believed this, he was stunningly naïve.

Unfortunately, Tilden's outgoing correspondence during these weeks is unavailable. Therefore, we cannot know what he was actually thinking, even though his public advice to militant Democrats suggests unflappable confidence. But the incoming mail and telegrams, which varied from optimistic to pessimistic, make it clear that he kept close tabs on developments in all three southern states. Two other things are clear from Tilden's mail in November and early December. First, many Democrats told Tilden that the decisive factor would not be what happened when the electoral college met on December 6 but how Congress counted the electoral votes in February 1877. Second, by mid-November, a week before any decision in the South, many Democrats told Tilden that the disputed electoral vote in Oregon was the key to the election no matter what happened in the South. As shown later, Tilden personally took action on the Oregon issue as the dispute in the South worked itself out.

South Carolina's canvassing board met on November 10, and in part because state law prohibited it from sitting for longer than ten working days, it completed its work first. There was a reason for its short tenure. The new legislature was due to meet on November 28, and in South Carolina, as in Louisiana, the legislature, not the returning board, determined the winner of the election for governor and lieutenant governor—races that South Carolina Democrats cared far more about than the presidential contest. The state canvassing board, in turn, determined who won the electoral vote, the congressional vote in each district, other statewide offices, and, crucially, the state legislative elections, which would determine the victor in the gubernatorial election between Wade Hampton and incumbent Republican Daniel Chamberlain. The canvassing board consisted of five elected state officials, all of whom were Republicans, and three of whom were seeking reelection in 1876: secretary of state, state treasurer, controller general, adjutant general, and attorney general.

Although both parties had claimed South Carolina by improbably large majorities on the basis of the fragmentary early returns, fuller results indicated a tight partisan deadlock. *On their face,* those returns, even including the clearly padded Democratic vote from Edgefield and other up-country counties, gave a majority to Hayes and most statewide Republican candidates. Yet they also showed that Hampton had won the governorship by the same margin. Equally important, if unchallenged, the reported Democratic victories in the state legislative races in the up-country counties would give Democrats the majority in the new state legislature and thus the ability to count Hampton in as governor.

As a result of these facts, both parties conceded South Carolina's electoral votes to Hayes early on. For this reason, far fewer northern Republican and Democratic politicians traveled to Columbia than to either Tallahassee or New Orleans. Republicans, however, refused to concede the governor's race. This is where the caveat *on their face* became critical, and this is why Grant's language about counting the votes actually cast became controversial in South Carolina, just as it did in Louisiana. There is little doubt that the Democratic votes reported from those counties had actually been cast. But many had been cast illegally by white South Carolinians and Georgians who voted repeatedly at different polling stations where the lack of a list of registered voters prevented supervisors from challenging them. In addition, even though U.S. election supervisors had been posted in those counties, there was no doubt that hundreds, possibly thousands, of blacks had been forcibly prevented from getting anywhere near the polls, where the federal supervisors were stationed.

South Carolina's election law, like Louisiana's, explicitly instructed the state returning board to examine returns from election districts where fraud or voter intimidation was charged and to exclude those returns from the final count if those charges proved true. Democrats immediately and accurately predicted that the Republicans on the state canvassing board would throw out the returns from Edgefield and other up-country counties. This action would not simply enhance Hayes's statewide majority; it would also deprive Hampton of his popular-vote majority and Democrats of their majority in the new legislature due to meet on November 28. Thus, forcing the canvassing board to simply count the votes actually reported and preventing it from examining and excluding disputed votes became the Democrats' top priority, just as it was in Louisiana. In the technical language of the day, this goal meant confining the board to a "ministerial" function and preventing it from exercising a "judicial" function. Irony abounds here, for the argument advanced by Democrats in South Carolina and Louisiana in November was the exact opposite of the one they would make in February before the Federal Electoral Commission created by Congress to determine who had won the disputed electoral votes from those two states and others. In February it was the Republicans who insisted that the electoral votes submitted by the states be accepted on their face, and the Democrats who insisted that the commission go behind the reported returns and reverse them should a recalculation of popular-vote totals warrant that action.

On November 12 the lawyer for the Democratic state committee, who was also the Democratic candidate for attorney general, filed a brief with the canvassing board asserting that the state law allowing the board to perform judicial functions was unconstitutional and demanding that it only sum up the returns submitted by county election supervisors. Two days later, Democrats petitioned the state supreme court, all of whose judges were nominally Republican, for an injunction prohibiting the board from adjudicating any contested results and a writ of mandamus ordering it to count the votes as submitted. Remarkably, the board agreed to await a ruling from the court on the constitutionality of the law creating it before it decided anything. More remarkably still, the court then announced that it would delay any such ruling until the board reported a preliminary summary of who had won the votes actually cast (except for governor and lieutenant governor).

On November 21 the board reported to the court that Hayes had won the electoral vote by some 900 votes and that Republicans had won all but two of the statewide offices, despite the heavy Democratic majorities in Edgefield, Laurens, and other up-country counties. If those votes were counted, the board said, Democrats had elected two state senators and eight assemblymen from Edgefield and Laurens; however, because reports of fraud and intimidation from those two counties were so numerous and credible, the board recommended that those returns be examined and reversed—a judicial determination of results for which the court had yet to give permission. In reply, two of the three supreme court justices (including Franklin J. Moses, the father of a former, notoriously corrupt, scalawag Republican governor of the state) ruled that the board must do nothing until the following day, when the court would rule on the constitutionality of the board's exercise of judicial powers.

This minuet would have qualified as farce, had its outcome not been so serious. Under the South Carolina Constitution, the state supreme court had absolutely no legal jurisdiction over what the canvassing board did. The following day, November 22, the Republican members of the canvassing board finally seemed to realize that fact, if only because they also believed that this was the final day they could legally sit as a canvassing board. Meeting on the morning of November 22, the canvassing board ordered the secretary of state, who was also the board's chairman, to award certificates of election to the seven Republican presidential electors, all the Republican statewide candidates except for Daniel Chamberlain and his running mate, all the congressional candidates it had declared winners, and all the state legislative candidates, with the exception of those Democrats from Edgefield and Laurens counties, whose returns were blatantly suspicious. Then the board summarily dissolved itself as a legal political entity, in accordance with state law.

As the board of canvassers was finally acting, the two hostile justices of the state supreme court, meeting elsewhere in Columbia, sent two writs of mandamus to the board, which were not delivered until after it had adjourned sine die. One ordered the board to award certificates of election to the Democratic legislators from Edgefield and Laurens counties, thereby virtually guaranteeing the defeat of Chamberlain. The other ordered the board to show cause on November 24 why it should not simply count the returns for presidential electors as submitted rather than investigating alleged fraud and intimidation in up-country counties. When the two judges learned that the returning board had already acted, in defiance of their order the previous day, they went ballistic. They jailed all the members of the canvassing board for contempt of court and awarded certificates of election to the Democratic legislative candidates from Edgefield and Laurens counties, even though state law explicitly gave that authority to the executive returning board. Republicans, in turn, quickly assembled a panel of Republican federal circuit judges who freed the canvassing board under writs of habeas corpus.

Still, this saga had not fully played out. Infuriated Democrats threatened to seize the statehouse by force, despite Hampton's pleas for calm. Grant sent orders through Secretary of War Don Cameron that Chamberlain was clearly the legal governor until a new one was chosen by the legislature and that troops in Columbia must protect him and the state capitol. When the legislature convened on November 28, the Republican majority of the assembly, all but one of whom were black, denied entry to the Democrats from Edgefield and Laurens counties because they lacked certificates of election from the secretary of state. Democrats then withdrew en masse and set up their own legislature. The Republicans, claiming to hold a legal quorum in both legislative chambers, declared Chamberlain the new governor on December 5, the day before the electoral college met. On December 7 the rival Democratic legislature named Hampton the new governor, a choice that was clearly popular with virtually every white South Carolinian and a minority of blacks who had voted for him to oust Republicans from power. Now federal troops had to keep the peace between rival Democratic and Republican governors as well as rival legislatures, a task they would perform until after the presidential election had finally been decided and Rutherford Hayes had been sworn in.

So what did this convoluted saga have to do with the disposition of South Carolina's seven electoral votes? Even the hostile majority of the state supreme court apparently accepted the canvassing board's conclusion that Hayes deserved them. Their obvious skepticism of the board's power to adjudicate contested returns was clearly meant to stop the investigation of returns in the state election. Nonetheless, their declaration that the canvassing board had acted in contempt of court and thus illegally by certifying the Republican electors on November 22 gave Democrats legal grounds for challenging the electoral vote. Even more important, the canvassing board's admission that it had acted without examining *any* contested votes allowed Democrats to claim that in some counties purportedly carried by Hayes, Republicans had rigged the vote and that Tilden, like Hampton, had carried South Carolina.

Thus, when South Carolina's electoral college assembled in Columbia on December 6, there were two sets of men claiming to be the state's legitimate electors. Republicans, with certificates signed by the secretary of state, awarded the state's seven electoral votes to Hayes. Republican Governor Chamberlain certified their count as correct and sent it under seal to the president of the Senate, as required by the Constitution. The Democratic electors claimed the state's electoral votes for Tilden and sent them to Washington without any official signature of certification whatsoever. Precisely because the returns, on their face, showed Hayes to be the winner of the state's electoral votes, these Democratic certificates apparently contained no listing of the popular-vote totals that gave Tilden a majority. This action flouted the Constitution's explicit requirement that such totals for all candidates be included with any certificates sent to the president of the Senate. South Carolina Democrats, one infers, sought primarily to give congressional Democrats grounds for challenging the Republican electoral votes.

Florida Democrats sought favorable court rulings to influence the outcome of the presidential race more directly and more persistently than did their fellow party members in South Carolina. Florida's population was small but widely dispersed. As a result, complete returns came in much more slowly than they did in the Palmetto State. Fully two weeks after election day, for example, seven of the state's thirty-nine counties had yet to be heard from. In anticipation of that delay, the 1868 law creating the state returning board gave it thirty-five days from the date of an election to determine its outcome and did not require it to meet until the last week in November. As in South Carolina, the state returning board consisted of elected state officials. One of its three members was the attorney general, a prewar southern Whig who had voted for Grant in 1872 but voted for Tilden in 1876. What is more, he publicly announced even before the board's first meeting that Tilden had carried Florida and was the next president. Thus in Florida, unlike in both Louisiana and South Carolina, Republicans did not monopolize the entire membership of the state returning board.[22]

Unlike in Louisiana and South Carolina, Florida's canvassing board could determine the winner of the gubernatorial race, but the law establishing the board did not explicitly give it authority to count the votes for presidential electors. That omission, together with the long delay in getting complete returns and the attorney general's premature pronouncement that Tilden had won, set the stage for legal conflict. From the day of the election, the two parties had charged each other with stealing ballot boxes and rigging favorable returns in different counties. By the third week of November, however, the squabbling focused on who would count the presidential votes and when that count would be made. Democrats pressed the returning board to begin the count before all the returns were in, but the two Republican members of the board refused to call it into session. Democrats' purpose here, Republicans charged, was to get an idea of the total claimed for Hayes so that the yet-to-be-heard-from counties, all lightly populated Democratic bastions, could report enough fictitious Democratic votes to overcome the Republican majority. Democrats, in turn, charged that under authority of an 1846 law, Governor Stearns intended to count the presidential vote himself to prevent the canvassing board, with its Democratic member, from giving Democrats a fair chance. Democrats therefore found a Democratic state circuit judge who lived some forty miles outside Tallahassee and brought him to the capital. They then filed briefs demanding that he issue an injunction prohibiting Stearns from attempting to count the vote and a writ of mandamus forcing the returning board to begin the count of the presidential vote at once. Out-of-state counsel for both parties argued the case. Stearns submitted an affidavit to the Democratic judge denying both that he had any intention of trying to count the vote himself and that the judge had any legal authority over his activities as governor. In any event, before the judge made a ruling, the Republican secretary of state called for the canvassing board, which he chaired, to begin its official meetings on November 27, apparently rendering the case moot.

Under the rules adopted by the board at its inaugural meeting, it would canvass all the returns for president except those from distant Dade County, which still had not reported, on the following day. Protests could be entered then, but none would be tried until after the initial count was completed. Six "visiting statesmen" from each party, their respective state chairmen, and gubernatorial candidates Stearns and Drew were invited to attend each board session. The following day, with Democrat Manton Marble and Republicans Edward Noyes, Lew Wallace, and William E. Chandler in attendance, the committee concluded that, on the face of the submitted returns, Hayes had defeated Tilden in the popular vote 24,327 to 24,284—a microscopic margin of 43 votes.

The board's work had only begun, however. Democrats challenged the vote in all ten counties with Republican majorities, the most heavily populated and blackest counties in Florida. Republicans, in turn, planned to challenge the Democratic majorities in the remaining twenty-nine counties, most of them thinly populated and heavily white, which Republicans disparaged as "cow-boy counties." Both parties claimed to have enough evidence of intimidation of election officials, ballot-box tampering, fictitious voting, and technical violations of the state's election law to force the canvassing board to alter the result in their favor. On this second inspection of the votes, significantly, the gubernatorial returns were also tallied.

Lack of space prevents a full analysis of the board's deliberations, which lasted until December 5, the day before Florida's electoral college met. Only one county's entire vote was thrown out, on the grounds that its commissioners had failed to make adequate preparations for the election. That decision was unanimous. Most were not; the two Republicans repeatedly outvoted Democratic Attorney General William A. Cocke. The board zeroed in on specific polling places within contested counties, and it used supposed technical violations by election supervisors at those polls to eradicate Democratic majorities. State law required that once all the ballots were in at any polling place, the ballot boxes were to be opened immediately, the votes tallied in public view, the ballots returned to their respective boxes, and the boxes sealed and carried under guard to the nearest clerk of court. Purported violations of that procedure, which was meant to prevent any tampering with the ballots before or after they were counted, cost Democrats significantly.

Three examples must suffice. The Jasper precinct in Hamilton County had given Democrats a 140-vote majority in the presidential and gubernatorial balloting. The board threw out its entire vote because the election inspectors, rather than counting the votes immediately after the poll closed, took a dinner break and left the boxes unattended while doing so. A 291 to 77 Democratic margin in a Jackson County precinct evaporated for the same reason. Finally, Democrats outpolled Republicans 401 to 59 in Key West, by far the most populous town in all south Florida. The board's majority threw out all those votes because the election inspectors had waited until the day after the election to count the votes and then had failed to do so in public view. Just in these three cases, the Republicans eliminated a net Democratic gain of 696 votes, which would have given the state's electoral vote to Tilden. Whether this technical nit-picking constituted the kind of fraud or steal Democrats had predicted lies in the eye of the beholder. In any event, Democrats would later argue that rejecting returns on these grounds, rather than for those reasons explicitly spelled out in the election law, was illegal.

Attorney General Cocke certainly believed that his colleagues were partisanly biased, if not blatantly dishonest, as other Democrats charged. The board announced on December 5 that its thorough canvassing of contested votes had expanded Hayes's margin over Tilden from 43 to 926 votes and had given Stearns a majority of 458 over Democrat Drew in the gubernatorial race, a race Democrats were certain they had won. Cocke publicly protested his colleagues' action on December 6, the day that Florida's presidential electors met. He protested the board's awarding of certificates of election to the Republican electors, statewide candidates, and congressional candidates, largely on the basis of legal technicalities. The board, he argued, should have accepted the votes from the three precincts identified above and thrown out the entire vote of heavily Republican Duval County because its probate judge had used improper legal procedures in forwarding its returns to the canvassing board. According to Cocke, the Democratic electors deserved certificates of election. His Republican colleagues on the board simply ignored his protest.

The four Democratic electors certainly believed that they had won, and on the morning of December 6 they secured writs of quo warranto from the same Democratic circuit judge who had earlier agreed to enjoin Governor Stearns from counting the vote. They served these writs on the four Republican electors just before they awarded their electoral votes to Hayes and Wheeler. But hearings where the Republicans would be required to show by what authority they held their office were not scheduled until December 18, long after Stearns had certified their votes as correct and sent them under seal to Washington. Unsurprisingly, the Democratic judge then ruled that the four Republicans did not legally hold the office of electors from Florida—the Democrats did. The Democrats, however, had not awaited that decision. Claiming to be acting as Florida's electoral college, on December 6 they sent their four votes for Tilden and Hendricks under seal to Washington, accompanied by Cocke's certification of their election and his legal opinion, but without any official certification by the governor.

The dispute over Florida's electoral votes and the judiciary's intervention in it was not yet over. In a suit brought by the Democratic gubernatorial candidate, the supreme court on December 23 issued a writ of mandamus ordering the board of canvassers to recount the vote for governor and other statewide officials using only the totals submitted by county officials. The board, insisted the court, had unconstitutionally appropriated judicial functions by selectively throwing out certain returns; its authority extended only to the ministerial function of adding up the votes sent to it. This new count showed that Drew and other Democratic candidates had narrowly won election, and all were peacefully sworn in on January 1, 1877. Democratic control of the new state legislature had been clear since November 7, so Democrats now controlled the entire state government.

The Democrats were quick to take advantage of that control. The ruling by the circuit court judge that the Republican electors had illegally cast the state's electoral vote, and the one by the supreme court that the board of canvassers had acted unconstitutionally in throwing out votes, along with Cocke's detailed protest, opened clear possibilities for Democrats, as Marble and other Democrats in New York were acutely aware. In early January the Democratic electors sought a writ of mandamus from the state supreme court to force the board of canvassers, now composed entirely of Democratic state officials, to recount the vote for president under the same rules it had imposed on the recount for governor. Even before the court acted, the legislature passed a law ordering the new board of canvassers to recount the presidential vote. Marble had written every word of this statute in New York and sent it by courier to Florida Democrats. That count awarded the certificates of election to the Democrats; they reassembled and once again sent four electoral votes for Tilden, this time certified by the new Democratic Governor George

Drew. The state legislature then passed another law affirming that Democrats had won the electoral vote. All these materials reached Congress on January 31, 1877, the day before the count of electoral votes began.

When the joint session of Congress met on February 1, 1877, to count the electoral votes, it thus confronted three sets of electoral votes from Florida—two for Tilden and one for Hayes. As would then become clear, the central issue was whether anything that happened in Florida after Stearns had certified the four Republican votes on December 6 had any legal bearing whatsoever on what would be decided in Washington.

The dispute over Florida's electoral votes lasted longer and was more convoluted, thanks to judicial interference, than that in the other two Deep South states. From the morning of November 8, however, northern Republicans and Democrats focused primarily on Louisiana. For that reason, far more northern politicos from both parties went to New Orleans than to Tallahassee or Columbia. Several things explain that focus. First, on their face, the returns submitted to the state returning board from Louisiana's parishes showed a majority of some 7,000 to 8,000 votes for Tilden. Both parties therefore knew that the outcome in Louisiana depended on whether the returning board was required to count those votes as cast or could throw out votes on the grounds that fraud, intimidation, or technical improprieties had prevented a full and fair vote in individual parishes and their electoral districts. On this question, Republicans and Democrats were at odds. The 1872 law establishing the state returning board explicitly gave it the authority to throw votes out, and Democrats clearly feared that the board would do so in the heavily Democratic East and West Feliciana and other parishes. Hence, just as in South Carolina and Florida, Democrats argued that the 1872 law unconstitutionally awarded judicial functions to an agency of the executive branch, whose powers were exclusively "ministerial," in violation of the separation of powers among distinct branches of the state government.

Second, and more important, Louisiana's state returning board was notoriously biased and corrupt. The state's Democrats had never accepted its ruling in 1872 that Republican William Pitt Kellogg rather than Democrat John McEnery had won the governorship, and even congressional Republicans had refused to count Louisiana's electoral votes submitted for Grant because they were obviously rigged. After the board declared in 1874 that Republicans had won a majority of the state house of representatives, a congressional investigating committee headed by William A. Wheeler, Hayes's running mate in 1876, had rejected those findings and insisted that Democrats be given control of the house. The same members of the returning board who had made that ruling in 1874, save for one, would determine the presidential results in 1876. Thus the chief function of the Republican "statesmen" sent to New Orleans, other than gathering affidavits and other evidence to defend or challenge the results submitted from individual parishes, was to attest that this widely discredited board acted on the up-and-up when counting the presidential votes. Democratic observers, in turn, were there to pressure or shame it into acting fairly, lest the Democratic House of Representatives throw out Louisiana's electoral votes once again.

The northerners in New Orleans—both Republican and Democrat—were largely trying to persuade the rest of the country rather than Louisiana's bitterly opposed party members. And from the standpoint of public relations, the Republican statesmen had the harder row to hoe. Unlike South Carolina and Florida, the members of Louisiana's returning board were not popularly elected statewide officials; rather, they were appointed by the Republican-controlled state senate. The 1872 law establishing the board specified that its five members should be divided among "all" political parties in the state, and the original board consisted of four Republicans and a single Democrat. In protest against the board's decision regarding the 1874 legislative elections, however, the lone, consistently outvoted Democrat had resigned in disgust. As of November 1876, he had not been replaced by another Democrat; nor would he be by the time the presidential vote was decided. Before December 6, Democratic lawyers submitted eighteen formal protests that the board was illegally constituted because it lacked a Democratic member and therefore had no legal standing. Nonetheless, the four Republicans insisted on deciding the vote without a Democratic member, and the Republican senate made no attempt to supply one. Here, then, were obvious grounds for a Democratic challenge to the Louisiana results when they came before Congress.

Nor were the reputations of the two black and two white Republicans on the board sterling. During November, unsubstantiated rumors swept New Orleans that the two black members had offered to count Tilden in for $100,000 apiece. That, the story went, was why Republicans refused to name a Democrat to the board: it would have produced a 3 to 2 vote for the Democrats. Undoubtedly the most dishonest member of the board, however, was its chairman, J. Madison Wells. Wells had been elected lieutenant governor of Louisiana on a Union Party ticket in

1864 under Lincoln's 10 percent Reconstruction plan. In 1865 Governor Michael Hahn had resigned to take a U.S. Senate seat that northern Republican senators would never let him fill. Wells then became governor and immediately used his extensive appointive powers to restore ex-Confederates to political control of the state at the expense of black and white members of the Union coalition. Betrayed by the beneficiaries of this policy, who continually rebuffed him, Wells swerved sharply in 1866 and tried to arrange an abortive constitutional convention that would enfranchise blacks. This move sparked the notorious New Orleans race riot in the summer of 1866 but earned Wells few points with Louisiana's black majority. In 1868, after blacks had been enfranchised by congressional statute, he was dumped unceremoniously from the Republican ticket. By the mid-1870s he had landed a job in the New Orleans customhouse, the epicenter of Republican corruption in Louisiana.

In November 1876 Wells's vote and influence with other members of the returning board were up for sale. For $100,000, he told first Democrats and then Republicans in New Orleans, he would count their man in. Apparently rebuffed by both parties' statesmen there, Wells then had the temerity to contact Tilden and Abram Hewitt. For $1 million, his agent told the appalled New Yorkers, Wells could make Tilden the next president. Tilden and Hewitt emphatically rejected this offer, yet evidence suggests that Colonel William Pelton, Tilden's nephew and personal secretary, was prepared to bargain with Wells for $200,000. No arrangement was finalized, however, before the board had to act to meet the December 6 deadline for the convening of the electoral college. Northern Republicans in New Orleans therefore faced a real challenge in trying to assure the northern public that these worthies on the returning board acted on the up-and-up when determining the outcome of the presidential race in Louisiana.

Those northern Republican statesmen may have attempted to use means other than hard cash to bribe the Republican members of the board to render a favorable decision. Possible evidence of such attempts exists in the Samuel J. Tilden Papers in New York's Public Library. *Possible* is the key word here, because the evidence consists of unauthenticated copies of purported contacts Ohio Senator John Sherman had with Wells and James Anderson, the other white member of the returning board. On November 20, the day the canvassing of the vote finally started, Anderson complained to Sherman that "your assurance that we shall be taken care of is scarcely specific enough." The Republicans on the board would have to leave the state if they counted in Hayes. "Will you, therefore, state in writing who we shall look to for the fulfillment of those promises?" On the same day, Sherman supposedly responded, "Neither Mr. Hayes, myself, the gentlemen who accompany me, or the country at large can ever forget the obligation under which you will have placed us should you stand firm in the position you have taken." He knew Hayes well enough, Sherman continued, that "I am justified in assuming responsibility for promises made and for guarantee that you shall be provided for as soon after the 4th of March as may be practicable."[23] A purported letter from Wells to Sherman, dated November 21, was an obvious attempt to extort a cash bribe from Republicans by threatening that board members might take Democratic money instead. "Let me, my esteemed sir, warn you of the danger. Millions have been sent here and will be used in the interest of Tilden, and unless some counter move, it will be impossible for me or any other individual to wrest its [the canvass's] productive results. . . . See our friends and act promptly or results will be disaster. A hint to the wise."[24] Apparently neither party, in short, was above dirtying its hands to capture Louisiana's eight electoral votes. Indeed, on the very day the electoral college met, one of the Republican electors publicly charged that Democrats had offered him $100,000 to cast his vote for Tilden.

Although almost all the visiting Democratic and Republican "statesmen" in New Orleans took rooms in the city's elegant St. Charles Hotel, relations between the two delegations were almost comically stiff and formal. Many of these men knew one another personally, either from common service in Congress or common service in Republican ranks during the 1860s. They easily could have met for discussions in someone's room, the lobby, or the hotel's bar. They apparently eschewed interpersonal conversation, however, and instead relied on letters to one another intended for publication in the northern press to score political points with the northern public.

Democrats launched this public relations campaign in a letter of November 14 that was instantly released to the press. Signed by John M. Palmer and Lyman Trumbull of Illinois and by Samuel J. Randall, Andrew Curtin, and William Bigler of Pennsylvania, among others, the letter was addressed to Judge Stanley Matthews, James A. Garfield, William D. Kelley, and other Republicans, some of whom had declined Grant's invitation to go to New Orleans. In this letter, the Democrats asked the Republicans to meet with them to mutually agree on the best way to secure a fair count of "the vote actually cast"—a phrase the Democrats managed to use three times in this short letter. On the same day that it published this epistle, the *New York Times* ran an angry editorial charging that this heavy-handed emphasis signaled the Democrats' intention to prevent the board from examining and discarding votes from parishes where bloated Democratic majorities reflected the successful prevention of black voting.[25]

Because northern Republicans arrived more slowly in New Orleans than did their Democratic counterparts, they did not reply until November 16. Signed by Senator John Sherman, Judge Matthews, Congressman Garfield, and twenty-two other Republicans, this letter rejected the Democrats' request for mutual consultation and launched some devastating partisan zingers. They were in New Orleans at the request of the president, wrote the Republicans, simply as private citizens to observe the count by the returning board. They had no authority to enter into negotiations with Democrats, especially to influence the actions of the returning board—as the Democrats' "votes actually cast" language implied. The 1872 election law, which Republicans quoted at length, explicitly *required* that board to throw out returns from parishes or election districts where conclusive evidence indicated that riot, fraud, armed force, intimidation, and other illegalities had prevented voters from registering or voting in sufficient numbers to affect the outcome. Republicans were right about this, for the language of the election law repeatedly used the imperative verb *shall* in detailing the duties of the state returning board. Then the Republicans twisted the partisan knife. The returning board, they insisted, clearly had judicial, not just ministerial, powers. "It would be a manifest interference with State rights and local self-government for persons, like ourselves, without official rights to attempt to influence or control its judicial action." If Louisianans had attempted to influence a corresponding board of New Yorkers in 1868 to overlook "the fraudulent returns of the City of New York, . . . such attempt would have been overwhelmingly condemned." Moreover, the powers of Louisiana's returning board were not "merely ministerial or clerical," unlike those of "the President of the Senate," whose sole duty was to count and announce the electoral votes for president and vice president sent to him from the states.[26] Already, Republicans were positioning themselves for an anticipated fight in February over who could count the electoral votes submitted to Congress.

Democrats parried this thrust in another letter. They denied that the president of the Senate could count the electoral votes. They had used the phrase "votes actually cast" with regard to Louisiana specifically because Grant had used it in his orders to Sherman. They had no intention of pressuring the returning board's course of action. All they sought was some mutual agreement between the two teams about how, physically, they could watch the proceedings of the returning board to ensure a fair count.

This exchange of letters occurred in part because Wells and other members of the returning board initially intended to hold all their sessions in private, with no witnesses whatsoever. Recognizing that this procedure would be a public relations disaster in the North, Garfield and other northern Republicans pressed Wells to change his mind and adopt a more transparent procedure. On November 17 Wells announced that five of the northern statesmen, along with a stenographer, from each party could witness the board's proceedings—or at least some of them. The board absolutely prohibited newspaper reporters from watching those sessions. It would proceed by first counting the votes from parishes that were uncontested in front of the two parties' delegations. Then it would take up contested parishes in alphabetical order. It would accept only written affidavits and legal briefs prepared in advance of each case; it refused to hear oral arguments by lawyers for either party. But it would accept oral testimony from witnesses Democrats and Republicans had recruited. Again, the two parties' observers could be there when the affidavits were opened and read and could listen to the witnesses' testimony. But—and this was a huge but—after all the disputed cases had been considered, the board would make its decision in secret session with no one but the four members in the room. The canvass itself would start on Monday, November 20.

Once the Democrats learned of this procedure, they selected their five observers: John M. Palmer and Lyman Trumbull of Illinois, William Bigler of Pennsylvania, George Smith of Wisconsin, and P. H. Watson of Ohio. Most of the others packed their bags and left for home before a single vote was counted. Many Republicans also left New Orleans before November 20; some, such as Judge Matthews, went home; others, such as his Ohio colleague E. F. Noyes, headed to Florida. Both Sherman and Garfield, however, remained in New Orleans until the board finished its open hearings, as did a number of other Republicans. Thus they decided to rotate their five observers from day to day; according to newspaper accounts, however, Garfield was there more frequently than any other Republican.

Before a single vote was counted, the counsel for the Democratic state committee submitted a brief to the board arguing, as did Democrats in South Carolina and Florida, that Louisiana's election law was unconstitutional because it required an agency of the executive branch to adjudicate contested results, a function properly reserved exclusively for courts. The Republican board members, needless to say, dismissed this argument out of hand.

More than half of Louisiana's seventy-one parishes were contested. Many of the witnesses who appeared before the board had probably been bribed. Many of the black witnesses who were expected to testify about white intimidation were so terrified about the prospect of retribution that they could be induced to come to New Orleans only under the protection of federal troops. More than one said that he could not return home and would be forced to leave the state after his testimony was completed. One woman testified that whites had murdered her husband because he intended to vote Republican, killed a child she held in her arms, and then stabbed and raped her. This brought Democrat John Palmer to his feet in sputtering outrage at so foul a crime.

These quasi-public hearings took considerable time, and it was not until December 5 that the board announced what it had decided in secret. It threw out the entire vote from Grant and East Feliciana parishes, as well as the results from individual polling districts in twenty-two others. Altogether it refused to count as legal some 15,000 ballots, 13,000 of which had reportedly been cast for Democratic candidates. Thus it wiped out a 6,000-vote majority for Tilden and an 8,000-vote majority for Francis Nichols, the Democrats' gubernatorial candidate, and gave Hayes and Stephen Packard majorities of between 3,000 and 4,000 votes. Democrats understandably cried fraud and foul, even though both they and Republicans alike had predicted for weeks that the board was certain to throw out some of the reported Democratic votes.

Thus in Louisiana, too, two groups claiming to be the state's legitimate electoral college met on December 6 and sent their conflicting electoral votes to Washington. Governor Kellogg certified the Republican votes, and the putative Democratic Governor John McEnery certified those of the Democrats. Only the state legislature could officially determine the outcome of the concurrent gubernatorial election, which both Packard and Nichols claimed to have won. As in South Carolina, that face-off would not be determined until after Hayes was inaugurated. Unlike Florida, however, the prolonged contest over the governorship had no bearing on the state's disputed electoral votes sent to Washington on December 6.

Weeks before any of the three southern states determined the outcome of the presidential race within them, Democrats discovered another way to get the single electoral vote they needed to prevent Hayes's election, even if Republican machines in all three of those states gave him their electoral votes. The U.S. Constitution explicitly prohibits anyone on the federal payroll from serving as a presidential elector, and technically, Americans voted for these often obscure men who served as electors. Within days of the November election, Democrats discovered that in both Vermont and Oregon one Republican elector had held the office of postmaster on election day. Thus both of them, Democrats eagerly announced, were constitutionally ineligible to receive the votes cast for them.

The two cases differed somewhat. The Republican postmaster in Vermont, a man named Henry N. Sollace, had sent a letter resigning his office on November 6, the day before the election, to the postmaster general in Washington. But that official did not acknowledge Sollace's resignation until after the election, so technically, he was still a postmaster when Vermont Republicans voted for him. John W. Watts, the fourth-class postmaster from Oregon who earned a grand annual salary of $240, did not send his letter of resignation until the day after the election, and the postmaster general did not officially acknowledge that resignation until November 14, a week after the election.

In both instances, Democrats argued, since the vote for the ineligible elector was a legal nullity, the governors of Vermont and Oregon should award a certificate of election to the elector receiving the next highest popular vote, that is, a Democratic elector in each state. There was no chance that Vermont's Republican governor would do that, even though Vermont Democrats sought court injunctions to force him to do so. Besides, Vermont, like many states, had a law that specifically dealt with vacancies occurring among the winning electors before the meeting of the electoral college. It allowed the remaining electors on the winning side to fill the vacancy themselves, and Vermont's Republicans picked the now officially resigned postmaster.

Oregon was another matter: its governor was a Democrat. On November 14 a Portland, Oregon, Democrat telegraphed New York Democratic

Congressman Samuel S. Cox, asking him whether Congress had any precedents "treating ineligible [electoral] candidates as disentitled to count & giving certificate to next highest."[27] The following day Cox forwarded that telegram to Tilden and urged him to send a prominent California Democrat to Oregon with a legal opinion arguing that a Democratic elector deserved the certificate. That day, Tilden asked New York Democratic Congressman Clarkson Potter, Tilden's next-door neighbor in Gramercy Park and a former judge, for his legal opinion on the matter. Potter told him that if Oregon's voters knew on election day that Watts was ineligible, a Democrat deserved the electoral vote. If they did not know, the vote for Watts was null, and Oregon should have only two, not three, electoral votes. What that meant, Potter explained to Tilden, was that Hayes could never get more than 184 electoral votes even if he got all 19 from the three southern states. The electoral vote would be a tie, and the Democratic House of Representatives would make Tilden president.

Armed with this opinion, Hewitt telegraphed the following instructions to Oregon's Governor Lafayette F. Grover that very day: "Upon careful investigation, the legal opinion is that the votes cast for a Federal office-holder are void, and that the person receiving the next highest number of votes should receive the certificate of appointment. This will force Congress to go behind the certificate, and open the way to get into the merits of all cases, which is not only just, but will relieve the embarrassment of the situation."[28] Hewitt's wording is exceedingly important. Clearly, he would have liked to transfer an electoral vote from Hayes's column to Tilden's if the Democrats could get away with it. But his wording strongly suggests that he hoped to use a dispute over Oregon's electoral vote primarily as a lever to force Congress to examine the certificates of election he now expected the returning boards from Florida, Louisiana, and South Carolina to give to Republican electors. Whatever Congress decided about that one electoral vote from Oregon, it could be used to force Congress to confront and reject what Democrats deemed fraudulent Republican vote counts from the Deep South.

Not surprisingly, not everyone agreed with Potter's legal opinion. Attorney General Alphonzo Taft, for example, told a meeting of Grant's cabinet that selection of presidential electors was exclusively each state's own affair and that Oregon should follow the precedent of most states and allow the two clearly elected Republican electors to fill the vacancy. He believed there was no precedent to allow one of the losing party's electors to claim that certificate. Oregon, in fact, had the same kind of law as Vermont; hence some Democrats urged Tilden to get Governor Grover to call the legislature, which Democrats controlled, into emergency session to repeal that law before the electoral college met. There is no evidence, at least in Tilden's papers, that he did so, but other Democrats from around the country, including Marble while he was still in Florida, certainly pressured Grover to make sure a Democrat got one of the state's electoral votes. "The subject is under careful examination," Grover telegraphed Marble on November 28.[29]

Grover wavered, but in the end he did as he was urged. On December 4 he awarded certificates of election to two Republicans and one Democrat. But the official legally responsible for canvassing the vote was the secretary of state, and even though a Democrat, he awarded certificates of election bearing the state seal to those two Republicans and the Republican Watts. The meeting of Oregon's electoral college on December 6 was the most bizarre in the nation. The two Republicans refused to allow E. A. Cronin, the Democrat certified by Grover, to act with them as the state's electoral college. Instead, they appointed Watts to the vacancy created by his former constitutional ineligibility, and the three sent their certificates of election for Hayes and Wheeler, signed and sealed by the secretary of state, to Washington. Simultaneously, Cronin announced that the two Democrats who had run with him as electors on November 7 had abdicated their seats, and under authority of state law, he appointed two other Democrats to their places. Those two Democrats cast their electoral votes for Hayes and Wheeler, while Cronin voted for Tilden and Hendricks. Grover certified this group as Oregon's official electoral college and sent their votes to Washington.

Thus, four states sent conflicting sets of electoral votes to Washington. Thus, twenty, not nineteen, electoral votes were still in dispute after the meeting of the electoral college on December 6. Thus, officials in Washington, not voters or returning boards in the states, would have to make the final determination about who had actually won the presidential election of 1876.

 **THE DISPUTE RESOLVED**

"If the House stands firm, all will come out right," one Democrat assured Tilden as early as November 22. "The democrats in the House have the power, if they have the nerve, to control the election," echoed another six days later.[1] Weeks before the second session of the Forty-fourth Congress opened on December 4, 1876, and the electoral college met two days later, Democrats counted on their huge majority in the House of Representatives to secure Tilden's victory no matter what the returning boards in Florida, Louisiana, and South Carolina did with their electoral votes. Most House Democrats were equally determined. At their caucus on December 3, they chose Philadelphia's Samuel J. Randall as their candidate for Speaker of the House, thereby assuring his election. He had been picked, Randall immediately wrote to Tilden, primarily to make sure that Tilden was counted in as president, and he promised to heed any instructions Tilden cared to send him to achieve that goal.

Democrats' faith in the House rested on three uneven pillars. One was its power to appoint investigating committees. On the session's opening day, Abram Hewitt introduced a resolution that the House send committees to Florida, Louisiana, and South Carolina to expose the fraudulent findings of the Republican returning boards. He then handed Randall a list of names, including the Republican members he had chosen without consulting any member of that party, for the South Carolina committee. The House adopted Hewitt's motion on a largely party-line vote, and committees with lopsided

Democratic majorities were dispatched to the three states. Unsurprisingly, those Democratic majorities later reported that Tilden deserved the electoral votes of Florida and Louisiana, and they deposited boxloads of affidavits, recalculated vote totals from different election districts, and other testimony to support their claims. In reply, minority reports from the committees' Republican members complained that Democrats had browbeaten or bribed witnesses, that Republicans had been denied the right to cross-examine those witnesses, and that Hayes and Wheeler had carried those two states. As one of the Republicans who had gone to Florida protested, Democrats had refused to let them see anything. "From the beginning to the end, not one particle of evidence that went before the canvassing board did we have."[2]

South Carolina was a special case. Even the Democrats on the investigating committee announced that Hayes had clearly carried it. Therefore, the case Democrats would make about South Carolina was not that Tilden deserved its votes but that Hayes did not deserve them either, because the intimidating presence of federal marshals and troops had prevented thousands of both blacks and whites from voting for Tilden. Voiding South Carolina's votes, not delivering them to Tilden, would be their strategy.

The Republican-controlled Senate also sought to reexamine the returns from the three southern states. It consigned the job to its standing Committee on Privileges and Elections, which originally planned to remain in Washington and summon witnesses from the South to appear before it. It quickly decided, however, to send subcommittees to all three southern states; the subcommittees' primary purpose, from Republicans' perspective, was to gather evidence that blacks had been prevented from voting by fraud and intimidation. Committee chairman Oliver P. Morton remained in Washington, where he focused his attention on Oregon's disputed electoral vote.

For much of December, however, Democrats, including Tilden himself, relied primarily on the continuing force of the Twenty-second Joint Rule, which would allow House Democrats to reject all the Republican returns from the South. That rule, as explained earlier, allowed any senator or representative to challenge any or all electoral votes from a state when its votes were opened before the joint meeting of Congress in February. Each chamber would then immediately go into separate session and vote, without any debate, to sustain or reject the objection. If either house by majority vote sustained the objection, the electoral votes would be thrown out, thus virtually guaranteeing that the House would choose the next president. Democratic confidence in that scenario grew when Congressman Abram Hewitt, still chairman of the Democratic National Committee, secured an interview with Grant at the White House on December 3 and then infuriated the president by announcing that Grant believed the House should throw out Louisiana's electoral votes.

This possibility is precisely why Morton had attacked the Twenty-second Joint Rule so passionately in early 1875 and again in early 1876 and tried to replace it with a law that would require a concurrent vote by both houses of Congress to reject any electoral votes. And that is why Morton had successfully persuaded his fellow Republican senators in 1875 and again in 1876 to rescind the joint rule. The House, however, had never considered Morton's new law or agreed to repeal the joint rule. Without that concurrence, House Democrats now argued in December 1876, the joint rule remained in effect. Indeed, in the first days of the congressional session, Speaker Randall found a pretext for ruling that all earlier joint rules were still in force. His Senate counterpart, Michigan Republican Thomas Ferry, the president pro-tem of the Senate (now serving as its president, because Vice President Henry Wilson had died), similarly found a pretext for ruling that no joint rules still existed.

For several reasons, Democrats had a tough case to make. For one thing, the constitutionality of automatically continuing joint rules from one Congress to the next was murky, to say the least. Reasonable men had disagreed during the Senate debates over repeal in early 1876, and by December of that year, inflamed partisan rancor had largely displaced reason. More important, the two leading legal minds among Senate Democrats, Ohio's Allen G. Thurman and Delaware's Thomas Bayard, had unequivocally declared on the Senate floor that the joint rule had ceased to exist once the Senate had voted to rescind it. House Speaker Randall and Tilden both relied too much on the continuing force of that rule, August Belmont warned Manton Marble on December 21. "Thurman & Bayard are themselves too much on record against it, besides which the Senate has already pronounced its determination for its abrogation." The best thing for Democrats, he added, was for both houses to enact into law Morton's earlier proposal.[3]

If the Twenty-second Joint Rule had indeed ceased to exist, there was no legal procedure for Congress to count the votes other than the sparse language of the Twelfth Amendment ordering the president of the Senate to open the votes and have them counted before a joint meeting of

Congress in February. As the Republican *New York Times* put it in a November 14 editorial entitled "A Weak Point in the Constitution":

> The rule being repealed, the fact remains that there is no distinct means provided by the Constitution for settling any questions which may arise on the counting of the votes. This state of things is extraordinary. The consequences of a dispute as to a Presidential election, with no means of determining it, are so obviously serious, and may be so full of peril for the country, that it seems impossible that such a dispute has not been provided for. But, as a matter of fact, it has not been.

This crisis was not Republicans' fault, the editorial continued. Republican senators had passed Morton's bill to replace the joint rule, but the Democratic House, obsessed with investigating Grant's administration, had not acted on it.[4]

This summary of the uncertain situation confronting Congress when it met was accurate. Where the *Times* saw a disgraceful crisis that should have been anticipated, however, hard-line Republicans in the Senate and House saw an opportunity. Long before Congress opened, they asserted that, with the Twenty-second Joint Rule now a dead letter, the president of the Senate had the exclusive power and authority to count the electoral votes and resolve disputes over contested returns from different states.

This claim was even more brazen than Democrats' assertion that the Twenty-second Joint Rule remained in effect. The language of the Twelfth Amendment to the Constitution was at once crystal clear and maddeningly vague about this point. It specified that on the day when representatives and senators assembled to hear the counting of electoral votes, "the President of the Senate shall, in the presence of the Senate and the House of Representatives, open all the certificates and the votes shall then be counted." But counted by whom? That question had repeatedly been asked by Republican and Democratic senators alike during the debates of 1875 and 1876. Now, among many Republicans in both congressional chambers, those doubts had conveniently dissolved; Hayes himself privately insisted that only Ferry could count the votes. Ferry and Ferry alone, they now claimed, could determine whether the disputed electoral votes from Florida, Louisiana, Oregon, and South Carolina belonged to Tilden or Hayes. The huge Democratic majority in the House had no say in the matter whatsoever.

Tilden's response to this Republican claim was to spend most of December overseeing the preparation of a legal tome, for which he wrote the introduction, entitled *The Presidential Counts*. It was published in early January. This hefty volume was a compilation of all historical precedents for counting electoral votes in Congress. For Tilden, its primary purpose was to cite the many speeches from Republican senators in early 1875 and 1876 denying that the president of the Senate alone could decide who had won disputed electoral votes. That is why, they had then argued, Morton's proposed law was needed. Tilden himself seemed content that his lengthy brief had spiked the Republicans' gun. Other Democrats deemed it insufficient for the emergency.

The effrontery of the Republicans' baldly partisan stance in fact outraged Democrats both inside and outside Congress. To them it represented the biggest of all Republican frauds, an outright attempt to steal the election. For one, it explains Democrats' insistence that the Twenty-second Joint Rule remained in effect because the House had never joined the Senate in rescinding it. Alternatively, the chairman of the House Judiciary Committee pushed for a new law specifying that the joint session of the Senate and House—where House Democrats alone would outnumber the combined force of Republicans from the House and the Senate—could decide disputed returns by majority vote.[5] Such a law, which had no prayer of passing the Republican Senate, would have assured Tilden's election. Still other House Democrats, however, threatened to deploy what we might call the "nuclear option." The Constitution stipulated that electoral votes must be opened and counted before members of the House and Senate. The Democratic majority in the House could stop any such assemblage simply by refusing to meet with the Senate unless and until Senate Republicans foreswore any attempt to have Ferry alone count the votes. A less extreme option was to filibuster when the House met alone to prevent completion of the count by inauguration day, March 4.[6] Either way, they believed, they could prevent Hayes from getting the necessary majority of electoral votes and throw the election into the House, where they could elect Tilden.

Democrats outside Washington reacted even more vehemently to the Republican stance. During December, January, and February, Democrats across the country became increasingly exasperated at the sphinx-like silence that emanated from Tilden's Gramercy Park mansion. Instead of marching orders for the Democratic troops or firm avowals that he had won and intended to fight to the end, they heard occasional pleas for calm and advice to read Tilden's legalese. As early as December 1, 1876, a Pennsylvania Democrat complained that both Tilden and the Democratic National Committee "have exhibited a weakness, at which the whole Democratic party have been quite shocked."[7] The Democratic National Committee, in fact, also failed to provide much direction. Chairman Hewitt, along with other leading Democrats in the House and Senate, wanted to issue a proclamation in December under the aegis of the national committee calling for simultaneous protest meetings in all the states on January 8, but the other members of the committee nixed that proposal.

Thus, many northern state Democratic organizations decided to rally public opinion on their own by calling public meetings in Springfield, Indianapolis, Columbus, and other state capitals in early January. Illinois Democrats denounced any attempt by Ferry alone to count the votes, "without the concurrence of both Houses of Congress," as "contrary to usage, revolutionary in character, and dangerous to the rights of the people." If the Senate and House could not agree on a "fair" method of counting the votes, "it will then become the duty of the House of Representatives immediately to choose a President." It should also investigate whether Grant deserved impeachment because he had used military force to pressure the returning boards in Florida, Louisiana, and South Carolina to illegally give those states' electors to Hayes.[8] Indiana Democrats similarly "denounce[d] the proposition that the President of the Senate has the power, not only to open, but to count the vote, as an innovation which the sentiment of the people will not tolerate." If Senate Republicans attempted that outrage, "we call upon the House of Representatives to exert all its constitutional power to defeat the usurpation, and we pledge it our support with all the resources which a people whose fundamental liberties are threatened can constitutionally command."[9] Ohio's incensed Democrats were blunter. "Any attempt to inaugurate a President simply upon the proclamation of the President of the Senate," they vowed on January 8, 1877, "will be an act of usurpation that will be resisted by the people to the last extremity, even should that extremity be an appeal to arms."[10]

All these public meetings, significantly, pledged to abide by any congressional decision in which both the House and the Senate had an equal voice. From the start of the congressional session, indeed, some Democrats and Republicans recognized that neither the Democratic claim that the Twenty-second Joint Rule remained in force nor the Republican claim that Ferry alone could resolve the dispute was tenable. They understood that some new arrangement that the public could accept must be devised. Surprisingly, one of these men was New York's Republican Senator Roscoe Conkling. As early as November 19, a Democrat from Utica, Conkling's hometown, excitedly wrote to Tilden that Conkling would never help Senate Republicans "succeed by fraud. . . . You may rely entirely upon his hearty *cooperation*."[11] Once Congress opened, Republicans also recognized, to their dismay, that Conkling would fight any attempt to have Ferry alone count the votes and would support efforts that gave the Democratic House an equal voice with the Senate. Pressure from businessmen in New York City eager for a peaceful resolution of the electoral crisis only increased Conkling's determination to resist the hard-ball tactics favored by many of his Senate colleagues. Ohio Republicans in Washington attributed Conkling's stance to personal jealousy of Hayes or to fear that the Republican reformers, whom Conkling hated, would dominate a Hayes administration. Conkling, however, was not the only Republican senator to oppose the scheme, and it is probable that any formal Senate resolution instructing Ferry to count the votes would have failed to achieve a majority.

George McCrary, a Republican representative from Iowa, was more important initially than Conkling. Obviously swayed by Democratic vows never to allow a joint meeting of Congress to convene and by threats of violence percolating around the country, McCrary introduced a resolution into the House of Representatives on December 7, 1876, that urged the creation of some tribunal "whose decision all will accept as final."[12] Thus he called on the House to create a committee of five men who, along with a like number of men from the Senate, could devise a "tribunal" with representation from both houses to resolve the disputed electoral votes. That House committee, he urged, should report "such a measure, either legislative or constitutional,"[13] that could satisfy the public without delay. The House sent McCrary's resolution to its Judiciary Committee. It enlarged McCrary's proposed committee to seven members and reported that recommendation to the House on December 14, when it was adopted on a voice vote without debate or dissent. A week later Speaker Randall, who came under intense pressure to appoint only Democratic hard-liners who would concede nothing to Republicans, named four Democrats—Ohio's Henry Payne, Virginia's Eppa Hunton, Illinois' William Springer, and Abram Hewitt—and three Republicans—McCrary, George F. Hoar of Massachusetts, and Michigan's

George Willard—to serve as the House committee. Hunton, Springer, and Hewitt were expected to be so intractable that the *New York Times* predicted that nothing would come of the committee's deliberations.

On December 18 the chairman of the Senate's Judiciary Committee, Vermont Republican George Edmunds (who had already introduced a constitutional amendment specifying that the Supreme Court alone should count the electoral votes), reported the House proposal to the Senate, where it was also adopted without dissent. Ferry then named four Republicans—Edmunds, Morton, New Jersey's Frederick Freling-huysen, and Illinois' John A. Logan—and three Democrats—Thurman, Bayard, and North Carolina's Matt Ransom—as the Senate committee. Logan, however, had not returned to Washington for the session. He had remained in Illinois to try, unsuccessfully, to secure his reelection from a legislature in which Democrats combined with Independents had a slight majority on the joint ballot. What happened in that Illinois Senate contest would soon prove decisive. For the moment, however, it meant that Logan could not serve, and Ferry named Conkling in his place.

Democrats cheered these developments, especially Conkling's in-clusion on the Senate committee, as evidence that Republicans were surrendering their insistence that Ferry alone could allot the twenty dis-puted electoral votes. Congress's action "in raising a committee to report a plan for 'counting' the electoral ballots," one exultant Democrat wrote on December 18, meant "that a check has been put upon the game of the Republican tricksters. Their 'infernal machine' with the President of the Senate set for the trigger, has turned out to be a very sorry device."[14] That inference proved decidedly premature. But Democrats also hoped that the two committees might create some body with authority to go behind the face of the electoral votes sent to the Senate and determine who actually deserved those votes.

On this point, the inclusion of Thurman and Bayard on the Senate committee—men who were clearly expected to be its dominant Demo-cratic voices—gave perceptive Democrats pause. Both had cheered the repeal of the Twenty-second Joint Rule precisely because both consid-ered it flatly unconstitutional. States alone, they maintained, had the ex-clusive power to appoint presidential electors. Once they were chosen, Congress had absolutely no constitutional power to dispute, challenge, or change what the states had done. To make such an attempt was a flagrant violation of states' rights and an unconscionable consolidation of power in Congress at the expense of those rights. What these and other Democrats had vociferously and repeatedly argued in 1875 and early 1876 would become Republicans' stance once a "tribunal" to settle the electoral vote dispute had been created. But even before its creation, that stance certainly seemed to jeopardize Democratic hopes of going behind the electoral returns sent to Congress.

After speaking with Bayard in Washington, however, Belmont reported to Marble on December 21 that Bayard "is willing to put aside some of his constitutional scruples *for the emergency,* his aid is of vital importance & we must not put unnecessary obstacles in his way." Belmont had far less faith in the other two Democrats on the Senate committee. "Thurman's [drinking?] habits are a terrible calamity. Ransom is not a match for Morton or Edmunds & so all our reliance must be on Bayard so far as the Senate Committee is concerned."[15]

Although the House and Senate committees readily exchanged ideas, initially they met separately from each other. Moreover, the two committees would vote separately on any plan, and no proposal could be adopted unless both committees accepted it. The Democratic-majority House committee thus had an effective veto power. No serious work began until early January because of the traditional holiday recess, although the House committee did order clerks to prepare a compendium of everything said in the House and Senate since the founding of the nation about counting electoral votes. This huge document anticipated much of what Tilden had gathered in his own tome, but both committees relied on it during January, when the real work was done.

Our knowledge of the deliberations of these committees depends almost exclusively on reminiscences by the participants written later— often years later. Nonetheless, their work can be reconstructed with reasonable confidence. From the start, both committees agreed that members of the Supreme Court should serve on the tribunal, and the Republican *New York Times,* for one, considered this judicial participation outrageous.[16] After a week of stalemate between mutually suspicious Democrats and Republicans on the House committee, McCrary presented a draft bill on January 10 that created a tribunal consisting exclusively of Chief Justice Morrison R. Waite and the four most senior associate justices on the Court, leaving Congress entirely unrepresented. Hewitt, whose later account is one of the chief sources historians possess, attributed this idea to President Grant, who, according to Hewitt, got Conkling to draft the bill that McCrary introduced. Democratic members met that night and the next day tried to force the House committee's

Republicans to openly acknowledge that this plan meant that Ferry could not count the votes. The Republicans adamantly refused. Then the Democrats stipulated that they could never accept Waite, who was too close personally to Hayes. Instead, they insisted on a tribunal consisting solely of the five senior associate justices: Nathan Clifford, a Democrat from Maine; Noah Swayne, a Republican from Ohio; Samuel F. Miller, an Iowa Republican; Stephen J. Field, a California Democrat; and David Davis of Illinois, whom almost everyone considered a genuine political independent. Democrats also stipulated that both houses of Congress must concur in accepting this tribunal's decision about disputed votes. If either house rejected it, the tribunal's recommendation would be ignored. As of the night of January 11, that was House Democrats' plan for a tribunal: Supreme Court justices alone would make the decision!

Meanwhile, Edmunds had presented a different plan to the Senate committee. He insisted that Senate and House members must be represented in equal numbers on any such tribunal, along with members of the Supreme Court. The House committee immediately acceded to the superiority of this scheme, but the next day, January 12, in a joint session of the two committees, Republicans and Democrats jousted over the size of the commission and the method of selecting its members. At first the committees inclined toward a nine-man commission—three representatives, three senators, and three associate justices. Soon, however, they opted for a fifteen-man commission composed of five men from each body. By mutual consent, three Republicans and two Democrats would represent the Senate, and three Democrats and two Republicans would represent the House.

The real question was how to pick five associate justices from the eight then sitting on the Supreme Court. Republican senators suggested naming six justices—Clifford, Field, Davis, Miller, Swayne, and William Strong—and then having them draw lots to see which one would be excluded. When word of this proposal reached the House, Speaker Randall exploded in outrage. "As soon as I heard of the Senate bill with six justices, I put my foot down and declared my condemnation of it," Randall wrote to Marble on January 15. "I think it is not only discreditable but positively disgraceful to talk about raffling off the Presidency! The plan of the Senate is about equal to my going on the street and asking the first colored boy I meet to toss pennies for it." Under that plan, Democrats could lose Clifford or Field or Davis, the only men on whom they could count for justice. They would then have "about the same chance as in submitting a Catholic doctrine for a decision to a Presbyterian synod or *vice versa*."[17]

Randall was not the only Democrat incensed by this possibility. The proposal had been made on January 13, a Saturday. At the request of one of the House Democrats, the two committees then recessed until Monday. That Saturday afternoon, Hewitt sent the draft plan by courier to Tilden (now freed of the governorship) in New York City to ascertain his views. Later that night he took the train to New York, planning to meet with Tilden on Sunday morning. Hewitt and his large family lived with his father-in-law, Peter Cooper, in a large house at the southern end of Lexington Avenue, only a three-minute walk from Tilden's Gramercy Park town house. At their meeting, Tilden adamantly opposed the process for picking the associate justices. He too called it a "raffle." But he also seemed hesitant to accept even the idea of a bipartisan election commission rather than relying on the Democratic House alone to elect him. Tilden and his closest advisers at that time were also toying with the idea of demanding that another presidential election be held immediately. As it turned out, Hewitt could get no clear commitment from Tilden by the time he left for Washington that Sunday night. In a telegram to Hewitt on Monday, January 15, Tilden said only, "Procrastinate to give days for information and consultation. The six Judge proposition [is] inadmissible."[18]

To a man, the Democratic majority on the House committee followed Tilden's wish. They made it plain at the joint meeting of the committees on January 15 that the "six Judge proposition" could never pass the House. For a while, the Senate committee threatened to present the plan to the Senate, no matter what the House committee did. Then a mutually acceptable compromise was reached, despite Tilden's lack of enthusiasm for the whole process. Had Tilden explicitly rejected the idea, nothing would have been done, but he failed to make his wishes clear. After the committees had completed their endeavors, Hewitt told one appalled Democrat that he had no idea whether Tilden agreed to the bill.[19]

Now, the bill would specify four associate justices, with a fifth to be chosen by those four men. The stated rationale for choosing the four was to achieve the widest geographical representation possible, although the absence of any southern justice on the Court in fact prohibited complete fairness. Thus the committees ostensibly picked the four justices to represent the federal circuit courts on which they still rode: Nathan Clifford from New England's First Circuit; William Strong, a Pennsylvania Republican, from the mid-Atlantic's Third Circuit; Iowa's Samuel F. Miller from the Eighth Circuit; and California's Stephen J. Field from the Ninth Circuit. The real objective, however, was achieving partisan balance.

The two committees agreed to this arrangement based on the assumption that these four men—four of the five most senior associate justices on the Supreme Court—would pick as the fifth judge the other most senior associate justice, David Davis of Illinois. A longtime Whig, Davis had joined the Republican Party in the 1850s and managed Lincoln's presidential campaign in 1860. Lincoln appointed him to the Supreme Court during the war, but in 1872 Davis was a leading contender for the Liberal Republican presidential nomination and was actually nominated by another dissident party, the National Labor Reform Party. This independent streak gave Democrats hope and Republicans the willies. But Davis's appointment was the sine qua non of any agreement between Republicans and Democrats.

On January 17 the committee members agreed, and Edmunds and Payne prepared a draft bill. The following day Edmunds submitted a report that he and Thurman had written to present with the bill. All but one of the fourteen men—Morton—signed on, and Edmunds presented the bill and the report to the Senate later that day, as did Payne in the House. The bill, which each house had to enact separately before anything could be done with regard to the electoral vote count, contained seven sections. The first moved up the date for the joint meeting of Congress to count the electoral votes from mid-February to February 1, in clear expectation of a prolonged process in adjudicating the disputed votes. Adopting the language of Morton's proposed but never passed law, it also stated that in all cases in which *only a single packet of electoral votes* had been sent to the Senate from a state, any senator or representative could object to any or all of the votes from that state (as had been the case under the Twenty-second Joint Rule). The House and Senate would then go into separate session, two hours would be allotted for debate, and then the two houses would vote whether to accept or reject the objection. But no state's electoral votes could be thrown out unless both chambers concurred in upholding the objection. This part of the subsequent act would be the lever used by dissident House Democrats to delay completion of the electoral vote count before inauguration day.

The second section explained the composition of the electoral commission and specified rules for replacing members who were unable to continue for reasons of health or death. It then directed that in all cases in which more than one return had been submitted by a state, and anyone objected to one or all of those returns, all the purported certificates naming the electors, the votes they had cast, "and papers so objected to, and all papers accompanying the same, and all such objections [which had to be written]" should be given to the commission, "which shall proceed to consider the same, with the same powers, if any, now possessed by the two Houses acting separately or together." It added that when determining who had won disputed electoral votes, the electoral commission "may . . . take into view such petitions, depositions, and other papers, if any, as shall by the Constitution and now-existing law, be competent and pertinent to such consideration."[20]

This language merits quotation at length because it points to the disputed powers of the commission to "go behind" the electoral returns sent to the Senate to determine the outcome. The crucial phrase about those powers, repeated twice, was "if any." Republicans and Democrats fundamentally disagreed about the reach of the proposed Federal Electoral Commission. Democrats insisted, and their proponents appearing before the commission would contend, that the commissioners must go behind the reported electoral votes to obtain a "fair," "just," or "moral" decision. Just as adamantly, Republicans contended that under the Constitution and existing federal law, the commission had no such power and that any attempt to go behind the certified returns reported from the states would necessarily take so long that the process could not possibly be completed by inauguration day. (Recall that under the Twenty-second Joint Rule, no time had been allowed for debate on an objection, let alone examination of any evidence relevant to it.) More important, Republicans asserted, any such attempt would be a flagrantly unconstitutional violation of states' rights.

This second section of the proposed bill also contained a provision of even greater importance. Once the commission submitted its ruling, in writing, on disputed votes to the two houses of Congress, written objections to those findings could be raised if they were signed by both senators and representatives. Only if both the Democratic House and the Republican Senate agreed by majority vote to such an objection could it be sustained. Otherwise, the ruling of the commission's majority would be final. This procedure was exactly the opposite of what Democrats on the House committee had originally sought; rather than requiring concurrence to accept the commission's rulings, it required concurrence to reject them. Democrats outside Congress would later howl that those insiders, especially Hewitt, had bungled away Tilden's chance of assuming the presidency with this concession to Republican demands. Whatever the commission ruled on the twenty disputed electoral votes, it was exceedingly unlikely that the two chambers would concur in rejecting its determination. Some sort of nonpartisan nirvana remained far beyond reach in the intensely partisan atmosphere of early 1877.

The next three sections of the bill were comparatively inconsequential. The third said that the president of the senate during joint sessions could not allow any debate after an objection to electoral votes or consider any motion other than for the two chambers to withdraw immediately into separate sessions. The fourth limited debate during those separate sessions to two hours. The fifth required the joint session to continue until a president had been chosen.

The sixth section, in contrast, was far more significant and must have been a Republican concession to House Democrats. Nothing in the bill, it said, would prevent "any citizen" from going to court, presumably to seek writs of quo warranto, to challenge the right of the president and vice president picked by Congress to legally hold those offices. The seventh section allowed the commission to make its own rules and ordered it to keep a record of its proceedings.

George Edmunds presented the bill and report to his Senate colleagues on January 18. In his brilliant speech defending them, he laid out with crystal clarity what was at issue between Republicans and Democrats, between the Senate and the House. Irony once again abounds here. Had Edmunds gotten his way in February 1875, Colorado would not have attained statehood in time to participate in the presidential election, and Tilden would have won with 184 electoral votes. Edmunds's printed report accompanying the bill sought to reassure both Democrats and Republicans that they would not be euchred out of the presidency by the operations of the committee. His speech, though also touting the bill's fairness, aimed primarily to reassure his Republican colleagues that Hayes was certain to emerge as the winner of the commission's deliberations.

To those who believed that the Constitution forbade Congress to adjudicate disputed votes, Edmunds's report cited the "necessary and proper" clause as giving Congress all the constitutional authority it needed to create such a commission. We have "endeavored to provide such lawful agencies of decision in the present case as shall be the most fair and impartial possible under the circumstances," the report continued. "It would be difficult, if not impossible, we think, to establish a tribunal that could be less the subject of party criticism than such a one." The report concluded by "impress[ing] upon Congress the necessity of a speedy determination upon this subject."[21]

In his speech, Edmunds repeatedly cited the bill's provision that the commission, in determining who had won disputed electoral votes, could "take into view such petitions, depositions, and other papers, if any, as shall, by the Constitution and now existing law, be competent and pertinent in such consideration." That was the crux of the disagreement between Republicans and Democrats, Edmunds frankly admitted. Democrats "desire . . . that this commission, if created, shall descend below the action of the State authorities and ascertain how many votes were given for this man and that man and the other, with a view, of course, to the success, as they suppose, of their own candidate if that were done." Republicans, in contrast, desired "that the law shall be so that they cannot descend behind the action of the authorities of a State, be that action right or wrong, lawful or unlawful." The members of the commission itself must resolve that question, said Edmunds. But they also must determine "the simple and obvious principle, not merely of justice and fair play, but of constitutional law, that would apply to such a case."[22]

Here, in a nutshell, was the gist of the arguments Republican and Democratic advocates would make before the commission. For Democrats, justice and fair play required the commission to go behind the submitted electoral returns. For Republicans, constitutional law allowed no such excursion because it would violate the sacrosanct right of states alone to choose presidential electors. Edmunds then made it clear that he accepted the Republican position. The selection of the next president, he averred, had occurred on December 6 when the electoral college met. The resolution of the disputed votes must be decided "by the law" as it existed on that day. "This would be a strange republic of law indeed, if after, according to one law, the candidate of one party had been elected, the Congress of the United States or anybody else [i.e., the Florida courts and state legislature], should make a new law by force of which the candidate of some other party got elected. Of course it would be an outrage upon the principles of government." Thus, the exclusive function of the commission was to ascertain "what the law and the fact was on that first Wednesday in December, 1876."

But there was more. If the two houses of Congress possessed the power to go behind the returns on December 6, 1876, the commission could do so as well. But if they did not—and Edmunds had clearly prejudged this question—then the commission had no such power. The commission was "commanded to decide what is the constitutional vote of a State; and, in doing that, it may take into view any evidence of any kind that the Constitution and the law, *as it is now,* makes appropriate to that subject, *and not any other.*"[23] For Republicans, in short, the letter of the law and justice were quite different things, but this was the position maintained by all the Republicans on the commission throughout its proceedings.

Edmunds was followed by Morton, the lone member of the two committees who had refused to sign onto the commission bill. He regarded the bill as a compromise just as insidious as the compromises of 1820 and 1850 that had benefited slaveholders. He believed that Hayes had clearly been elected and would be inaugurated with "no violence and no revolution." The Constitution conferred on the states the exclusive right to choose presidential electors; Congress had no authority to challenge their choices once made. To attempt to do so, as this bill contemplated, would be a "revolution which will ultimately be the end of presidential elections." Yet the language of the bill allowing the commission to consider petitions, depositions, and other papers clearly gave it that authority, one that Congress itself did not possess. Democrats would never have supported this bill "except that it gave them a chance for the only thing that can count Mr. Tilden in, and that is, to go behind the returns. Outside of that, he has no chance, no hope." Democrats might assert that they supported "a bill which at the very beginning cuts off and shuts out this their only hope, [but] I must be excused for saying I don't believe it."[24]

Conkling then tried to defend the committees' handiwork, and Massachusetts Republican Henry Dawes joined Morton in attacking it. The debate was on, and a similar one occurred in the House. From the start it was clear that many Republicans, such as Ohio's James Garfield in the House, opposed the bill on constitutional grounds or simply because it made unnecessary concessions to Democrats when, by their assessment, Hayes had clearly and constitutionally won. Convinced that Ferry alone had the authority to settle the dispute, Hayes himself considered the bill a fatal "surrender" of the Republican position.[25]

In contrast, most Democrats embraced the bill, although a minority of southerners in the House remained cool; they wanted the House to count Tilden in without regard to the Senate. In January, however, those naysayers were a distinct minority among Democrats. On January 24, for example, Pennsylvania's William Bigler excitedly wrote to Tilden that the commission bill assured his election. "It recognizes the right of the Commission to go behind the certificates on allegation of fraud. Besides I have special confidence in one of the judges who will be selected as a Republican. He will be just and impartial in his action, with slight inclinations to our side."[26] Here, Bigler must have been referring to Pennsylvanian William Strong, who had served two terms as a Democratic congressman in the early 1850s. Democrats' eagerness to obtain the election commission, as well as Republicans' objections to it, would be reflected in the votes by which the two chambers finally passed the electoral commission bill.

Before those votes occurred on the afternoon of January 26, however, a bombshell reached Washington by telegraph from Illinois. The preceding night, Democrats and the five Independents in the Illinois legislature, who outnumbered Republicans by only two votes on a joint ballot, had elected Justice David Davis to succeed Republican John A. Logan as U.S. senator from Illinois. Evidence suggests that Colonel William T. Pelton, Tilden's nephew and private secretary, had worked with Cyrus McCormick, chairman of the Illinois Democratic state committee and himself an aspirant for the Senate seat, to arrange this result, although Tilden knew nothing about it. Unlike his uncle, Pelton was a loose partisan cannon. As noted earlier, he had been willing to buy the votes of the Louisiana returning board, and in 1878 conclusive evidence (the so-called cipher telegrams) revealed that he had also attempted to bribe a few Republican electors in South Carolina to cast their votes for Tilden, an attempt that Tilden somewhat shakily denied any knowledge of in 1878. Now, in 1877, Pelton tried to tilt the Illinois election in favor of Davis, possibly with still more bribes, on the assumption that the grateful Davis—the fifth associate justice on the electoral commission— would award enough disputed electoral votes to Tilden to make him the winner. If so, his gambit backfired. Upon receiving telegraphic word of his election to the Senate, Davis immediately announced his refusal to serve on the commission because he could not be properly independent in his judgment.

When the House and Senate voted on January 26, however, many congressmen did not know of Davis's decision. He would remain an associate justice of the Supreme Court until his Senate term began on

One of the two Democratic legal titans who served on the Federal Electoral Commission: Senator Thomas F. Bayard of Delaware. (Courtesy of the Library of Congress. LC-DIG-cwpbh-00461.)

The other legal titan on the Federal Electoral Commission was Senator Allen G. Thurman of Ohio. (Courtesy of the Library of Congress. LC-DIG-cwpbh-00488.)

March 4, 1877, and thus could still serve on the electoral commission. Consequently, the votes in the two chambers to adopt the measure revealed a decided Democratic preponderance in favor of the new law. In the Senate, Republicans supported the measure 24 to 16; Democrats did so 23 to 1. Morton, Dawes, James G. Blaine (now a senator), Maine's Hannibal Hamlin, and Ohio's John Sherman were all in the minority. Aside from Morton, all the Republican senators who had served on the committee that devised the bill supported it. The partisan imbalance was far sharper in the House. There, in what Garfield told his diary was "the largest House I have ever seen in this session,"[27] Republicans opposed the bill 33 to 68, and Democrats supported it 154 to 18.[28]

According to the measure passed by the two houses and signed by President Grant on January 29, both the Senate and the House were to choose their five members of the commission by voice vote on January 30, two days before they would meet to count the electoral votes. Caucuses of the two parties could select these representatives, whereas the presiding officers of the House and Senate had appointed the committee members who devised the electoral commission bill. In the Senate, Democrats chose their acknowledged heavyweights Thurman and Bayard; Republicans chose Edmunds, Frelinghuysen, and Morton, all of whom had served on the earlier committee. That Morton had opposed the bill and had already announced his conviction that Hayes was president only punctuated what everyone knew: the House and Senate members were expected to be partisan advocates, not impartial judges. House Democrats chose Payne, Hunton, and Josiah Abbott of Massachusetts, while Republicans picked George F. Hoar and Garfield, who had voted against the commission plan. Of great significance, Garfield had also signed a report that Sherman had submitted to Grant from the Republican observers in Louisiana, attesting to the honesty and accuracy of its returning board's decision to award Louisiana's electoral votes to Hayes. Garfield, in short, was hardly impartial. For this reason, 23 Democrats refused to support him and defiantly identified themselves when the House chose its members of the commission by voice vote; for the same reason, in the earlier House Republican caucus, Garfield had received all but 2 votes from the 91 Republicans. Again, no one expected the representatives and senators on the commission to do anything but advance their respective parties' interests.

Nor did anyone expect the four associate justices on the commission to be anything but partisan advocates. In his cutting speech to the Senate on January 18, Morton had exposed the idea that they had been chosen to achieve geographical representation for the fig leaf that it was. That fact, in essence, left the vote of the commission up to the fifth justice. Once it was clear that Davis would not serve, the most senior of the remaining associate justices was Noah Swayne, but like Chief Justice Waite, he hailed from Ohio, Hayes's home state. After fractious debate among themselves, according to Garfield's diary, the four justices chose Joseph Bradley of New Jersey, whom Grant had appointed to the Court, along with William Strong, in 1870 and who rode the vast circuit encompassing the former Confederacy.

Though clearly disappointed by Davis's unwillingness to serve, leading Democrats were initially relieved by the choice of Bradley. He had once unsuccessfully sought a congressional seat as a Republican and had served as a Republican presidential elector. Yet he was known primarily as a first-rate lawyer who had, for years, been one of the leading lights of the New Jersey bar. Abram Hewitt, who had made a fortune manufacturing iron and steel in New Jersey, had known Bradley for years and considered him "an able lawyer and a man of the highest integrity." Tilden, who had served as a director of many of Hewitt's widespread business enterprises, fully agreed with this assessment.[29] Knowledgeable Republicans concurred, somewhat more worriedly, about Bradley's integrity and nonpartisanship. As the Republican *Chicago Tribune* opined on February 14, "The fear that Republicans have is that Bradley is an intensely legal man, even more legal than Republican, and that he will not hesitate to give the Presidency to Tilden if the technical points shall be in his favor. . . . These persons fear that he is more lawyer than Republican, and the Democrats fear that he is more Republican than lawyer."[30] Even earlier a New Jersey Democrat had assured Tilden that the leading Republicans in his state feared Bradley's stubborn independence "and will not feel safe until his last vote is cast."[31]

With Nathan Clifford, the senior associate justice, presiding, the electoral commission held its first meeting on January 31 in the Supreme Court chambers, the former Senate chambers in the basement of the Capitol. First it appointed support staff and adopted rules of procedure. Of the latter, two were most important. The law allowed numerous representatives and senators to offer objections in writing to the disputed Republican and Democratic electoral vote certificates. The commission would, of course, consider all written objections, but it limited oral testimony to two objectors from each party. Similarly, although each party had hired a number of lawyers to submit written briefs on each disputed case, the commission chose to hear oral arguments from only two at-torneys on each side, and those arguments would be limited to a total of two hours for each side. In the Florida case, in fact, the commission al-lowed oral arguments from three lawyers on each side, but their allotted time remained two hours each. Both Republicans and Democrats care-fully chose their objectors with an eye toward maximizing their impact on the commission, and especially its five judges.

On Thursday, February 1, the count of electoral votes before the as-sembled Congress began in the House chamber. Certificates were opened in alphabetical order by state. All went smoothly until the three returns from Florida were reached. Democrats objected to the Hayes returns, Republicans to the two for Tilden. Those written objections; the certificates and the papers accompanying them from ex-Governor Stearns, Democratic Attorney General Cocke, and new Democratic Gov-ernor Drew; and the law the new Democratic legislature had passed at-testing to the legitimacy of the Democratic electors were duly sent to the electoral commission. The joint meeting of the House and Senate then adjourned until word of the commission's decision was sent to Speaker Randall, whose job it was to invite the Senate back into the House cham-ber to resume the count of votes. In other words, if the Speaker refused to recall the joint meeting, the vote count could be blocked. That was House Democrats' leverage in the proceedings.

Both parties had used considerable care in picking their objectors who might testify before the commission about the Florida case. Repub-licans chose two Iowa representatives, McCrary and John Kasson, both of whom knew Justice Samuel F. Miller intimately. McCrary, indeed, had once clerked for him in Iowa, while Kasson had watched Florida's returning board count the votes. One of the Democratic objectors to the Hayes return who testified was Congressman Joseph R. Tucker of Vir-ginia. More important was Congressman David Dudley Field of New York City, Justice Stephen Field's brother. A renowned attorney who had, in the 1840s, assumed responsibility for codifying New York's laws of civil procedure, Field had never before held elective office. A prewar Jacksonian Democrat, Field had actually voted for Hayes in 1876 but fervently believed that Tilden had won and deserved to be counted in. Thus, when Democratic Congressman Smith Ely resigned his seat in December after being elected mayor of New York City, Tilden prevailed on Field to run in a special election in an overwhelmingly Democratic district so that he could represent Tilden's interests. Elected on January

2, Field appeared in Washington on January 11 and immediately made it clear that he considered himself Tilden's legal counsel in the electoral vote dispute.

Both parties also recruited teams of distinguished lawyers to make their case before the commission. The Democratic attorneys who made oral arguments on Florida were Charles O'Conor and Jeremiah Sullivan Black. For years a leading lawyer in New York City, O'Conor had worked to free Jefferson Davis from military imprisonment after the Civil War. He had also been the straight Democratic candidate for president in 1872, run by dissident Democrats who refused to accept Horace Greeley as their nominee. Once a judge on Pennsylvania's supreme court, Black had served as attorney general for most of James Buchanan's administration.[32] Black, not coincidentally, was also the co-owner, with Garfield, of a large farm in Virginia that the two men were currently trying to sell. The Republicans who made oral arguments were William M. Evarts of New York, a former attorney general, and U.S. District Judge Stanley Matthews of Ohio.

The Florida case set the precedent for all the disputes addressed by the electoral commission. Therefore, it is the only one treated here in some detail. Because the printed report of the electoral commission's proceedings ran to more than a thousand pages, however, even that detail must be highly selective. It bears repeating that in all the cases of disputed electoral votes from the South, the central question was whether the commission could or should "go behind the returns," that is, admit evidence beyond the different certificates and accompanying papers sent to the president of the Senate, such as the boxes of affidavits gathered by the Democratic-controlled House committees.

Both the Democratic objectors to the Hayes returns and the Democratic lawyers argued that the commission must go beyond the returns. The majority of the nation's voters clearly preferred Tilden, they asserted. Hence, the commissioners must pay heed to that majority opinion. At the very least, they must take into account the findings in quo warranto proceedings in the Florida courts against the legitimacy of the Republican electors, the law passed by the Florida legislature in 1877 attesting that the new findings of the canvassing board gave Florida's electoral votes to Tilden, and the certification of their election by Democratic Governor Drew as evidence of the genuine sentiment of Florida's electorate. In addition, the Democratic protagonists insisted, the evidence gathered by the House investigating committee clearly showed that there had been so much fraud in the casting and reporting of Republican votes that Hayes's supposed majority of Florida's popular vote was utterly fictitious. Contrary to what Edmunds had told the Senate, Democrats contended—and Justice Field embraced this argument in his opinion on the Florida case—the presidential election did not end when the electoral college met on December 6. It did not end until Congress counted the electoral votes in February. Consequently, all evidence about developments in Florida between December 6 and February 1 must be considered. According to this evidence, Tilden clearly deserved Florida's four electoral votes.

Finally, Democrats alleged that one of the Republican electors was constitutionally ineligible because he had been a federally appointed and paid shipping commissioner on the day of the election. If nothing else, they contended, the commission must declare his election void and award the electoral vote to one of the Democrats. Here, Democrats advanced the same case used in the dispute over the vote in Oregon.

Reduced to its essence, the Republicans' rebuttal rested on three prongs. First, they insisted that nothing occurring in Florida after the Republican electors had sealed their certificates on December 6 had any legal standing in the matter. Everything after that moment was post facto or post hoc and legally inadmissible; this included the subsequent supreme court rulings about the gubernatorial vote and quo warranto judgments, the findings of a new canvassing board in January, the laws passed that month ordering a new canvass and attesting to the accuracy of the new findings, and certainly any evidence gathered by a biased House committee in December and early January.

Second, Republicans insisted that any attempt to go behind the returns, as Democrats demanded, would necessitate weeks if not months of intensive labor to investigate not only county returns but also polling district returns. Such an endeavor was simply impossible if Congress were to name the new president by inauguration day. Failure to have a president chosen by that date would inevitably create chaos and probably invite armed violence. Thus the very safety of the nation and its people mandated that the commission not attempt to go behind the returns.

Third, and most important, Republicans embraced states' rights theory, so dear to Democrats, to stymie any such move by the commission. The Constitution, they averred, explicitly gave to the states, by whatever means their respective legislatures devised, the exclusive power to select presidential electors. Florida law allowed a popular election of presidential electors and thus required a canvassing board to determine which of those electors had been legally elected. Just as any attempt by the two houses of Congress to challenge or replace the men chosen by that canvassing board, on whatever grounds, would be a massively unconstitutional violation of the rights explicitly granted to states by the Constitution, so would any attempt by this commission, a creature of Congress. Congress could not delegate powers that it did not constitutionally possess on the day the electoral college met.

The corollary of this argument strikes this observer as by far the most ingenious part of the Republicans' argument in the Florida case, as well as in the other two cases from the South. States alone had the authority to pick presidential electors, but those states alone, without any post hoc interference from federal authorities, newspapermen, or anyone else, also had the *responsibility* to make sure that the selection of those presidential electors was honest and aboveboard. In essence, the Republican objectors and lawyers conceded that there may have been fraudulent voting, manipulation of returns submitted to the canvassing board, and bribery of those who testified before it, but it was the responsibility of the state legislature—and only the state legislature— to prevent such illegalities. It could have passed laws before the election or between the election and the meeting of the electoral college to remedy such wrongs. But Florida's legislature had not done so. Rulings by Florida's state courts, moreover, were irrelevant, for the Constitution explicitly gave the state legislature the exclusive authority to pick presidential electors. No matter how much fraud and chicanery had marred the casting and counting of votes in Florida, it was simply too late, not to mention unconstitutional, for a federal commission to try to rectify it. Accordingly, the votes cast for Hayes on December 6 were the only votes the commission could sanction.

Two brief remarks by Republicans illustrate the contempt with which they greeted the case advanced by Democrats. David Dudley Field had led off the Democratic assault on the Hayes certificates by arguing that evidence of Republican fraud in Florida was so massive that the commission simply must go behind the returns. In his diary later that day, Garfield dismissed Field's presentation as "sophomoric and far below the level of the occasion."[33] Jeremiah Black also contended that fraud was so flagrant that the commission must consider the later actions by Florida's courts and legislature to redress it. "Fraud vitiates everything," Black intoned. "No, it does not," snapped Stanley Matthews in rebuttal.[34]

Oral arguments in the Florida case began on the morning of February 2 and closed in the midafternoon on Monday, February 5. The members then went into private session to discuss the issue before them. This issue was *not* who should receive Florida's electoral votes. Rather, it was whether the commission should allow the admission of extrinsic evidence, as Democrats had pleaded. After several hours of discussion, Joseph Bradley asked for a recess until the following morning so that he could study the matter more fully. Everyone knew that Bradley's would be the decisive vote, so the recess was agreed to.

The following day Edmunds, Morton, Thurman, Hunton, Bayard, Garfield, and all the other congressional members of the commission voiced their opinions, save for Ohio's Payne. None of them wavered from the partisan lines voiced by their parties' objectors and attorneys. Some of these opinions lasted more than an hour, so at 7:45 PM the commission adjourned until Wednesday. All the Supreme Court justices had yet to be heard from, and no one had a clue where Bradley stood. He apparently remained undecided.

Exactly what Bradley did on the night of February 6 and in the early-morning hours of February 7 has generated more controversy than any other aspect of the commission's work, in part, one suspects, because his ruminations on the case during the preceding night, February 5, are totally unknown. Undocumented rumors about what Bradley did on the night of the sixth appeared almost immediately in the press and more fully a year later. For years, however, historians relied on the credibility of a "Secret History" of the disputed vote count that Hewitt first jotted down in 1878 and then revised in 1895. This manuscript remained undiscovered in Hewitt's private papers until it was found by historian Allan Nevins, who endorsed it as uncontestable truth in his 1935 biography of Hewitt. According to Hewitt, John G. Stevens, a New Jersey friend of Bradley's, was staying at Hewitt's Washington house on the night of February 6. Stevens visited Bradley at his home that night and returned to Hewitt's about midnight, where he told other house guests that he had read Bradley's opinion and that it was favorable to Tilden's position. Thus Hewitt fully expected Tilden to get Florida's votes. Supposedly, however, Stevens also told Hewitt later that, after he left Bradley's house, Frelinghuysen, a fellow New Jersey member of the commission, and Navy Secretary George Robeson, another New Jersey man, had visited Bradley and, together with Bradley's wife, persuaded him to change his opinion, or at least its conclusion, and to rule against any attempt to go behind the returns.[35]

Associate Justice Joseph Bradley provided the decisive vote on the Federal Electoral Commission. (Courtesy of the Library of Congress. LC-DIG-cwpbh-00616.)

Later in 1877 and in 1878 embellishments were added to this story. Some time between Tuesday evening and the following morning when the commission reassembled, the tale now went, Bradley had actually *read* his already written pro-Democratic opinion to Justices Clifford and Field. Exactly where or when this reading supposedly occurred was not specified. In a San Francisco newspaper interview in 1878 Field denied that Bradley had ever *read* anything to him, while implying that Bradley had indeed told Field that he favored the Democratic position about going behind the returns. Others said that scores of carriages had surrounded Bradley's house in the early morning of February 7, one of them belonging to Tom Scott, who opposed Tilden's election because he would oppose federal subsidies for Scott's still-unbuilt Texas and Pacific Railroad. Still others described Mrs. Bradley descending the stairs in her nightgown, falling on her knees, and praying to God that her husband would keep Tilden out of the White House. Who, one wonders, actually saw and later blabbed about that juicy tidbit?

No other member of the commission subsequently received such withering criticism from the Democratic press, and in September 1878, while on vacation in Vermont, Bradley wrote a public letter that was published in a Newark, New Jersey, newspaper.[36] After the commission recessed on February 6, Bradley maintained, he had spoken to no one outside or inside his home—not Stevens, not Field and Clifford, not Republican heavyweights, not bullying businessmen, and, presumably, not his fervently praying wife. Nor had he read any opinion to Clifford and Field, for he had been genuinely undecided. To help him make a decision, he had indeed written out opinions on both sides of the question. In this letter, Bradley left unclear exactly when he finally made up his mind. Other evidence suggests that it was not until the actual meeting of the commission on Wednesday, February 7.

That day, Payne and the justices voiced or read their opinions on whether they should go behind the returns. Again, some of these opinions took more than an hour to deliver. Field, who had indeed visited Bradley's home on February 4 to try to persuade him to uphold the Democratic case, led off for the justices. The commission's session began at 11 AM, but Bradley, Garfield noted in his diary, did not rise to speak until 2:13 PM. At the start of the session, Senator Edmunds, who was later charged with browbeating Bradley, told him that because his opinion was bound to be decisive, he should write it out rather than giving an extemporaneous oral delivery. Bradley did so—forgoing the careful notes on others' presentations he had taken at every previous session of the commission. It was only then, I believe, that Bradley reached a final decision, so impressed had he been by the plausibility of arguments on both sides.

"All were intent" when Bradley rose, "because B. held the casting vote," Garfield wrote in his diary. "All were making a manifest effort to appear unconcerned. It was a curious study to watch the faces as he read. It was ten minutes before it became evident that he was against the authority to hear extrinsic evidence."[37] Bradley began by flatly denying the right of the president of the Senate alone to count the votes, a tack that apparently raised Democratic hopes. But then he veered and repeated the arguments that Democrat after Democrat had made in 1875 and 1876 and that Republican lawyers were making now: The Constitution gave states the exclusive power to pick presidential electors. Aside from naming the day for the meeting of the electoral college, Congress had no power to investigate, challenge, or change those votes—so long as the named electors were constitutionally eligible. Even if clear evidence of fraud existed, Congress lacked the constitutional jurisdiction to remedy it. Quite unlike contested elections of representatives and senators, Bradley added, Congress had no role in a presidential election other than counting the electoral votes states had submitted. Since the electoral commission was a creature of Congress, it too lacked the constitutional authority to investigate the returns.[38] Thus Bradley joined the other Republicans on the commission to vote 8 to 7 against going behind the returns. But then, as Garfield noted in the same diary entry, Bradley "surprised us all by holding that we could hear testimony as to the [constitutionality] of [Republican elector Frederick C.] Humphreys."[39] Here, Bradley joined the seven Democrats in defeating the seven other Republicans by voting that all evidence relevant to this question, none of which had ever been submitted to the president of the Senate, must be admitted to adjudicate this fellow's eligibility as a Republican elector.

Thus the Florida case remained unsettled. Thus Democratic objectors to Humphreys's vote and Democratic and Republican lawyers again had to try to persuade the fifteen commissioners. Ultimately, this rehearing made no difference. Evidence clearly showed that Humphreys had resigned his federal job before November 7, 1876. On February 9, Bradley joined the seven other Republicans, over the negative votes of the seven Democrats, in awarding Florida's four electoral votes to Hayes. That decision was officially reported to the joint session of Congress on Saturday, February 10.

David Dudley Field immediately presented a written objection to this decision signed by six Democratic senators and twelve representatives, including Hewitt. Eight grounds of objections were listed, among them that the commission had refused to recognize the right of Florida's courts to review and overrule the findings of the state's canvassing board. The House and Senate immediately went into separate session, and the Senate quickly voted to accept the commission's decision by a party-line vote of 44 to 24. Furious House Democrats, in contrast, began a stall that would escalate with each passing day. The majority voted to adjourn until Monday, February 12, and when the House met then, hours were wasted on parliamentary motions before the two-hour clock for consideration of the commission's decision, mandated by the law, started. Finally, the House voted on Field's motion to reject the commission's finding. It passed 168 to 103, "almost strictly on party grounds," as Garfield tersely reported to his diary.[40] The Senate vote, however, ensured that Florida's four votes went to Hayes.

On the afternoon of February 12 Randall summoned the Senate back into the House chamber to acknowledge that result and continue the count. Georgia's votes for Tilden were accepted without comment. When Illinois was reached, however, Republicans fully expected Democrats to challenge one of their electors on the grounds of constitutional ineligibility. But Conkling had warned Hewitt that raising this objection would require going behind the reported returns to see whether that elector was indeed ineligible, thus jeopardizing the case Democrats hoped to make with regard to Oregon. So Democrats held their fire, and the count proceeded without incident until Ferry read the two returns from Louisiana. They were sent to the commission, and again the joint meeting recessed until its decision was reported.

Bradley would join the Republicans on the commission in awarding all 20 disputed electoral votes to Hayes by an 8–7 vote. Democratic objections to the Republican returns from Louisiana, Oregon, and South Carolina differed slightly from those advanced in the Florida case, as did the personnel among objectors and lawyers who appeared before the commission. In the Louisiana case, for example, Democrats protested, quite accurately, that the canvassing board that had awarded certificates to Republican electors was illegally constituted because it lacked a Democratic member and thus acted illegally when counting the votes. They also maintained that two of the Republican electors were constitutionally ineligible. Changing its rules as it went along, the commission voted to give counsel for each side in this case four hours. Matthew Carpenter, ex-Senator Lyman Trumbull, and former Supreme Court Justice John A. Campbell represented the Democrats; Evarts and ex-Congressman Samuel Shellabarger, in an argument that especially impressed Garfield, retorted for the Republican lawyers. On Friday, February 16, the commission met for eleven hours to mull over these arguments, but in the end, the eight Republicans rejected the Democratic objections. Once again, significantly, no one on the commission knew beforehand how Bradley might rule. Once his position became clear, Garfield told his diary, "There was a long breath of relief, up or down, but actual relief to all from the long suspense."[41]

This decision was reported to the Speaker on February 17, when the representatives and senators reconvened. Again, Democrats presented written objections, and the two houses went into separate session. Again, the Senate immediately accepted the commission's decision by a vote of 41 to 28. Again, the Democratic House stalled by postponing any action until Monday, the nineteenth. "It is manifest that the Democrats intend to delay the decision as long as possible," Garfield told his diary on February 13.[42] Once it did vote, the House futilely rejected the commission's decision on Louisiana by a vote of 173 to 77. That vote indicated that some Republicans could not stomach what had happened in Louisiana, secure in the knowledge that the Senate's action had already guaranteed the votes for Hayes.

Even Democrats knew that their claim to the one electoral vote from Oregon, where Republicans had clearly won a majority of the popular vote, was their weakest case. Oregon state law explicitly ordered the secretary of state to canvass the returns in the presence of the governor, award certificates of election to the winning electors, and attach the seal of the state to those certificates. That official had awarded certificates to all three Republicans, including Watts. To Garfield, this case seemed so open and shut that he characterized the Democratic effort to get that one vote as "a perfectly absurd proposition" and fully expected a unanimous commission vote on behalf of the Republicans.[43] When the commission finally voted on Friday, February 23, however, it again split 8 to 7. Ohio Democrat Thurman had taken sick, and the vote occurred in the bedroom of his house. Citing his illness, Thurman then resigned his place on the commission, and Senate Democrats chose New York Senator Francis Kernan to replace him for the hearings on South Carolina.

The following day the Senate voted once again to accept the decision on Oregon, and the House voted to reject it.

On Tuesday, February 27, the reconstituted commission heard conflicting testimony on South Carolina's disputed electoral votes and reached a decision later that day. Here, Democrats objected that because South Carolina's Republican legislature had ignored a provision of the 1868 state constitution ordering it to enact a voter registration law, the entire election of November 7 was void, and no electoral votes from South Carolina should be counted. Democrats also contended that the presence of federal marshals and troops in South Carolina on that day had intimidated potential Democratic voters and thus deprived South Carolina of a republican form of government. Because the Constitution explicitly required Congress to provide such republican government to every state, its creature, the electoral commission, must rule that South Carolina's electoral votes were null and should not be counted by Congress. Here, Democrats did not rely on pleas for justice and fair play, largely, one suspects, because the returns on their face gave South Carolina's votes to Hayes. Instead, they relied on the letter of the South Carolina Constitution and of the U.S. Constitution as they stood on election day.

Stanley Matthews and Samuel Shellabarger were the Republicans' legal counsel on the South Carolina case. Montgomery Blair, once postmaster general in Lincoln's cabinet, and Jeremiah Black spoke for the Democrats. In his closing argument, Black angrily denounced the commission's clear partisan bias. Acknowledging that any argument before these men was "a forlorn hope," he railed that the commission's refusal to hear extrinsic evidence guaranteed that "we can never expect such a thing as an honest election again." "At present, you have us down and under your feet," he raged. "But . . . wait a little while . . . retribution will come in due time." Garfield characterized this frustrated outburst as "bitter and insulting."[44] And of course, it did no good. Near 7 PM the commission awarded South Carolina's electoral votes to Hayes by the now predictable 8–7 margin.

The following day, February 28, Democrats just as predictably objected to this decision when the two chambers reconvened, and they quickly dispersed to separate sessions. House "Democrats filibustered with all their might to prevent the completion of the count," Garfield reported to his diary.[45] But the Republican Senate again quickly accepted the commission's decision on South Carolina, thereby rendering nugatory the

Democratic House's predictable rejection of it. House Democrats stalled so long before casting that vote, however, that the two houses did not reassemble together until after 6 PM. Nor would they finally complete the count of the electoral vote until after 4 AM on March 2, scarcely thirty-six hours before the winner was due to be sworn in on Sunday.

Congress had begun the count of electoral votes on February 1. There were returns from only thirty-eight states to consider, yet it had taken a full month to complete the count. Why? Granted, the suspension of the count while the electoral commission heard testimony about and deliberated on the disputed returns from Florida, Louisiana, Oregon, and South Carolina delayed it. But aside from the Florida case, the commission had actually operated with relative dispatch. Instead, House Democrats who challenged the constitutional eligibility of individual Republican electors from Michigan, Nevada, Pennsylvania, Vermont, and Wisconsin were primarily responsible for the slow count. Republicans lost none of those electoral votes because the Republican Senate steadfastly refused to agree to any of the Democratic objections. But each such objection allowed the House to go into separate session, where Democrats consumed as much time as possible to delay or prevent the completion of the vote count. This Democratic stalling is what Garfield at the time and subsequent historians have called "filibustering."[46]

Democrats in the House were clearly successful in mobilizing a majority of their members to sustain this attempted filibuster, but southern Democrats were obviously more militant than their northern colleagues. The reason is clear. Southern Democrats were desperate to deprive the Republican Party of its control over the army and U.S. marshals. "My poor Southern Country is looking to you as their only hope for their constitutional rights," one Virginian wrote to Tilden in December. "We are looking to you as our political savior."[47] "What the South has expected from Gov. Tilden's election no man who does not live in the South can be made to know," Alabama's Leroy Pope Walker told Manton Marble. "It sees resurrection after burial. And what our disappointment will be at his failure is beyond the possibilities of language to express. It is to have been resurrected only to be reinterred."[48] Southern Democrats, in short, had ample reason to fight against Hayes's election until the bitter end.

In fact, however, southern Democrats' militancy in February marked a significant shift since December. Then, the issue before House Democrats was not whether to delay an already started count of electoral votes. Rather, it was whether House Democrats should prevent the constitutionally mandated meeting of the two houses altogether and confront Republicans in other ways. Then, as Garfield noted in his diary, and as both Democratic and Republican newspaper correspondents reported from Washington, southern Democrats were far more moderate and conciliatory than their northern colleagues. When New York's former Mayor Fernando Wood urged in a Democratic caucus that the House launch formal impeachment proceedings against Grant, for example, southern Democrats led in quashing the proposal. Similarly, when some midwestern Democrats spoke wildly of installing Tilden as president by armed force, southern Democratic congressmen firmly spurned any resort to violence. Unlike northern Democratic vaporers, they announced, they had personally experienced hard fighting and wanted no more of it.

More important, rumors circulated in Washington during December that a substantial number of southern Democratic congressmen were willing to cut a deal with Republicans who were close enough to Hayes to know his intentions regarding policy toward the South. They would oppose any motions in the House to block a joint meeting if those men could guarantee that Hayes would remove the remaining troops from South Carolina and Louisiana so that the Democratic administrations of Wade Hampton and Francis Nichols could govern unimpeded. On December 13, 1876, a Washington Democrat sent nearly identical warnings to Tilden and to Charles Dana, editor of the Democratic *New York Sun*. "There is danger of serious defection among southern democratic leaders. Certain of Hayes' friends are making proposals to certain southern democrats and they are entertained and may be accepted. There is a potential combination enlisted in this movement—Jay Gould, [Collis P.] Huntington, and Tom Scott—the Union Pacific, Central Pacific, Texas Pacific and Penna Railroad. There is a deep undercurrent unseen by the gentlemen managing your case here."[49] Five days later R. B. Radford also warned Tilden from Washington that forty to fifty southern Democrats might cut a deal with Hayes. Hayes had "already assured them of his intention to admit them into his confidence," for Hayes's purpose was to win over former Whigs in the South who "have recently been with us as a consequence of the war and republican outrage. . . . The machinery has already to my certain knowledge been set in motion for that object. Hayes is a much wiser man than he is popularly regarded."[50]

During December most Ohio Republicans in Washington were so confident that Ferry alone would count the votes that they saw no need for help from southern Democrats to give Hayes 185 electoral votes. But like Hayes himself, they were very much interested in pursuing the objective aired when Hayes was composing his letter accepting the Republican nomination—namely, splitting former southern Whigs away from southern Democrats and bringing them into a reconfigured southern Republican coalition. Achieving that goal would make Hayes's job of dealing with Congress and governing infinitely easier. When Garfield learned that southern Democrats had killed the impeachment proposal in a House Democratic caucus, for example, he told his diary that "wise management may break the strength of the Southern Democracy. We ought to have the old Whig element with us." Three days later he reported that he had been urged "to sound the Democrats in regard to their policy and bring Hayes to the determination of finding some earnest Southern Union men to help him build up the Republican Party in the South."[51]

Republican newspapermen quickly learned that some southern Democrats were putting out feelers toward northern Republicans. Ironically, they were many of the same men who had first learned of Blaine's questionable railroad dealings—Henry Van Ness Boynton, Washington correspondent of the *Cincinnati Gazette,* and his editor Richard Smith; Murat Halstead, editor of the *Cincinnati Commercial;* Joseph Medill, editor of the *Chicago Tribune;* and William Henry Smith, president of the Western Associated Press. Now, however, an important new player joined the group. This was Andrew Kellar, the editor of a Democratic newspaper in Memphis, Tennessee. Smith had befriended Kellar, a habitually dissatisfied Democratic ingrate who was eager to bring about a realignment in southern politics, at the St. Louis national convention. With Hayes's implicit blessing,[52] these men took on the role of intermediaries between southern Democrats and northern Republicans in Washington.

Halstead, Medill, and Kellar all visited the capital city in December to advance the rapprochement. Of these, Kellar, whom Boynton immediately took under his wing, was the most important because potential southern Democratic defectors trusted him more than they did Republican newspapermen or congressmen. Thus Kellar explained—and in some cases personally formulated—the terms necessary to cause former southern Whigs to abandon the Democratic ship. In addition to the removal of federal troops still in Louisiana and South Carolina, they wanted guarantees from Ohio Republicans that Hayes would fulfill his promise to eliminate the color line in southern politics by purging carpetbaggers and blacks from federal appointive offices and pledge in his inaugural address that federal attempts to enforce Reconstruction legislation in the South would cease. They also insisted that Hayes appoint at least one southern Democrat to his cabinet, who would in turn appoint Democrats to at least half the patronage slots under his control in southern states. Furthermore—and here, Kellar's residence in Memphis was crucial—the ex-Whigs among southern Democrats demanded that Hayes endorse and work for congressional subsidies for rebuilding levees along the Mississippi River and for building Scott's proposed Texas and Pacific Railroad from Marshall, Texas, to San Diego, California. In return for these concessions, southern Democrats supposedly promised to block any House effort to prevent the joint meeting that would count the electoral votes. At that time, it must be stressed, most Republicans still expected Ferry alone to count the votes. But these southern Democrats also allegedly promised that if Hayes and his allies upheld their end of the bargain, they would provide enough votes to elect Ohio Republican James A. Garfield Speaker of the House when the new Forty-fifth Congress met in December 1877, a promise that the cagey Garfield never believed.[53]

Sherman, Garfield, and other Republicans in Washington, along with William Henry Smith, kept Hayes informed of these negotiations with southern Democrats. Still convinced that Ferry alone should count the electoral votes—indeed, he strongly opposed the creation of the electoral commission—Hayes responded cautiously, if not coolly. As for the southerners' demands about economic policy, he wrote to Smith on December 24, "I do not wish to be committed to details. It is so desirable to restore peace and prosperity to the South that I have given a good deal of thought to it. The two things I would be exceptionally liberal about are education and internal improvements of a national character."[54] In early January, however, Hayes informed Smith that he did not believe "in the trustworthiness of the forces you hope to rally. After we are in, I believe a wise and liberal policy can accomplish a great deal. But we must rely on our own strength to secure our rights."[55] To demands that he make more explicit pledges about his policy toward the South, he repeatedly told correspondents that he stood by his acceptance letter.

Despite Hayes's attempts to distance himself from the December negotiations in Washington, they had occurred. And the terms that were broached, according to one distinguished American historian, constituted a "Compromise of 1877"—a compromise every bit as real and significant as the Compromise of 1850.[56] What must be stressed, however, is that most of these preliminary negotiations occurred in December, when there was still a possibility that House Democrats might flout the Constitution and attempt to prevent any joint meeting of the House and Senate to count the electoral votes. The appointment of committees by the House and Senate in late December to create a tribunal that could resolve the electoral vote dispute, and the adoption of the recommended bill by both houses of Congress on January 26, 1877, temporarily relegated these talks to the back burner.

The electoral commission's decision about Florida and what it portended for the other disputed cases restarted these talks. By then, it also seemed clear that Grant intended to prop up the Republican administrations in Louisiana and South Carolina with federal troops until he left office. Hence, Democrats from those states pressed southern Democrats in the House to exert whatever leverage they could to get Hayes's closest friends to commit him to removing troops from those states if he was inaugurated. In February, therefore, southern Democrats pushed the House Democratic caucus to filibuster to prevent Hayes's inauguration in order to extort those concessions. The chairman of Louisiana's Democratic state committee, Edward A. Burke, came to Washington so that he could personally orchestrate the stall. Conversely, by the last week of February, some of the northern Democrats who had been most militant in December, including Speaker Randall, now conceded Hayes's election and opposed delay.

Nonetheless, southern Democrats' efforts so endangered the completion of the count before March 4 that a conference between Ohio Republicans and southern representatives was convened by Stanley Matthews at his rooms in the Wormley House hotel on the night of February 26 to finalize terms. Aside from Matthews, Senator John Sherman, former Ohio Governor William Dennison, and Congressmen Garfield and Charles Foster represented Hayes's interests. Burke, Louisiana Democratic Congressman Ezekiel Ellis, and Henry Watterson, the Louisville, Kentucky, newspaperman who had been elected to fill an empty House seat the previous August, represented the southerners. Earlier that day, Burke had promised Grant that Francis Nichols was pledged to protect blacks' constitutional rights should the federal troops guarding the statehouse in New Orleans be removed. He repeated that pledge to the five Ohioans. Watterson offered similar pledges on behalf of South Carolina's Wade Hampton. Was that pledge sufficient, they asked, to get Hayes to remove the remaining federal troops?

Garfield's diary entry for that day makes no mention whatsoever of any economic terms involved in a bargain. He did note, however, that exchanges between Burke and Matthews "led me to believe that there had been former consultations, and that a compact of some kind was meditated." Garfield emphatically told the other participants that no one there from Ohio had a right to speak for Hayes and that he wanted no part of an unseemly bargain to end the Democratic filibuster. "I thought Matthews did not like my remarks, but I made them to prevent any misunderstanding so far as I was concerned," Garfield wrote.[57]

Nor was Congressman Foster pleased with Garfield's intervention. He immediately wrote a letter, dated February 27 and cosigned by Matthews, which was addressed to John Gordon, a Georgia Democrat, and John Brown, a Kentucky Democrat. "We can assure you in the strongest possible manner of our great desire to have him [Hayes] adopt such a policy as will give to the people of the States of South Carolina and Louisiana the right to control their own affairs in their own way," subject only to the Constitution and federal laws pursuant to it, Foster wrote. "We feel authorized, from our acquaintance with and knowledge of Gov. Hayes and his views on this question," the letter continued, "to pledge ourselves to you for him and that such will be his policy." That same day Matthews sent a separate note to Congressman Ellis pledging that Hayes would indeed remove the troops from Louisiana.[58]

What impact these assurances had on southern Democrats in the House is unclear. What is clear is that most of them tried to delay the completion of the count until the bitter end; that it was primarily northern Democrats, not southerners, who voted with Republicans to force the House to resume joint meetings with the Senate; and that the vote could not be completed until 4 AM on March 2. On Monday, March 5, Hayes was publicly sworn in as the next president.

Evidently embarrassed by the way he had won that office, Hayes added several paragraphs about the proceedings of the electoral commission to the end of his inaugural address. Noting that only "the peculiar circumstances" of the 1876 election had required the creation of a "tribunal" to decide its outcome, he praised its members as "men of long-established reputation for integrity and intelligence" whose decisions were "entitled to the fullest confidence of the American people." Nonetheless, he admitted, "For the present, opinion will widely vary as to the wisdom of the several conclusions announced by that tribunal." Such disagreement was inevitable "in every instance where matters of dispute are made the subject of arbitration under the forms of law. Human judgment is never unerring, and is rarely regarded as otherwise than wrong by the unsuccessful party in the contest." Still, he concluded, the fact that the "conflicting claims to the Presidency" had been "amicably and peaceably adjusted" was "an occasion for general rejoicing."[59]

Most Democrats never accepted such a rosy conclusion. Throughout Hayes's presidency, they insisted that it was illegitimate. Long before the count of the electoral vote was completed, the bitterness and rage among Democrats had already exploded. Most blamed the foolishness of congressional Democrats, especially Hewitt, for agreeing to the creation of the electoral commission, particularly once they knew that David Davis refused to serve on it. "If the Democratic House have been foolishly 'fleeced' by a Republican 'confidence game,'" a Vermont Democrat wrote to Tilden on February 20, "neither you nor the Democratic party behind you are bound by the fraud." "The defeat of the Democratic party is due measurably to the manipulation of inexperienced or overconfident directors," concurred a New Yorker two days later. "There has been too much willingness on the part of the democrats to compromise & Senator Kernan [by agreeing to replace Thurman on the commission] to say the least has acted unwisely." "If the chairman of our National Committee had not wavered and hesitated, at a decisive moment, and thereby awakened doubts as to your purpose, the spirit and courage of the democracy, then showing a bold front, would have precluded the possibility of the electoral commission and its decision," added an Illinois Democrat. "To the imbeciles who allowed the consummation of this wicked scheme . . . the democracy . . . point the finger of contempt," raged a Vermonter on March 2. "The timid, weak, vacillating, balking, hesitating course of Mr. Hewitt et id omnes genus has robbed us of our rights," summarized a Philadelphian on March 4. "One bold, resolute determined man could have saved the fight."[60]

Although many Democrats had earlier complained of Tilden's seeming passivity during the struggle, they now, at the last moment, called on him to lead the party in resistance to the commission's decisions. "It is your duty to call upon your party immediately to inaugurate you, and they will swarm from every section of the country to carry out your wishes," vowed a Chicago Democrat on February 21. "They await only a reason, and a leader, to rise up in arms." "I would never submit to the damnable fraud," echoed a Rochester, New York, supporter three days later. "I would advise the friends to resist to the last extremity &

until eternal justice prevails." "Counsel resistance. We dare not submit to fraud," New Jersey's James M. Scovel telegraphed from Philadelphia on February 26.[61]

Cooler heads urged Tilden to employ the section of the electoral commission act that authorized court challenges against the winners announced by Congress. "Why can you not proceed against Hayes by Quo-warranto and make him show cause why he holds the office of President?" a Tennessean asked Tilden on March 2. "Then the court could not refuse to receive evidence and by this means you may yet be placed in possession of your right." "We think it is your imperative duty to contest the title of the Presidency, before the Supreme Court," urged a Pennsylvanian in February. "The House of Reps threw away a certainty for an uncertainty, and got it, but you can certainly win by judicial investigation. For the sake of pure & good government we hope you will contest and fight it to the bitter end."[62]

By far the most bitter, and unwittingly the funniest, advice along these lines came in a letter from Baltimore dated March 1. "My Dear Sir, enter suit at once against Rutherford B. Hayes in the name and in behalf of the People of the United States forbidding him the exercise of that office and keep him in court the whole of the next four years and you will save your country." This Democratic soldier advised his putative commander to be in Washington on inauguration day so that Tilden could personally "serve the writ on him [Hayes], if he takes the oath on Sunday, the first thing on Monday morning, if he waits till Monday to take the oath. Serve the moment afterward before he makes his [inaugural] speech."[63] Now *that* would have been a scene for the history books!

The purpose of this brief conclusion is not to summarize everything said in the foregoing chapters. Rather, it is to assess the significance of the election. What should people remember about it? Did it make any difference in the short term that Rutherford Hayes rather than Samuel Tilden was the victor?

In some important ways, the presidential election of 1876 was unique. No other presidential election in American history was decided by so close a margin in the electoral vote (see table 8 in appendix A). No other election produced anything like the Federal Electoral Commission of 1877 to determine who won the electoral vote. And none evoked so high a participation rate by potential voters.

Some fraction of those recorded votes, and not just in the South, was undoubtedly fraudulent. Nonetheless, the unprecedented and thereafter unequaled turnout rate is perhaps the election's most surprising feature. Certainly, the correspondence received by Hayes and Tilden failed to predict it. By the last two months of the campaign, moreover, there was little to distinguish Republicans from Democrats on issues such as reform, specie resumption, and even the Catholic school question once House Democrats and Senate Republicans had offered quite similar, yet distinctive, constitutional amendments on that issue. How, a modern reader might justly ask, could an election that produced yet another in a string of bearded, seemingly unprepossessing Republican presidents possibly evoke so much interest among voters?

Historians cannot get inside the minds of nineteenth-century voters. We can, however, infer why men bothered to vote and how they voted when they did. Continuing hard times, still vivid memories of Civil War sacrifices, and white southerners' determination to reestablish white supremacy in their region probably best explain the astonishing turnout in 1876. Nineteenth-century elections were primarily referenda on competing political parties, not their presidential candidates, because few if any voters ever personally saw or heard those candidates. The first presidential election in American history that brought more than four-fifths of the potential electorate to the polls occurred in 1840, a year also mired in deep depression. In terms of absolute numbers, turnout in that contest was fully 60 percent higher than in 1836. Three-fifths of those new voters supported the "out" Whigs rather than the incumbent Democrats, in part because Whigs promised that their programs would bring about economic recovery and relief. In 1876 Democrats, especially in the North, undoubtedly benefited from a similar determination to throw the discredited "ins" out, although their campaign's focus on reform rather than relief may have cost Tilden some votes. Yet northern Republicans possessed a weapon of even greater potency. It is absolutely clear that fear of ex-Confederates recapturing control of the federal government in Washington, thereby betraying more than 300,000 dead Union soldiers, constituted the Republican Party's most telling appeal in the North. That their candidate, unlike the priggish Tilden, had repeatedly demonstrated valor on the battlefield only added to their advantage. Yet memories of the war and more recent experience with Republicans' Reconstruction programs also best explain the breathtaking jump in white support for Democrats in the South that year.

These aspects of the 1876 election were time-specific. Nonetheless, a number of its characteristics *were* eerily similar to the long dispute over Florida's result in 2000, even beyond the fact that Republicans garnered its electoral votes in both years. Of these, perhaps the most important was the resort to both state and federal courts by both Democrats and Republicans to gain a partisan edge, although in 1876 this occurred in South Carolina as well as Florida. Democrats in 2000 who ranted about the outrageous and unprecedented intervention of the U.S. Supreme Court in resolving the Florida dispute, in part by overruling decisions of the state supreme court, simply did not know American history very well. In 1875 and 1876 scores of both Democratic and Republican representatives and senators maintained that the Supreme Court alone should count the electoral votes and decide any disputes over them. What bothered them most was the idea that Congress itself, without any explicit constitutional authorization, should attempt to do so. This background helps explain why almost everyone in January 1877 assumed that Supreme Court justices must sit on any tribunal that decided the disputed electoral votes. Recall, moreover, that as of January 11, 1877, a membership consisting exclusively of the five most senior associate justices of the Court was House Democrats' preferred composition of any tribunal that determined the winner of the twenty disputed electoral votes.

Although the body eventually created by Congress was called the Federal Electoral Commission, the preliminary use of the term *tribunal* in the debates prior to its creation was hardly accidental. Republicans feared and Democrats expected it to perform "judicial" as opposed to merely "ministerial" functions, because judicial functions entailed examining evidence. In Florida, Louisiana, and South Carolina, Democrats had argued strenuously that the state returning boards had only the latter power, not the former one. In Washington during the winter of 1876–1877, the two parties reversed their partisan stances on that question. And once it became clear that the electoral commission was going to count Hayes in, furious Democrats once again urged Tilden to go to court to save his bacon. That political parties might seek judicial rulings to gain a partisan advantage in elections was hardly unprecedented in 2000.

That said, as a historian with no legal training whatsoever, I wonder what has become of the ancient doctrine of quo warranto—that is, by what legal right does a public official hold the office he (or she) claims to hold?—which Florida Democrats used in 1876 and some Democrats wanted Tilden to employ. Granted, judges probably would have denied personal "standing" to "any citizen" empowered by the language of the 1877 law to seek such writs in federal courts. But Tilden in 1876, just like Al Gore in 2000, surely had such "standing," even if neither chose to pursue such suits. The point here is that I know of no evidence that Democratic lawyers in 2000 ever considered using this doctrine.[1]

Whatever the fate of quo warranto, some might still protest that the most egregious aspect of the Supreme Court's intervention in 2000 was its overruling of decisions by the Florida supreme court that favored Gore. In 1877 Democratic lawyers arguing before the Federal Electoral Commission advanced the same case. They demanded that the commission honor state court rulings on elections held under the aegis of state authority. But just as the Supreme Court ruled in 2000 that the U.S. Constitution delegated all authority over presidential elections to state legislatures, not their courts, so did the majority of the electoral commission, with its three Republican associate justices, rule in 1876.

Beyond the uniqueness of the 1876 election and its parallels to the 2000 contest, what should history books say about that election's outcome? Did it make any real difference that Hayes rather than Tilden was counted in? With regard to Reconstruction, it made little difference, in my opinion. That congressional experiment—dependent as it was on Republican control of southern state governments, or at least on Republicans' ability to recapture that control having lost it—had already ended in eight of the eleven former Confederate states. The huge Democratic majorities in those eight states demonstrated that fact. Once Democrat George Drew assumed Florida's governorship in early 1877, President Grant removed federal troops from that state. And after Hayes was finally elected in the early morning of March 2, Grant ordered the troops in South Carolina and Louisiana to return to their barracks. That order guaranteed the instant collapse of the administrations of Daniel Chamberlain and Stephen Packard. For unknown reasons, however, the order went astray. Thus it was left to Hayes, within weeks of his inauguration, to issue similar orders that guaranteed Democratic control of state governments in all the former Confederate states. Yet can anyone seriously believe that Tilden would have acted differently or that the fortunes of African Americans in the South would have been any better under a Tilden administration than a Hayes administration?

The same conclusion holds for the other issues that dominated the rhetoric of the 1876 election. On January 1, 1879, during Hayes's presidency, the United States did resume specie payments. Tilden was firmly committed to specie resumption, but one doubts that he could have achieved it any sooner had he been president. At the same time, continued Republican control of the Senate would have negated any further attempts by House Democrats to repeal the Specie Resumption Act even if Tilden had been counted in.

The same is most likely true of civil service reform. Hayes appointed pro-reform Republicans such as William M. Evarts and Carl Schurz to his cabinet. Those appointments infuriated regular Republican titans in Congress, but they did little to diminish those politicos' control over the allotment of federal patronage jobs. Given the hunger of thousands of ravenous Democrats for federal pap after sixteen years out of power, one doubts that Tilden would have been any more successful in changing the system, despite the Democratic mantra of reform.

Tilden, quite unlike Hayes, had ignored the Catholic school question in his letter accepting the Democratic nomination. One suspects that he had no interest in this question. After all, he had signed New York Republicans' repeal of the "Gray Nun Act" just as readily as he had signed the Democrats' bill enacting it. Hayes, in contrast, obviously cared deeply about the Catholic school question. Because Senate Republicans lacked the two-thirds majority necessary to enact their own version of the Blaine Amendment throughout Hayes's term—and indeed, for the remainder of the nineteenth century—there was no attempt to amend the Constitution on that matter. Instead, Congress, often with the support of Democrats, required those seeking statehood to incorporate so-called little Blaine amendments in their state constitutions as the price of admission. It seems unlikely that Tilden would have attempted to stop this policy. In any event, between 1877 and 1881, no additional western states were admitted to the Union.

Only one final policy area requires counterfactual investigation here. One of the most controversial actions by Hayes as president was to deploy federal troops to break up a massive and massively destructive strike by railroad workers against their employers in 1877. Would a President Tilden—who had earned millions of dollars as an attorney for railroad corporations and who had appointed a state commission that, in 1877, recommended the disfranchisement of non–property owners in New York City's municipal elections—have responded any differently to this crisis? One doubts it. The protection of private property rights was simply too dear to Tilden.

Outside of any policy differences between a President Hayes and a President Tilden, did the closely contested elections of 1876 have any impact on partisan politics that the history books should note? Aside from a few thousand Liberal Republicans in the North and erstwhile white Republicans in the South, there is little evidence that those elections produced a major voter realignment in the United States. What they did, however, was return millions of American voters to the polls who had sat out the elections of 1872 and 1874 but whose partisan inclinations were already formed. Within the South, moreover, blacks continued to vote heavily Republican until they began to be disfranchised in the 1880s and 1890s. Once Democrats regained control of southern state legislatures and returning boards, however, they negated black voting power except in a few municipalities and state legislative and congressional districts.

Nonetheless, Democrats' astounding remobilization of previously apathetic white voters both in the North and especially in the South in 1876, along with Republicans' miraculous comeback after the 1874 debacle in most northern states, brought Democrats and Republicans to a competitive equilibrium that had not existed since the 1850s and would continue until the 1890s. That political achievement of the elections of 1876 constitutes their major historical significance, not the fact that Hayes was counted in and Tilden was not. That equilibrium, it bears repeating, depended on the return of hundreds of thousands of northern Republican voters to the polls. And their return testifies to the grip that the hatred and fear aroused by the Civil War still held over the majority of the northern electorate.

Table 1. Partisan Division of Congressional Seats Filled in 1872 and 1874

Region	1872			1874		
	Democrat	Republican	Independent	Democrat	Republican	Independent
New England	0	21	0	4	14	3
Mid-Atlantic	14	53	0	40	27	0
Midwest	17	67	0	38	43	3
Far West	2	4	0	1	1	0
Border states	24	8	1	33	0	0
Confederate states	29	43	1	51	14	2

Source: Michael J. Dubin, *United States Congressional Elections, 1788–1997: The Official Results* (Jefferson, N.C.: McFarland, 1998).

This table does not include Connecticut and New Hampshire, which voted in the spring of 1873 and 1875, or California and Mississippi in 1874.

Table 2. Swings in the Republican and Democratic Popular Vote by Region, 1872–1876

Region* and Party	President 1872	1872 to 1874–1875	1874–1875 to 1876	1872–1876
New England				
Republican	337,866	−87,290	+126,960	+39,670
Democratic	181,907	+32,098	+85,397	+117,495
Mid-Atlantic				
Republican	881,981	−201,830	+296,757	+94,927
Democratic	675,778	+59,802	+217,928	+346,253
Midwest				
Republican	858,226	−227,636	+445,391	+217,755
Democratic	619,021	+59,802	+286,552	+346,354
Plains/West				
Republican	159,629	−26,820	+84,340	+57,520
Democratic	95,466	+21,646	+37,095	+58,741
Border states				
Republican	318,152	−115,000	+163,812	+48,812
Democratic	358,773	−6,014	+164,465	+158,431
Ex-Confederate upper South				
Republican	315,265	−82,734	+99,679	+16,945
Democratic	294,066	+34,786	+127,640	+162,426
Ex-Confederate Deep South				
Republican	444,181	−48,548	+17,343	−31,203
Democratic	364,793	+76,764	+200,782	+277,546
National				
Republican	3,597,132	−789,858	+1,234,282	+444,426
Democratic	2,834,125	+333,421	+1,119,859	+1,447,266

* Unlike in table 1, Kansas and Nebraska are grouped with California, Oregon, and Nevada (Plains/West), not with the Midwest.

Table 3. Results of Congressional Elections by Region, 1874–1876

Year and Region	Democratic Seats	Republican Seats	Independent Seats
1874–1875			
North	92	87	8
Border states	33	0	0
Ex-Confederate states	56	14	3
1876			
North	61	126	0
Border states	29	4	0
Ex-Confederate states	63	8	2

These figures are based on the authoritative election returns contained in Michael J. Dubin, *United States Congressional Elections, 1788–1997: The Official Results* (Jefferson, N.C.: McFarland, 1998). Special elections required by the deaths of congressmen-elect before the new Congress opened changed the partisan balance slightly in Republicans' favor in each case. According to Dubin, the partisan count at the start of the Forty-fourth Congress in December 1875 stood at Democrats, 176; Republicans, 106; and various independents, 10. For the start of the Forty-fifth Congress in October 1877, it stood at Democrats, 150; Republicans, 141; and Independents, 2. In short, in 1876 and subsequent special elections, Republicans reduced a 70-seat Democratic majority to only 9 seats.

Table 4. Estimated Proportions of Whites and Blacks Voting Republican and Democratic in Louisiana Presidential and Gubernatorial Elections, 1868–1876

Race and Party	Whites (%)	Blacks (%)
1868 president		
Republican	0	58
Democratic	75	14
Not voting	25	28
1872 governor		
Republican	3	79
Democratic	61	5
Not voting	36	16
1876 governor		
Republican	0	84
Democratic	94	0
Not voting	6	16

This table is based on regression estimates calculated in a remarkable senior thesis written under my supervision at the University of Virginia by Stuart Delery, "One Supreme and Final Effort: Redemption in Louisiana, 1868–1877" (1990).

Table 5. Popular Vote for President by State, 1872 and 1876

State	1872 Grant	1872 Greeley	1876 Hayes	1876 Tilden	1876 Cooper
New England					
Connecticut	50,638	46,084	59,034	61,934	774
Maine	61,422	29,087	66,300	49,917	663
Massachusetts	133,472	59,260	150,063	108,777	779
New Hampshire	37,168	31,524	41,539	38,509	76
Rhode Island	13,665	5,329	15,787	10,712	68
Vermont	41,481	11,520	44,428	20,350	0
Mid-Atlantic					
New Jersey	91,656	77,086	103,517	115,962	712
New York	440,736	388,735	489,207	521,949	1,987
Pennsylvania	349,589	212,041	384,184	366,204	7,187
Midwest					
Illinois	241,944	187,966	278,232	258,601	9,533
Indiana	186,147	165,049	208,011	213,601	17,233
Iowa	131,566	73,417	171,326	112,121	9,901
Michigan	138,455	81,216	166,534	141,095	9,060
Minnesota	55,117	34,639	72,962	48,799	2,311
Ohio	281,852	245,484	330,698	323,182	3,057
Wisconsin	104,997	87,311	130,070	123,926	1,509
Plains/West					
California	54,020	41,786	78,322	76,468	44
Kansas	67,048	33,566	78,322	37,907	1,944
Nebraska	18,329	7,812	31,916	17,554	2,320
Nevada	8,413	6,236	10,383	9,308	0
Oregon	11,819	8,302	15,206	14,149	510
Border states					
Delaware	11,115	10,693	10,752	13,381	0
Kentucky	88,766	102,369	97,156	159,656	1,944
Maryland	66,760	67,706	71,981	91,780	33
Missouri	119,196	153,853	145,029	203,077	3,498
West Virginia	32,315	30,051	42,046	56,495	1,373
Ex-Confederate states					
Alabama	90,272	79,444	68,708	102,989	0
Arkansas	41,373	37,927	38,669	58,071	289
Florida (R)	17,764	15,427	23,849	22,927	0
Florida (D)	—	—	24,340	24,434	0
Georgia	62,550	80,356	50,446	130,088	0
Louisiana (R)	71,663	57,029	75,315	70,508	0
Louisiana (D)	—	—	77,174	83,723	0
Mississippi	82,175	47,288	52,605	112,173	0

Table 5 (*continued*)

State	1872		1876		
	Grant	Greeley	Hayes	Tilden	Cooper
North Carolina	94,769	70,094	108,417	125,427	0
South Carolina	72,290	22,790	91,870	90,896	0
Tennessee	85,655	94,391	89,566	133,166	0
Texas	47,468	69,126	44,803	104,803	0
Virginia	93,468	91,676	95,558	139,670	0

In 1872 a dissident straight Democratic candidate, Charles O'Conor, garnered fewer than 30,000 votes nationwide and more than 3,000 votes in only two states, Georgia and Illinois. Thus, I added his total in each state to Greeley's to better measure the growth of the Democratic vote between 1872 and 1876 in each state. In 1872 Louisiana Democrats and Republicans submitted different returns for Grant and Greeley. As a result, Congress refused to count any electoral votes from that state, but here I used the Republican returns for 1872. In 1876 Republicans and Democrats submitted different vote counts from Florida and Louisiana. For that year I listed both Republican (R) and Democratic (D) totals. Only the Republican returns were sent to Congress from South Carolina, but Democrats there vigorously protested their legitimacy.

Table 6. Turnout Rates in 1872 and 1876, Winning Margins of the Major Party Vote in 1876, and Winning Party's Percentage of the Total Vote in 1876, by State

State	Turnout Rate		Winning Margin in 1876 (Party)	Winning Party's Percentage in 1876
	1872	1876		
North				
California	57.9	72.9	1,854 (R)	50.6
Connecticut	71.3	82.0	2,900 (D)	50.7
Illinois	75.0	87.5	19,635 (R)	50.9
Indiana	85.3	94.6	5,515 (D)	48.6
Iowa	79.0	99.1	59,205 (R)	58.4
Kansas	65.7	77.8	40,415 (R)	66.2
Maine	57.9	71.5	16,383 (R)	56.7
Massachusetts	62.0	72.3	41,286 (R)	57.8
Minnesota	67.5	71.3	24,163 (R)	58.8
Nebraska	43.7	57.0	14,362 (R)	59.8
Nevada	74.1	90.0	1,075 (R)	52.7
New Hampshire	80.9	92.0	3,030 (R)	53.9
New Jersey	81.4	91.8	12,445 (D)	52.6
New York	80.5	89.6	32,742 (D)	51.4
Ohio	84.4	94.4	7,516 (R)	50.2
Oregon	60.5	70.4	1,057 (R)	50.9
Pennsylvania	68.6	83.5	17,980 (R)	50.6
Rhode Island	49.2	49.4	5,075 (R)	59.3
Vermont	69.1	83.3	24,078 (R)	68.6
Wisconsin	70.6	83.9	6,144 (R)	50.9
Border states				
Delaware	73.3	73.4	2,629 (D)	55.4
Kentucky	66.2	80.9	62,540 (D)	61.5
Maryland	75.0	82.7	19,799 (D)	56.0
Missouri	66.6	76.6	58,048 (D)	57.7
West Virginia	61.2	83.6	14,449 (D)	56.5
Ex-Confederate states				
Alabama	79.6	73.8	34,281 (D)	60.0
Arkansas	67.6	64.7	19,402 (D)	59.8
Florida (R)	77.0	93.5	862 (R)	51.0
Florida (D)	—	—	94 (D)	50.1
Georgia	55.2	63.5	79,642 (D)	72.1
Louisiana (R)	76.4	77.9	4,807 (R)	51.6
Louisiana (D)	—	—	6,549 (D)	52.0
Mississippi	71.7	79.9	59,568 (D)	68.1
North Carolina	71.9	90.1	17,010 (D)	53.6
South Carolina	60.4	101	974 (R)	50.3

Table 6 (*continued*)

State	Turnout Rate		Winning Margin in 1876 (Party)	Winning Party's Percentage in 1876
	1872	1876		
Tennessee	66.2	74.6	43,590 (D)	59.8
Texas	56.3	54.6	60,000 (D)	70.0
Virginia	66.2	77.6	44,312 (D)	59.4

The turnout percentages were calculated by Professor Walter Dean Burnham and were taken from the U.S. Census Office's *Historical Guide to United States Statistics*. I listed both the Republican (R) and Democratic (D) returns reported from Florida and Louisiana; I do not know which set Burnham used to estimate the 1876 turnout rates in those states, but in both, Democrats reported more total votes cast.

Table 7. Differentials in the Major Parties' Proportion of the Popular Vote by Region, as Measured by the Republican Margin

Region*	1872	1874–1875	1876
New England	+29.8	+7.2	+13.0
Mid-Atlantic	+13.0	−7.1	−1.3
Midwest	+13.2	−1.2	+5.6
Plains/West	+24.6	+4.1	+15.4
Border states	−6.8	−27.2	−17.5
Ex-Confederate upper South	+3.4	−17.0	−15.7
Ex-Confederate Deep South	+8.8	−6.3	−22.6

This table excludes third-party votes in 1876 but counts them (except for a tiny Prohibitionist vote) in the anti-Republican column in the congressional elections of 1874–1875. The differential is deciphered as follows: If Republicans garnered 55 percent of the two-party popular vote and Democrats garnered 45 percent in a region, the score would be +10. If the proportions of the vote were reversed, the score would be −10.

* New England includes Maine, New Hampshire, Vermont, Massachusetts, Connecticut, and Rhode Island. The mid-Atlantic region includes New Jersey, New York, and Pennsylvania. The Midwest includes Ohio, Indiana, Illinois, Michigan, Wisconsin, Minnesota, and Iowa. The Plains/West region includes Nebraska, Kansas, Nevada, Oregon, and California. The border states include Delaware, Maryland, West Virginia, Kentucky, and Missouri. The ex-Confederate upper South includes Virginia, North Carolina, Tennessee, and Arkansas. The ex-Confederate Deep South includes South Carolina, Georgia, Florida, Alabama, Mississippi, Louisiana, and Texas.

Table 8. Final Vote of the Electoral College in 1876

State	Hayes and Wheeler	Tilden and Hendricks
Alabama	—	10
Arkansas	—	6
California	6	—
Colorado	3	—
Connecticut	—	6
Delaware	—	3
Florida	4	—
Georgia	—	11
Illinois	21	—
Indiana	—	15
Iowa	11	—
Kansas	5	—
Kentucky	—	12
Louisiana	8	—
Maine	7	—
Maryland	—	8
Massachusetts	13	—
Michigan	11	—
Minnesota	5	—
Mississippi	—	8
Missouri	—	15
Nebraska	3	—
Nevada	3	—
New Hampshire	5	—
New Jersey	—	9
New York	—	35
North Carolina	—	10
Ohio	22	—
Oregon	3	—
Pennsylvania	29	—
Rhode Island	4	—
South Carolina	7	—
Tennessee	—	12
Texas	—	8
Vermont	5	—
Virginia	—	11
West Virginia	—	5
Wisconsin	10	—
Total	**185**	**184**

RUTHERFORD B. HAYES'S INAUGURAL ADDRESS, MARCH 5, 1877

Fellow Citizens: We have assembled to repeat the public ceremony begun by Washington, observed by all my predecessors, and now a time-honored custom, which marks the commencement of a new term of the Presidential office. Called to the duties of this great trust, I proceed, in compliance with usage, to announce some of the leading principles, on the subjects that now chiefly engage the public attention, by which it is my desire to be guided in the discharge of those duties. I shall not attempt to lay down irrevocably principles or measures of administration, but rather to speak to the motives which should animate us, and to suggest certain important ends to be attained in accordance with our institutions and essential to the welfare of our country.

At the outset of the discussions which preceded the recent Presidential election it seemed to me fitting that I should fully make known my sentiments in regard to several of the important questions which then appeared to demand the consideration of the country. Following the example, and in part adopting the language of one of my predecessors, I wish now, when every motive for misrepresentation to pass away, to repeat what was said before the election, trusting that my countrymen will candidly weigh and understand it, and that they will feel assured that the sentiments declared in accepting the nomination for the Presidency will be the standard of my conduct in the path before me, charged as I now am, with the grave and difficult task of carrying them out in the practical administration of the Government so far as depends, under the Constitution and laws, on the Chief Executive of the nation.

The permanent pacification of the country upon such principles and by such measures as will secure the complete protection of all its citizens in the free enjoyment of all their constitutional rights is now the one subject in our public affairs which all thoughtful and patriotic citizens regard as of supreme importance.

Many of the calamitous effects of the tremendous revolution which has passed over the Southern States still remain. The immeasurable benefits which will surely follow, sooner or later, the hearty and generous acceptance of the legitimate results of that revolution have not yet been realized. Difficult and embarrassing questions meet us at the threshold of this subject. The people of those States are still impoverished, and the inestimable blessing of wise, honest, and peaceful local self-government is not fully enjoyed. Whatever difference of opinion may exist as to the cause of this condition of things, the fact is clear that in the progress of events the time has come when such government is the imperative necessity required by all the varied interests, public and private, of those States. But it must not be forgotten that only a local government which recognizes and maintains inviolate the rights of all is a true self-government.

With respect to the two distinct races whose peculiar relation to each other have brought us the deplorable complications and perplexities which exist in those States, it must be a government which guards the interests of both races carefully and equally. It must be a government which submits loyally and heartily to the Constitution and the laws—the laws of the nation and the laws of the States themselves—accepting and obeying the whole Constitution as it is.

Resting upon this sure and substantial foundation, the superstructure of beneficent local governments can be built up, and not otherwise. In furtherance of such obedience to the letter and spirit of the Constitution, and in behalf of all that its attainment implies, all so-called party interests lose their apparent importance, and party lines may well be permitted to fade into insignificance. The question we have to consider for the immediate welfare of those States of the Union is the question of government or no government; of social order and all the peaceful industries and the happiness that belong to it, or a return to barbarism. It is a question in which every citizen of the nation is deeply interested, and with respect to which we ought not to be, in a partisan sense, either Republicans or Democrats, but fellow-citizens and fellow-men, to whom the interests of a common country and a common humanity are dear.

The sweeping revolution of the entire labor system of a large portion of our country and the advance of 4,000,000 people from a condition of servitude to that of citizenship, upon an equal footing with their former masters, could not occur without presenting problems of the gravest moment, to be dealt with by the emancipated race, by their former masters, and by the General Government, the author of the act of emancipation. That it was a wise, just, and providential act, fraught with good for all concerned, is now generally conceded throughout the country. That a moral obligation rests upon the National Government to employ its constitutional power and influence to establish the rights of the people it has emancipated, and to protect them in the enjoyment of those rights when they are infringed or assailed, is also generally admitted.

The evils which afflict the Southern States can only be removed or remedied by the united and harmonious efforts of both races, actuated by motives of mutual sympathy and regard; and while in duty bound and fully determined to protect the rights of all by every constitutional means at the disposal of my Administration, I am sincerely anxious to use every legitimate influence in favor of honest and efficient local *self*-government as the true resource of those States for the promotion of the contentment and prosperity of their citizens. In the effort I shall make to accomplish this purpose I ask the cordial cooperation of all who cherish an interest in the welfare of their country, trusting that party ties and prejudice of race will be freely surrendered in behalf of the great purpose to be accomplished. In the important work of restoring the South it is not the political situation alone that merits attention. The material development of that section of the country has been arrested by the social and political revolution through which it has passed, and now needs and deserves the considerate care of the National Government within the just limits prescribed by the Constitution and wise public economy.

But at the basis of all prosperity, for that as well as for every other part of the country, lies the improvement of the intellectual and moral condition of the people. Universal suffrage should rest upon universal education. To this end, liberal and permanent provision should be made for the support of free schools by the State governments, and, if need be, supplemented by legitimate aid from national authority.

Let me assure my countrymen of the Southern States that it is my earnest desire to regard and promote their truest interests—the interests of the white and of the colored people both and equally—and to put forth my best efforts in behalf of a civil policy which will forever wipe out in our political affairs the color line and the distinction between North and South, to the end that we may have not merely a united North or a united South, but a united country.

I ask the attention of the public to the paramount necessity of reform in our civil service—a reform not merely as to certain abuses and practices of so-called official patronage which have come to the sanction of usage in the several Departments of our Government, but a change in the system of appointment itself; a reform that shall be thorough, radical, and complete; a return to the principles and practices of the founders of the Government. They neither expected nor desired from public officers any partisan service. They meant that public officers should owe their whole service to the Government and to the people. They meant that the officer should be secure in his tenure as long as his personal character remained untarnished and the performance of his duties satisfactory. They held that appointments to office were not to be made nor expected merely as rewards for partisan service, nor merely on the nomination of members of Congress, as being entitled in any respect to the control of such appointments.

The fact that both the great political parties of the country, in declaring their principles prior to the election, gave a prominent place to the subject of reform of our civil service, recognizing and strongly urging its necessity, in terms almost identical in their specific import with those I have here employed, must be accepted as a conclusive argument in behalf of these measures. It must be regarded as the expression of the united voice and will of the whole country upon this subject, and both parties are virtually pledged to give it their unreserved support.

The President of the United States of necessity owes his election to office to the suffrage and zealous labors of a political party, the members of which cherish with ardor and regard as of essential importance the principles of their party organization; but he should strive to be always mindful of the fact that he serves his party best who serves the country best.

In furtherance of the reform we seek, and in other important respects a change of great importance, I recommend an amendment to the Constitution prescribing a term of six years for the Presidential office and forbidding a reelection.

With respect to the financial condition of the country, I shall not attempt an extended history of the embarrassment and prostration which we have suffered during the past three years. The depression in all our varied commercial and manufacturing interests throughout the country, which began in September 1873, still continues. It is very gratifying, however, to be able to say that there are indications all around us of a coming change to prosperous times.

Upon the currency question, intimately connected, as it is, with this topic, I may be permitted to repeat here the statement made in my letter of acceptance, that in my judgment the feeling of uncertainty inseparable from an irredeemable paper currency, with its fluctuation of values, is one of the greatest obstacles to a return to prosperous times. The only safe paper currency is one which rests upon a coin basis and is at all times and promptly convertible into coin.

I adhere to the views heretofore expressed by me in favor of Congressional legislation in behalf of an early resumption of specie payments, and I am satisfied not only that this is wise, but that the interests, as well as the public sentiment, of the country imperatively demand it.

Passing from these remarks upon the condition of our own country to consider our relations with other lands, we are reminded by the international complications abroad, threatening the peace of Europe, that our traditional rule of noninterference in the affairs of foreign nations has proved of great value in past times and ought to be strictly observed.

The policy inaugurated by my honored predecessor, President Grant, of submitting to arbitration grave questions in dispute between ourselves and foreign powers points to a new, and incomparably the best, instrumentality for the preservation of peace, and will, as I believe, become a beneficent example of the course to be pursued in similar emergencies by other nations.

If, unhappily, questions of difference should at any time during the period of my Administration arise between the United States and any foreign government, it will certainly be my disposition and my hope to aid in their settlement in the same peaceful and honorable way, thus securing to our country the great blessings of peace and mutual good offices with all the nations of the world.

Fellow-citizens, we have reached the close of a political contest marked by the excitement which usually attends the contests between great political parties whose members espouse and advocate with earnest faith their respective creeds. The circumstances were, perhaps, in no respect extraordinary save in the closeness and consequent uncertainty of the result.

For the first time in the history of the country, it has been deemed best, in view of the peculiar circumstances of the case, that the objections and questions in dispute with reference to the counting of the electoral votes should be referred to the decision of a tribunal appointed for this purpose.

That tribunal—established by law for this sole purpose; its members, all of them, men of long-established reputation for integrity and intelligence, and, with the exception of those who are also members of the supreme judiciary, chosen equally from both political parties; its deliberations enlightened by the research and the arguments of able counsel—was entitled to the fullest confidence of the American people. Its decisions have been patiently waited for, and accepted as conclusive by the general judgment of the public. For the present, opinion will vary widely as to the wisdom of the several conclusions announced by that tribunal. This is to be anticipated in every instance where matters of dispute are made the subject of arbitration under the forms of law. Human judgment is never unerring, and is rarely regarded as otherwise than wrong by the unsuccessful party in the contest.

The fact that the two great political parties have in this way settled a dispute in which good men differ as to the facts and the law no less than as to the proper course to be pursued in solving the question in controversy is an occasion for general rejoicing.

Upon one point there is entire unanimity in public sentiment—that conflicting claims to the Presidency must be amicably and peaceably adjusted, and that when so adjusted the general acquiescence of the nation is sure to follow.

It has been reserved for a government of the people, where the right of suffrage is universal, to give to the world the first example in history of a great nation, in the midst of the struggle of opposing parties for power, hushing its party tumults to yield the issue of the contest to adjustment according to the forms of law.

Looking for the guidance of that Divine Hand by which the destinies of nations and individuals are shaped, I call upon you, Senators, Representatives, judges, fellow-citizens, here and everywhere, to unite with me in an earnest effort to secure to our country the blessings not only of material prosperity, but of justice, peace, and union—a union depending not upon the constraint of force, but upon the loving devotion of a free people; "and that all things may be so ordered and settled upon the best and surest foundations that peace and happiness, truth and justice, religion and piety, may be established among us for all generations."

Source: James D. Richardson, ed., *Messages and Papers of the Presidents, 1789–1897,* vol. 8 (Washington, D.C.: Government Printing Office, 1897), 442–447.

NOTES

AUTHOR'S PREFACE

1 This in fact is the title of one of the books written since the 2000 election mentioned above. Roy Morris Jr., *Fraud of the Century: Rutherford B. Hayes, Samuel Tilden, and the Stolen Election of 1876* (New York: Simon and Schuster, 2003).

CHAPTER 1 REPUBLICANS' FALL FROM GRACE

1 Furious at the endorsement of Greeley, dissident Democrats had run New York's Charles O'Conor as a "straight Democratic" candidate. He received fewer than 30,000 votes nationwide.

2 Godkin quoted in Eric Foner, *Reconstruction: America's Unfinished Revolution, 1863–1877* (New York: Harper and Row, 1988), 500.

3 James L. Whitmire to Richard T. Yates, Metamora, Illinois, April 27, 1872, Richard T. Yates Papers, Illinois State Historical Library, Springfield, Illinois.

4 A Democratic newspaper had run an exposé about the Crédit Mobilier in the fall of 1872, before the presidential election, but it was only during the subsequent short session of Congress that the extent of the scandal drew national attention.

5 Grant and the *New York Herald* both quoted in William Gillette, *Retreat from Reconstruction, 1869–1879* (Baton Rouge: Louisiana State University Press, 1979), 182.

6 Quoted ibid., 37.

7 I am excruciatingly aware that many modern readers find the postwar "Money Question" not just convoluted but also mind-numbing. Nonetheless, it was so central to the 1876 presidential campaigns that it is impossible to understand that election without confronting its complexities.

8 In the Senate, 41 percent of Democrats supported and 59 percent opposed the measure, while 57 percent of Republicans favored it and 43 percent were against it. In the House, Democrats split 48 percent in favor and 52 percent against; Republicans divided 62 percent in favor and 38 percent against.

CHAPTER 2 A PIVOTAL CONGRESSIONAL SESSION

1 Throughout Reconstruction, New Orleans, not Baton Rouge, served as Louisiana's state capital.

2 James D. Richardson, ed., *Messages and Papers of the Presidents, 1789–1897* (Washington, D.C.: Government Printing Office, 1897), 6:313.

3 John R. Lynch, *The Facts of Reconstruction* (New York, 1913), 135, as quoted in Brooks D. Simpson, *The Reconstruction Presidents* (Lawrence: University Press of Kansas, 1998), 181.

4 As quoted in Simpson, *The Reconstruction Presidents,* 177.
5 *Appleton's Annual American Cyclopaedia for 1875* (New York: D.S. Appleton, 1876), 153. Except where noted otherwise, I relied on this source, which provides an extensive but excerpted account of Congress's actions, for the evidence in this chapter.
6 Ibid., 146.
7 Ibid.
8 Ibid., 147.
9 Ibid., 150.
10 In the Senate, for example, all but one of the votes in favor of the measure were cast by Republicans; the exception was Missouri's Liberal Republican Carl Schurz, who refused to caucus with Republicans. All but two of the negative votes came from Democrats.
11 *Appleton's Annual American Cyclopaedia for 1875,* 187.
12 I have not examined the 1865 debate over this rule, but I assume its purpose was to allow furious congressional Republicans to throw out the electoral votes for Lincoln cast by Tennessee and Louisiana, whose state governments had been reorganized under Lincoln's "10 percent" plan.
13 *Appleton's Annual American Cyclopaedia for 1875,* 198.
14 For the Colorado story I relied on the *Congressional Globe,* read on the Library of Congress's Web site, rather than *Appleton's Annual American Cyclopaedia for 1875.* The latter utterly ignores the bill in its coverage of Congress, providing evidence that no one at the time recognized how consequential this would be for the 1876 presidential election.
15 It is impossible to ascertain from the record of the congressional debates why no Democrat complained, but the fact is that none did, at least in this Congress.
16 *Congressional Globe,* 43rd Cong., 1st sess., 4692.

CHAPTER 3 PREVIEWS

1 Ulysses S. Grant to General Harry White, May 29, 1875, in *Appleton's Annual American Cyclopaedia for 1875,* 743. In this public letter, Grant himself said that he had been charged with "Caesarism."
2 Ibid.
3 *Appleton's Annual American Cyclopaedia for 1875,* 218, 478.
4 Ibid., 402, 562, 618.
5 Ibid., 763.
6 Ibid., 468.
7 Ibid., 618.
8 Ibid., 562–564.
9 Ibid., 562, 617.
10 Ibid., 472.
11 Ibid., 563.
12 Southern party leaders seemed indifferent to the money question, quite unlike those in the North. In 1875 Mississippi was the only former Confederate

state where Democrats and Republicans adopted state platforms, and neither said anything about resumption. Nor did a Louisiana Democratic state convention held in January 1876.

13 *Appleton's Annual American Cyclopaedia for 1875,* 471–472, 467–468, 478–479.

14 Ibid., 402, 416, 606, 763.

15 Ibid., 607.

16 Ibid., 563.

17 Ibid., 468.

18 Ibid., 467, 544, 562.

19 Ibid., 478.

20 Ibid., 477.

21 Ibid., 477–478.

22 Ibid., 509, 467, 478, 403.

23 Ibid., 100–101.

24 In 1872 a Republican had won the House seat by 751 votes over his Democratic opponent.

25 *Appleton's Annual American Cyclopaedia for 1875,* 610.

26 Ibid., 610, 563, 98.

27 Ibid., 744.

CHAPTER 4 THE EMERGENCE OF A REPUBLICAN CONTENDER

1 P. M. Wagenhals to Rutherford B. Hayes, March 31, 1875; General J. Kilpatrick to Hayes, June 5, 1875; R. M. Stimson to Hayes, June 14, 1875, Rutherford B. Hayes Papers, Rutherford B. Hayes Presidential Center, Fremont, Ohio.

2 General James M. Comly to Hayes, Columbus, April 4, 1875, Hayes Papers. The Republican postmaster in Columbus, Comly edited the most influential Republican newspaper in the state, the *Ohio State Journal.*

3 Diary entry for April 14, 1875, in *Diary and Letters of Rutherford Birchard Hayes, Nineteenth President of the United States,* vol. 3, *1865–1881,* ed. Charles Richard Williams (Columbus: Ohio State Archeological and Historical Society, 1924); hereafter cited as *Hayes Diary and Letters.*

4 See, for example, Hayes to James G. Blaine, June 16, 1875, typescript copy, Hayes Papers.

5 Diary insert for May 18, 1873, *Hayes Diary and Letters,* 243.

6 Hayes to General J. M. Comly, April 7, 10, 1875; Hayes to Clark Waggoner, May 17, 1875, typescript copies, Hayes Papers.

7 *Catholic Telegraph* quoted in the *Summit County Beacon,* September 8, 1875, which is quoted in Jack D. Morton, "Ohio's Gallant Fight: Northern State Politics during the Reconstruction Era, 1865–1878" (Ph.D. diss., University of Virginia, 2004), 180.

8 *Appleton's Annual American Cyclopaedia for 1875,* 606–607.

9 Diary entry for June 3, 1875, *Hayes Diary and Letters,* 274; emphasis in original. Hayes undoubtedly underlined the italicized words in his handwritten

diary, but I have followed the style of the published edition of the diary in italicizing them.

10 Hayes to James G. Blaine, June 16, 1875, typescript copy, Hayes Papers.

11 Hayes to Captain A. T. Wikoff, July 8, 1875, typescript copy, Hayes Papers.

12 Hayes to Major W. D. Bickham, July 10, 1875, typescript copy, Hayes Papers.

13 James A. Garfield to Hayes, June 24, 1875, Hayes Papers.

14 *Hayes Diary and Letters*, 248.

15 William McKinley to Hayes, June 8, 1875, Hayes Papers.

16 Edward D. Mansfield to James Williams, August 4, 1875, copy, Hayes Papers.

17 Hayes to Horace Austin, August 22, 1875, typescript copy, Hayes Papers.

18 *Cincinnati Daily Gazette*, October 9, 12, 1875, quoted in Morton, "Ohio's Gallant Fight," 188–189.

19 *Cincinnati Enquirer*, October 11, 1875, quoted ibid., 194.

20 Diary entry for October 12, 1875, *Hayes Diary and Letters*, 295.

21 Rutherford Hayes to Lucy Hayes, January 30, 1876, ibid., 301.

22 *Appleton's Annual American Cyclopaedia for 1875*, 79–80.

23 Ibid., 80.

24 *Messages and Papers of the Presidents, 1789–1897*, 7:334.

CHAPTER 5 REPUBLICANS' NOMINATION

1 William M. Gwin to Manton Marble, Washington, D.C., January 8, 1876, Samuel J. Tilden Papers, New York Public Library. Gwin had served a term in the House representing Mississippi in the early 1840s, but he moved to California in 1849 and represented that state in the Senate during the decade of the 1850s.

2 I used the copy of the 1876 Republican national platform printed in Arthur M. Schlesinger Jr., ed., *History of U.S. Political Parties*, 4 vols. (New York: Chelsea House and R. W. Bowker, 1973), 2:1371–1373. For the Missouri state platform, see *New York Times*, May 25, 1876.

3 Quoted in Keith Ian Polakoff, *The Politics of Inertia: The Election of 1876 and the End of Reconstruction* (Baton Rouge: Louisiana State University Press, 1973), 16.

4 Edwin Casserly to Manton Marble, San Francisco, May 5, 1876, Manton Marble Papers, Library of Congress.

5 Quoted in Polakoff, *The Politics of Inertia*, 20.

6 "Convention Notes," dispatch to the Associated Press, June 14, 1876, in *New York Times*, June 15, 1876, 1.

7 Quoted in Polakoff, *The Politics of Inertia*, 37.

8 Rutherford B. Hayes to Capt. D. K. Smith, March 9, 1876, typescript copy; Z. F. Miller to A. E. Lee (Hayes's secretary), March 27, 1876, Hayes Papers.

9 John Sherman to R. B. Hayes, Senate Chamber, March 18, 1876, Hayes Papers.

10 Cincinnati correspondence, June 11, 1876, in *New York Times*, June 12, 1876.

11 *New York Times*, May 16, 1876.

12 My account of the famous Mulligan letters episode is based on Polakoff, *The Politics of Inertia*, 50–52.

13 Edward F. Noyes to Rutherford B. Hayes, June 3, 1876, Hayes Papers; *New York Times*, June 3, 1876, 1.

14 Quoted in Polakoff, *The Politics of Inertia*, 51.

15 Quoted ibid., 52.

16 Quoted in *New York Times*, May 17, 1876, 4.

17 *New York Times*, May 16, 1876.

18 Here I rely on Polakoff, *The Politics of Inertia*, 43, only because the print in the May 17, 1876, *New York Times* account is so microscopic that my aging eyes cannot decipher it.

19 A. E. Lee to Hayes, June 12, 1876, Hayes Papers.

20 M. F. Force to Hayes, June 12, 1876, Hayes Papers.

21 A. E. Lee to Hayes, June 14, 1876, Hayes Papers.

22 Rutherford Hayes to General R. P. Buckland, June 14, 1876, typescript copy, Hayes Papers.

23 *New York Times*, May 24, 1876.

24 Smith to Hayes, May 27, 1876, Hayes Papers.

25 "Latest Aspect of the Contest," *New York Times*, June 14, 1876, 1.

26 "Convention Notes," dispatch to Associate Press, *New York Times*, June 14, 1876, 5.

27 "The Permanent Organization," *New York Times*, June 15, 1876, 1.

28 Ibid. The Republican Reform Club of New York City was distinct from the Fifth Avenue Hotel conclave, which had also called for an honest candidate and civil service reform.

29 "Second Day of the Convention," *New York Times*, June 16, 1876, 1. The editors of the *Times* strongly opposed Blaine's nomination, and the reporters it dispatched to Cincinnati undoubtedly shared this anti-Blaine bias. Nonetheless, there is no reason to doubt the accuracy of this report.

30 "The Platform," *New York Times*, June 15, 1876, 1.

31 "The Platform," *New York Times*, June 16, 1876, 2.

32 Ibid.

33 For the debate on the platform, see *New York Times*, June 16, 1876, 2; Schlesinger, *History of U.S. Political Parties*, 2:1373–1375.

34 All the nominating speeches can be found in *New York Times*, June 16, 1876; see also Schlesinger, *History of U.S. Political Parties*, 2:1375–1385.

35 Given McPherson's support for Blaine, he must have believed this information, whether it was true or not.

36 *New York Times*, June 16, 1876, 5.

37 William Dennison to Rutherford B. Hayes, June 15, 1876, telegram, Hayes Papers.

38 M. F. Force to Hayes, June 16, 1876, typescript copy, Hayes Papers.

39 My account of the convention's final day is taken from Schlesinger, *History of U.S. Political Parties*, 2:1385–1405. See also the numerous reports in the June 17, 1876, issue of the *New York Times*.

40 It is impossible to tell from the published reports of the convention's proceedings why the four Pennsylvania delegates who had protested the unit rule joined the rest of the Pennsylvania delegation in allowing a chance for McPherson's ruling to be overturned.

41 John W. Herron to Hayes, June 16, 1876, Hayes Papers.

42 William Henry Smith to Hayes, Chicago, June 21, 1876, Hayes Papers.

43 Benjamin H. Bristow to John M. Harlan, Washington, June 16, 1876, telegram; John W. Bell to Hayes, June 17, 1876, Hayes Papers. Bell's letter reflected another contribution of the 1876 presidential election to American political history: that was the first year that Republicans were nicknamed the Grand Old Party, or GOP.

44 Michael C. Kerr to Manton Marble, June 17, 1876, Marble Papers.

CHAPTER 6 DEMOCRATS ARE FORCED TO STRADDLE

1 T. J. Hudson to J. H. Harmon, May 16, 1876, Tilden Papers.

2 Newspaper clipping of letter dated May 6, 1876, with W. L. Washington to Samuel J. Tilden, May 10, 1876, Tilden Papers.

3 *Appleton's Annual American Cyclopaedia for 1876* (New York: D. S. Appleton, 1877), 648.

4 *Baltimore Gazette* quoted in *New York Times*, May 19, 1876, 4.

5 Rutherford B. Hayes to H. S. Noyes, May 20, 1876, and Alphonzo Taft, May 22, 1876, typescript copies, Hayes Papers.

6 James A. Beck to Montgomery Blair, Lexington, Kentucky, May 19, 1876, Tilden Papers.

7 *Appleton's Annual American Cyclopaedia for 1876*, 409.

8 August Belmont to Manton Marble, February 14, 1876, Marble Papers.

9 Michael C. Kerr to Marble, March 31, 1876, Marble Papers.

10 Ibid.

11 George L. Miller to Marble, March 20, 1876, Marble Papers.

12 S. L. M. Barlow to Manton Marble, n.d., Marble Papers.

13 Thomas Bayard to Manton Marble, January 16, 1876, Marble Papers.

14 Francis Kernan to Colonel William Pelton, May 16, 1876, Tilden Papers.

15 Although Republicans still controlled the state governmental machinery in Louisiana and Florida, as well as South Carolina, by 1876, most Democrats—certainly most northern Democrats—were confident of carrying them in November.

16 J. D. B. to Manton Marble, New Orleans, May 29, 1876, Marble Papers.

17 For the Democratic platform, see *New York Times*, June 29, 1876, 1; *Appleton's Annual American Cyclopaedia for 1876*, 785–786. The *Times* has a fuller account of the debate over the platform at the Democratic convention; *Appleton's* has a more complete rendition of the platform itself.

18 The key document here is Manton Marble to Samuel J. Tilden, July 1876, Bedford, New York, Marble Papers.

19 I used the account of these speeches in the *New York Times*, June 29, 1876. The account in the Democratic *New York World* differed slightly. See Polakoff, *The Politics of Inertia*, 89–90.

20 Marble to Tilden, June 28, 1876, telegram, Marble Papers.

21 See "Hendricks in a State of Doubt," *New York Times*, June 30, 1876, 1.

22 Robert B. Minturn to Samuel J. Tilden, Staten Island, July 3, 1876, Tilden Papers.

23 Duncan's angry letter is quoted in the *New York Times*, July 7, 1876, 2.

CHAPTER 7 THE CAMPAIGN

1 Recent research suggests that thousands, perhaps tens of thousands, of blue-collar workers in large cities, though often loyal to their preferred party, had little if any knowledge of the issues involved in elections. See Richard Franklin Bensel, *The American Ballot Box in the Mid-Nineteenth Century* (New York: Cambridge University Press, 2004).

2 John M. Harlan to W. D. Bickham, June 19, 1876; John Andrews to Rutherford B. Hayes, June 30, 1876; W. M. Dickson to Hayes, June 30, 1876, Hayes Papers.

3 L. F. S. Foster to Hayes, July 1, 1876, Hayes Papers.

4 Carl Schurz to Hayes, July 5, 1876, Hayes Papers.

5 Charles Nordhoff to Hayes, June 22, 1876, Hayes Papers.

6 William H. Smith to Hayes, July 1, 1876, Hayes Papers.

7 George William Curtis to Hayes, June 30, 1876, Hayes Papers.

8 Charles Nordhoff to Hayes, June 22, 1876, Hayes Papers.

9 Edward L. Pierce to Hayes, June 23, 1876, Hayes Papers.

10 Walter Allen to Hayes, June 30, 1876, Hayes Papers.

11 J. W. Clark to Hayes, June 26, 1876, Hayes Papers.

12 George W. Curtis to Hayes, June 30, 1876, Hayes Papers.

13 Hayes to Major W. D. Bickham, June 25, 1876, typescript copy, Hayes Papers.

14 W. M. Dickson to Hayes, June 30, 1876, Hayes Papers.

15 John Andrews to Hayes, Columbus, Ohio, June 30, 1876, Hayes Papers.

16 J. B. Ridenour to Hayes, June 23, 1876; Charles M. Walker to Hayes, June 22, 1876, Hayes Papers.

17 For Hayes's letter, I relied on *Appleton's Annual American Cyclopaedia for 1876*, 783–785.

18 Hayes to James A. Garfield, August 5, 1876, typescript copy, Hayes Papers.

19 Hayes to James A. Garfield, August 12, 1876, typescript copy, Hayes Papers.

20 *New York Times*, July 20, 1876, 1.

21 The Liberal Republican National Committee had called for this presidential nominating convention at a meeting in New York City on May 9. This committee was separate from the Fifth Avenue Hotel conclave that met on May 15 and made no attempt to nominate a candidate of its own.

22 Hayes to Schurz, July 24, 1876; Hayes to Smith, August 10, 1876; Hayes to R. C. McCormick, September 8, 1876, typescript copies, Hayes Papers.

23 *New York Times,* July 6, 1876, 5.

24 *New York Times,* July 19, 1876, 4.

25 Hayes to James A. Garfield, August 5, 1876, Hayes Papers.

26 *New York Times,* August 12, 1876, 1.

27 Leroy Pope Walker to Manton Marble, July 27, 1876, Marble Papers.

28 W. G. Sumner to Manton Marble, July 10, 1876, Marble Papers.

29 *New York Times,* July 1, 1876, 4.

30 R. Henning to Samuel J. Tilden, July 18, 1876, Tilden Papers.

31 William R. Morrison to Abram Hewitt, July 1876, Tilden Papers.

32 August Belmont to Manton Marble, July 29, 1876, Marble Papers.

33 Samuel J. Tilden to Abram Hewitt, July 15, 1876, Tilden Papers.

34 Ibid.

35 Hugh McDermott to Tilden, July 18, 1876, Tilden Papers.

36 Ticknor Curtis to Tilden, July 10, 1876, Tilden Papers.

37 Tilden's acceptance letter can be found in *Appleton's Annual American Cyclopaedia for 1876,* 787–790.

38 Hendricks's letter can be found in *New York Times,* August 5, 1876, 1.

39 Hayes to James G. Blaine, September 14, 1876, typescript copy, Hayes Papers.

40 Hayes to John A. Bingham, September 5, 1876, typescript copy, Hayes Papers.

41 Diary entry for November 1, 1876 in *Hayes Diary and Letters,* 371–372.

42 Horatio Seymour to Tilden, October 25, 1876, Tilden Papers.

43 *Appleton's Annual American Cyclopaedia for 1876,* 133, 172.

44 Hayes to Garfield, August 5, 1876, typescript copy, Hayes Papers.

45 Hayes to John Sherman, August 7, 1876, typescript copy, Hayes Papers.

46 *Appleton's Annual American Cyclopaedia for 1876,* 174–176.

47 Ibid., 176.

48 Hayes to Garfield, August 12, 1876, typescript copy, Hayes Papers.

49 Hayes to John A. Bingham, September 5, 1876, typescript copy, Hayes Papers.

50 Abram Hewitt to Samuel J. Tilden, August 6, 1876, Tilden Papers.

51 Diary entry for September 14, 1876, in *Hayes Diary and Letters,* 357.

52 Hayes to R. C. McCormick, October 14, 1876, ibid., 366–367.

53 Hayes to William H. Smith, October 20, 1876, ibid., 369.

54 In his October 25 letter warning Tilden that Irish Catholic laborers disliked Democrats' stress on reform rather than relief, Horatio Seymour also noted that Republicans had dropped their anti-Catholic rhetoric by then.

55 *New York Times,* August 14, 1876, 2.

56 *New York Times,* August 4, 1876, 4.

57 *New York Times,* October 12, 1876, 4.

58 William Bigler to Samuel J. Tilden, October 25, 1876; Theodore P. Cook to Tilden, October 25, 1876; C. J. Godwin to Tilden, October 26, 1876, Tilden Papers.

59 Samuel Bowles to David A. Welles, October 25, 1876, Marble Papers.

60 *Messages and Papers of the Presidents*, 8:376.

61 *New York Times*, October 10, 1876, 1.

62 Samuel Dickson to Manton Marble, October 26, 1876, Marble Papers.

CHAPTER 8 THE ELECTIONS OF 1876

1   *New York Times*, August 15, 1876, 1.

2   August Belmont to Samuel J. Tilden, October 3, 1876, Tilden Papers.

3   *Appleton's Annual American Cyclopaedia for 1876*, 410–411.

4   Hayes to John Sherman, July 24, 1876, typescript copy, Hayes Papers.

5   Hayes to James P. Root, August 22, 1876, typescript copy, Hayes Papers.

6   Ingersoll quoted in Polakoff, *The Politics of Inertia*, 145–146.

7   Hayes to William H. Smith, September 9, 1876, typescript copy, Hayes Papers.

8   Diary entry for October 15, 1876, in *Hayes Diary and Letters*, 368–369.

9   Hayes to R. C. McCormick, October 14, 1876, typescript copy, Hayes Papers.

10 George W. Morgan to Samuel J. Tilden, October 21, 1876, Tilden Papers.

11 *New Orleans Picayune*, August 16, 1876, quoted in *New York Times*, August 20, 1876, 7.

12 "Wade Hampton's Canvass," *New York Times*, October 13, 1876, 1.

13 George W. Morgan to Samuel J. Tilden, November 8, 1876, Tilden Papers.

14 If one counts the eight anti-Republican Independents elected in 1874–1875, the Republican minority in the House shrank from seventy-eight to nine seats.

15 Quoted in Polakoff, *The Politics of Inertia*, 202. My account of these proceedings relies entirely on Polakoff's study.

16 *New York Times*, November 8, 1876, 4.

17 Both quotations from Polakoff, *The Politics of Inertia*, 204.

CHAPTER 9 THE DISPUTED RESULTS

1   Report in *New York Sun*, November 9, 1876, quoted in Polakoff, *The Politics of Inertia*, 205.

2   Diary entry for November 12, 1876, in *Hayes: The Diary of a President, 1875–1881*, ed. T. Harry Williams (New York: David McKay, 1964), 50–51.

3   Manton Marble to George W. Smith, November 10, 1876, Marble Papers.

4   August Belmont to Samuel J. Tilden, November 9, 1876, Tilden Papers.

5   Henry Watterson to Tilden, November 9, 1876, Tilden Papers.

6   Ulysses Grant to William T. Sherman, November 10, 1876, telegram, in *The Papers of Ulysses S. Grant*, vol. 28, ed. John Y. Simon et al. (Carbondale: Southern Illinois University Press, 2005), 19–20.

7   *New York Times*, November 11, 1876, 1.

8   U. S. Grant to Philip H. Sheridan, November 11, 1876, telegram, in *Papers of Grant*, 36–37.

9   J. Dickson Burns to Manton Marble, November 11, 1876, Marble Papers.

10 Henry Watterson to Samuel J. Tilden, November 13, 1876, Tilden Papers.

11 Hayes to Carl Schurz, November 13, 1876; Hayes to John Sherman, November 27, 1876, typescript copies, Hayes Papers.

12 The electoral college, of course, was not a common assemblage of electors from all the states in a single place. Rather, the presidential electors who had received a majority of the popular vote from each state met in their respective state capitals to cast their votes, which were then sent under seal to Washington.

13 Rutherford Hayes to Carl Schurz, November 13, 1876, typescript copy, Hayes Papers.

14 For an egregious example written after the 2000 election, see Morris, *Fraud of the Century.*

15 Wallace quoted in Polakoff, *The Politics of Inertia,* 216.

16 *New York Times,* November 10, 1876, 8.

17 *New York Times,* November 14, 1876, 5. The language quoted here is from the dispatch sent to the *Times* from Greensboro on November 13.

18 J. Dickson Burns to Manton Marble, November 11, 1876, Marble Papers.

19 C. Gibson to Samuel J. Tilden, November 28, 1876, Tilden Papers. A Missourian, Gibson was one of the Democratic observers sent to Florida.

20 Hayes to John Sherman, November 27, 1876, typescript copy, Hayes Papers.

21 Diary entry for December 5, 1876, in *Hayes: The Diary of a President,* 54–55; Hayes to Carl Schurz, December 6, 1876, typescript copy, Hayes Papers.

22 The official titles of these panels differed among the three states. In South Carolina and Florida it was the Board of State Canvassers. In Louisiana it was the State Returning Board. I use the two terms interchangeably.

23 James Anderson to John Sherman, November 20, 1876; John Sherman to D. A. Weber and James Anderson, November 20, 1876, copies with no indication of who made them, Tilden Papers.

24 J. Madison Wells to ?, November 21, 1876, unauthenticated copy, Tilden Papers. Wells began this message with the words "My Dear Senator." Since Sherman was the only sitting Republican senator among the Republicans in New Orleans, I assume that he was the recipient if Wells actually wrote such a note.

25 *New York Times,* November 15, 1876; the report from Louisiana is on p. 1, the editorial on p. 4.

26 *New York Times,* November 17, 1876, 1.

27 H. H. Effenger to Samuel S. Cox, November 14, 1876, telegram, Tilden Papers.

28 Quoted in Polakoff, *The Politics of Inertia,* 226–227.

29 Lafayette Grover to Manton Marble, November 28, 1876, telegram, Marble Papers.

CHAPTER 10 THE DISPUTE RESOLVED

1 H. B. Stanton to Samuel J. Tilden, November 22, 1876; C. Gibson to Tilden, November 28, 1876, Tilden Papers.

2 Speech of Minnesota Congressman Mark H. Dunnell on February 12, 1877, quoted in Charles Fairman, *Five Justices and the Electoral Commission of 1877*, supplement to vol. 7 of the *Oliver Wendell Holmes Devise History of the Supreme Court of the United States* (New York: Collier Macmillan, 1988), 115.

3 August Belmont to Manton Marble, December 21, 1876, Marble Papers.

4 *New York Times*, November 14, 1876, 4.

5 Whether the gathering of senators and representatives in the same chamber was in fact a joint session, analogous to those held by many state legislatures to elect U.S. senators, was itself a point of considerable partisan contention that winter. Republicans staunchly insisted that it was not.

6 The Constitution stipulated that presidents were to be inaugurated on the fourth day of March following the November presidential election. In 1877 March 4 fell on a Sunday. Hayes would be privately sworn in on that day, but the public ceremony took place on Monday, March 5.

7 John B. Deis to Samuel J. Tilden, December 1, 1876, Tilden Papers.

8 *Appleton's Annual American Cyclopaedia for 1876*, 393–394.

9 Ibid., 411.

10 *The Diary of James A. Garfield*, vol. 3, *1875–1877*, ed. Harry James Brown and Frederick D. Williams (East Lansing: Michigan State University Press, 1973), 413 n14.

11 Thomas Springs to Samuel J. Tilden, November 19, 1876, Tilden Papers.

12 Fairman, *The Electoral Commission of 1877*, 47.

13 *Appleton's Annual American Cyclopaedia for 1877* (New York: D. S. Appleton, 1878), 137.

14 James C. Welling to Manton Marble, December 18, 1876, Marble Papers.

15 August Belmont to Manton Marble, December 21, 1876, Marble Papers.

16 See, for example, the two uncaptioned editorials in *New York Times*, January 13, 1877, 4. At this time, the staunchly Republican editors of the *Times* still insisted that only the president of the Senate could count the votes.

17 Samuel J. Randall to Manton Marble, January 15, 1876, Marble Papers.

18 Quoted in Allan Nevins, *Abram S. Hewitt with Some Account of Peter Cooper* (New York: Harper and Brothers, 1935), 353.

19 On this point, see J. C. Welling to Manton Marble, March 10, 1877, Marble Papers. According to Welling, "On the morning that the Bill was reported to Congress, Mr. Hewitt told me in reply to an inquiry of mine, that he did not know what Mr. Tilden thought of the bill, because Mr. Tilden's views on the matter had not been consulted."

20 The language of the bill, which eventually passed without amendment, is quoted in full in *Appleton's Annual American Cyclopaedia for 1877*, 137–138.

21 Ibid., 139.

22 Ibid., 143.

23 Ibid., 143–144; emphasis added.

24 Ibid., 144–147.

25 Diary entry for January 21, 1877, in *Hayes: The Diary of a President*, 69.

26 William Bigler to Samuel J. Tilden, January 24, 1877, Tilden Papers.

27 *Diary of Garfield*, 3:414.

28 For the partisan breakdown of these votes, I relied on Polakoff, *The Politics of Inertia*, 279, and Michael Les Benedict, "Southern Democrats in the Crisis of 1876–77: A Reconsideration of *Reunion and Reaction*," *Journal of Southern History* 64 (November 1980): 510–511. Polakoff lists 158 Democratic votes in favor in the House. Southerners cast 13 of the negative Democratic votes there.

29 Nevins, *Hewitt*, 367.

30 Quoted in Fairman, *The Electoral Commission of 1877*, 124.

31 Joseph T. Crowell to Samuel J. Tilden, February 8, 1877, Tilden Papers.

32 When a number of Buchanan's cabinet members, including Secretary of State Lewis Cass, resigned during the secession crisis, Buchanan moved Black to the State Department and named Edwin M. Stanton, another Pennsylvanian, as attorney general.

33 Diary entry for February 2, 1877, in *Diary of Garfield*, 3:430.

34 Fairman, *The Electoral Commission of 1877*, 74.

35 For this excerpt from Hewitt's "Secret History," see Nevins, *Hewitt*, 371–372.

36 The letter, dated September 2, 1878, and published in the *Newark Advertiser* on September 5, is reprinted in full in Fairman, *The Electoral Commission of 1877*, 135–136. I made no attempt to delve into the facts of this incident and instead relied on previous accounts. But among those involved in this truly contentious historiographical debate, I far prefer Fairman's account, which vigorously defends Bradley's judicial integrity and utterly demolishes Nevins's skewed pro-Democratic account.

37 Diary entry for February 7, 1877, in *Diary of Garfield*, 3:435.

38 Bradley's opinion and its similarity to previous Democratic arguments are carefully examined in Fairman, *The Electoral Commission of 1877*, 95–106.

39 Diary entry for February 7, 1877, in *Diary of Garfield*, 3:435.

40 Diary entry for February 12, 1877, ibid., 439.

41 Diary entry for February 16, 1877, ibid., 442.

42 Diary entry for February 13, 1877, ibid., 440–441.

43 Diary entry for February 21, 1877, ibid., 445.

44 Fairman, *The Electoral Commission of 1877*, 118; diary entry for February 27, 1877, in *Diary of Garfield*, 3:450.

45 Diary entry for February 28, 1877, in *Diary of Garfield*, 3:451.

46 Diary entry for March 1, 1877, ibid., 452.

47 D. J. Goodwin to Samuel J. Tilden, December 12, 1876, Tilden Papers.

48 Leroy Pope Walker to Manton Marble, December 19, 1876, Marble Papers.

49 A. M. Gibson to Samuel J. Tilden, December 13, 1876, Tilden Papers. Gibson's letter to Dana is also in the Tilden Papers. Here we see the kernel of

C. Vann Woodward's famous thesis about a "Compromise of 1877" in his *Reunion and Reaction: The Compromise of 1877 and the End of Reconstruction* (Boston: Little, Brown, 1951).

50 R. B. Radford to Samuel J. Tilden, December 18, 1876, Tilden Papers.

51 Diary entries for December 7 and 10, 1876, in *Diary of Garfield*, 3:392–393.

52 Hayes to William H. Smith, December 24, 1876, and January 3, 1877, typescript copies, Hayes Papers.

53 See Garfield's expression of doubt at Boynton's assurance that he would be the next Speaker in his diary entry for March 29, 1877, in *Diary of Garfield*, 3:466. In the congressional elections held in 1876, Republicans, by rewinning a majority of northern House seats, had reduced Democrats' majority in the House to fewer than sixteen seats. (All lists of partisan balance in the House in the nineteenth century must be tentative. Because elections were held a full year before congressmen took office, the cold fact is that a few men who won election died or resigned before they ever took their seats.) Thus it appeared in December that it would take only nine southern Democratic defectors to make Garfield Speaker. The Democrats' margin at the start of the next Congress was in fact only nine seats, meaning that only five southern Democratic votes could make Garfield Speaker. He was assumed to be Republicans' candidate for that slot in December 1876 because they had run him that month against the Democrats' Samuel Randall. The death of Michael Kerr, the Democratic Speaker elected in the first term, after that session adjourned, is what necessitated a new election for Speaker in December 1876.

54 Rutherford B. Hayes to William H. Smith, December 24, 1876, typescript copy, Hayes Papers.

55 Hayes to Smith, January 3, 1877, typescript copy, Hayes Papers.

56 See Woodward, *Reunion and Reaction*, and his "Yes, There Was a Compromise of 1877," *Journal of American History* 60 (June 1973): 215–223. Woodward's influential thesis that northern Republicans cynically abandoned the voting rights of southern African Americans, and thus the experiment of Reconstruction, to obtain the help of former Whigs among southern Democratic congressmen in having Hayes counted in has been challenged and, in my opinion, utterly demolished by the following works: Polakoff, *The Politics of Inertia*; Benedict, "Southern Democrats in the Crisis of 1876–77," 489–524; and Allan Peskin, "Was There a Compromise of 1877?" *Journal of American History* (June 1973): 65–75. Peskin subsequently published a biography of Garfield. Three questions are at issue in this debate. Did Hayes's ultimate election kill Reconstruction, as Woodward maintains, or was it already long dead? Surely, it was already dead in eight of eleven former Confederate states. Did these negotiations between northern Republicans and southern Democrats occur in February 1877, when House Democrats tried to delay the electoral vote count, or in December, when the question was whether the Democratic House would agree to a joint session to *start* the count of electoral votes? The evidence points to the earlier date. Did

southern Democratic House members, as Woodward alleges, actually oppose Democratic filibusters in the House to allow Hayes's election as their part of the bargain? No; the evidence gathered by subsequent historians shows that southern Democrats in fact led the filibuster, and it was northern Democrats who sought to stop it.

57 Diary entry for February 26, 1877, in *Diary of Garfield*, 3:448–450.

58 Ibid., 466 n103.

59 *Messages and Papers of the Presidents*, 7:446.

60 James M. Johnson to Samuel J. Tilden, February 20, 1877; Thomas Cottman to Tilden, February 22, 1877; John A. McClernand to Tilden, March 2, 1877; Albert Schofield to Tilden, March 4, 1877, Tilden Papers.

61 Albert Maher to Samuel J. Tilden, February 21, 1877; Henry L. Fish to Tilden, February 24, 1877; J. M. Scovel to Tilden, February 26, 1877, Tilden Papers.

62 S. B. Franks to Samuel J. Tilden, March 2, 1877; H. H. Jacobs to Tilden, February 22, 1877, Tilden Papers.

63 John Randolph to Samuel J. Tilden, March 1, 1877, Tilden Papers.

CONCLUSION

1 Conversations with several faculty members from the University of Virginia School of Law, as well as a federal circuit court judge for whom my daughter once clerked, suggest that most lawyers today have never heard of quo warranto.

BIBLIOGRAPHIC ESSAY

Because the literature on the topics covered in this book is vast, I have confined this bibliography to the primary and secondary sources I used to write it. The massive collection of Rutherford B. Hayes Papers is housed at the Hayes Library of the Rutherford B. Hayes Presidential Center in Fremont, Ohio. It contains both outgoing correspondence from Hayes, usefully separated in typescript copies, and incoming correspondence, which understandably ballooned considerably once Hayes won the Republican nomination in 1876. For those unable to travel to northwestern Ohio, these latter letters are available through interlibrary loan on microfilm. The main collection of the Samuel Jones Tilden Papers is housed in the Manuscript Division of the New York Public Library, an institution that the wealthy Tilden helped found. As far as correspondence is concerned, this collection consists almost exclusively of incoming letters. The papers of Manton Marble, a close associate of Tilden and onetime owner and editor of the *New York World,* the nation's most influential Democratic newspaper, are located in the Manuscript Division of the Library of Congress. The fourteen-month span of letters I examined was primarily incoming correspondence, but there are also important copies of letters and telegrams that Marble sent to others.

Students of the 1876 presidential election can also consult printed versions of diaries compiled at the time by the key actors. There are two published editions of the diary that Rutherford B. Hayes kept during the years covered in this book, and the original manuscript version is housed at the Hayes Presidential Center. These are Charles R. Williams, ed., *Diary and Letters of Rutherford Birchard Hayes: Nineteenth President of the United States,* vol. 3, *1865–1881* (Columbus: Ohio State Archaeological and Historical Society, 1924), and T. Harry Williams, ed., *Hayes: The Diary of a President, 1875–1881* (New York: David McKay, 1964). Harry J. Brown and Frederick D. Williams, eds., *The Diary of James A. Garfield,* vol. 3, *1875–1877* (East Lansing: Michigan State University Press, 1973), is valuable on Garfield's role in the 1876 campaign, as a "visiting statesman" in Louisiana, and especially as a member of the Federal Electoral Commission. John Y. Simon et al., eds., *The Papers of Ulysses S. Grant,* vols. 27–28 (Carbondale: Southern Illinois University Press, 2005), provides much information on Grant's role in the disputed election. Especially valuable are the lengthy editorial notes that reprint many of the letters sent to Grant from southern Republicans about the obstacles they faced in attempting to vote.

Newspapers, of course, also followed these political events. I relied exclusively on the daily editions of the then-Republican *New York Times.* The paper's partisan bias, as well as its obvious tilt in favor of reform elements within the Republican Party against regulars such as Roscoe Conkling, Oliver P. Morton, and James G. Blaine, clearly shades its editorials and the reports of some of its correspondents.

Nonetheless, no newspaper in 1876 and 1877 had so many regular correspondents stationed in so many places, and by 1876 the *Times* (rather than the *New York Tribune*, then owned by Jay Gould) clearly had the greatest impact on the rest of the Republican press across the country. The scores of articles quoted by the *Times* from around the nation echoing its own stories and its own attacks on Tilden during the 1876 campaign clearly attest to that fact.

I also relied heavily on *Appleton's Annual American Cyclopaedia* (New York: D. S. Appleton, 1876, 1877, 1878). These inexplicably underutilized volumes are a treasure trove of information. The entries for individual states usually contain reports on parties' state conventions and platforms as well as election results. There are also long sections on events and debates in Congress and national political developments. Aside from private letters and some newspaper accounts, my treatment of how returning boards treated disputed votes in Florida, Louisiana, Oregon, and South Carolina is taken almost exclusively from this extraordinary source.

The tables in appendix A illustrating the results of the congressional elections held between 1872 and 1876 are derived from Michael J. Dubin's authoritative *United States Congressional Elections, 1788–1997: The Official Results* (Jefferson, N.C.: McFarland, 1998). Finally, the lengthy appendices to the essays by David Herbert Donald, "The Republican Party, 1864–1876," and Leon Friedman, "The Democratic Party, 1860–1884" in *History of U.S. Political Parties*, vol. 2, *1860–1910 The Gilded Age of Politics*, ed. Arthur M. Schlesinger Jr. (New York: Chelsea House and R.W. Bowker, 1973) contain valuable primary material. Donald's appendix includes lengthy reports on the Republican national conventions in 1872 and 1876 as well as state-by-state returns for the elections in those years. Friedman's provides a lengthy excerpt from Abram Hewitt's "Secret History of the Disputed Election of 1876–1877."

The cartoons of Thomas Nast were another key primary source. Most of these originally appeared in *Harper's Weekly*, but many of the best ones are usefully reproduced in Morton Keller, *The Art and Politics of Thomas Nast* (New York: Oxford University Press, 1968).

A number of previous books have been written about the presidential election of 1876. The oldest, based largely on newspaper accounts, is Paul Leland Haworth, *The Hayes-Tilden Disputed Presidential Election of 1876* (Cleveland: Burrows Brothers, 1906). The most famous is C. Vann Woodward, *Reunion and Reaction: The Compromise of 1877 and the End of Reconstruction* (Boston, Little, Brown, 1951). Woodward says very little about the 1876 campaign itself. Instead, he focuses on the resolution of the disputed electoral votes to advance his thesis about a Compromise of 1877 in which Republicans sold out Reconstruction in the South to get Hayes counted in. This thesis has subsequently been challenged by Allan Peskin, "Was There a Compromise of 1877?" *Journal of American History* 60 (June 1973): 215–223, and Michael Les Benedict, "Southern Democrats in the Crisis of 1876–1877: A Reconsideration of *Reunion and Reaction*," *Journal of Southern History* 64 (November 1980): 489–524. It is also challenged in Keith Ian Polakoff, *The Politics of Inertia: The Election of 1876 and the End of Reconstruction* (Baton Rouge: Louisiana State University Press, 1973), which is by far the best existing study of the 1876 election. Even though Polakoff's focus differs from my own—he is interested in how the decentralized nature of political parties affected the outcome—I drew on his extensive research in virtually every chapter of this book. The disputed Bush-Gore election of 2000 spawned two recent books on the 1876 election. The very title of Roy Morris Jr., *Fraud of the Century: Rutherford B. Hayes, Samuel Tilden, and the Stolen Election of 1876* (New York: Simon and Schuster, 2003), indicates his slant on the election. That his index contains not a single entry for Liberal Republicans also indicates how much our approaches to this election differed. Nonetheless, he unearthed evidence, apparently missed by Polakoff, about Louisiana Republicans' erasure of potential Democratic voters from the New Orleans registration rolls before the 1876 election, which I incorporated in my account. Finally, former Chief Justice William H. Rehnquist's *Centennial Crisis: The Disputed Election of 1876* (New York: Alfred A. Knopf, 2005) is a thinly disguised attempt to defend the intervention of the Supreme Court in the 2000 election by citing the bipartisan agreement in 1877 that gave Supreme Court justices a major role in settling the dispute over electoral votes that year.

Biographies exist for every Republican and Democratic contender for their parties' presidential nomination in 1876, but I consulted only those for the two eventual nominees. For Hayes, see Harry Barnard, *Rutherford B. Hayes and His America* (Indianapolis: Bobbs-Merrill, 1954); Ari Hoogenboom, *Rutherford B. Hayes: Warrior and President* (Lawrence: University Press of Kansas, 1995); and Hans L. Trefousse, *Rutherford B. Hayes* (New York: Times Books, Henry Holt, 2002). For Tilden, see John Bigelow, *The Life of Samuel J. Tilden*, 2 vols. (New York: Harper and Brothers, 1895), and Alexander C. Flick, *Samuel Jones Tilden: A Study in Political Sagacity* (New York: Dodd, Mead, 1939). Two other books are far more astute about certain aspects of Tilden's career than either of these adoring biographies. For Tilden's relationship with Boss William M. Tweed and his role in bringing the Tweed Ring down, Kenneth D. Ackerman's *Boss Tweed: The Rise and Fall of the Corrupt Pol Who Conceived the Soul of Modern New York* (New York: Carroll and Graf, 2005) is superb. David Quigley, *Second Founding: New York City, Reconstruction, and the Making of American Democracy* (New York: Hill and Wang, 2004), offers persuasive evidence that Tilden's political views were fundamentally antidemocratic. Finally, Allan Nevins, *Abram S. Hewitt* (New York: Harper and Brothers, 1935), contains useful information about the 1876 campaign and its aftermath, even if it verges on hagiography.

I believe that the competition for Liberal Republican support constituted the strategic fulcrum of the 1876 campaign, but the literature on the Liberal Republican movement and party is surprisingly thin. Although several useful articles have been published, the standard history of the party, Earl D. Ross, *The Liberal Republican Movement* (New York: AMS Press, 1919), is dated. The latest attempt at a book-length analysis, Andrew L. Slap, *The Doom of Reconstruction: The Liberal Republicans in the Civil War Era* (New York: Fordham University Press, 2006), is not wholly persuasive. Happily, excellent discussions of Liberalism as a mind-set opposed to activist government can be found in Eric Foner, *Reconstruction: America's Unfinished Revolution, 1863–1877* (New York: Harper and Row, 1988), and David Montgomery, *Beyond Equality: Labor and the Radical Republicans* (New York: Alfred A. Knopf, 1967). For the bolt of Massachusetts Republicans to the Liberal Republican Party, however, one must consult Dale Baum, *The Civil War Party System: The Case of Massachusetts, 1848–1876* (Chapel Hill: University of North Carolina Press, 1984).

Similarly, there is no useful single-volume analysis of the Greenback Party, but for a penetrating discussion of that party and its base in the electorate, see Paul Kleppner, *The Third Electoral System, 1853–1892: Parties, Voters, and Political Cultures* (Chapel Hill: University of North Carolina Press, 1979).

Each of the issues discussed in the 1876 campaign has generated a literature of its own. On the movement for civil service reform, see Ari Hoogenboom, *Outlawing the Spoils: A History of the Civil Service Reform Movement, 1865–1883* (Urbana: University of Illinois Press, 1961), and John G. Sproat, *"The Best Men": Liberal Reformers in the Gilded Age* (New York: Oxford University Press, 1968). Mark Wahlgren Summers, *The Era of Good Stealings* (New York: Oxford University Press, 1993), is by far the best study of corruption as a political issue in the 1870s ever written.

The standard study of the complex topic of specie resumption is Irwin Unger, *The Greenback Era* (Princeton, N.J.: Princeton University Press, 1964). But see also Robert Sharkey, *Money, Class, and Party: An Economic Study of the Civil War and Reconstruction* (Baltimore: Johns Hopkins University Press, 1959), and Walter T. K. Nugent, *The Money Question during Reconstruction* (New York: W. W. Norton, 1967). For the federal government's use of its surplus revenue after the war to buy back bonds rather than accumulate gold for specie resumption, see Jeffrey Williamson, "Watersheds and Turning Points: Conjectures on the Long-Term Impact of Civil War Financing," *Journal of Economic History* 34 (September 1974): 636–661.

The potency of anti-Catholicism as a political issue in 1875 and 1876 is demonstrated in Kleppner, *The Third Electoral System*; Paul Kleppner, *The Cross of Culture: A Social Analysis of Midwestern Politics, 1850–1900* (New York: Free Press, 1970); and Ward M. McAfee, *Religion, Race, and Reconstruction: The Public School in the Politics of the 1870s* (Albany: State University of New York Press, 1998). For New Jersey, see Samuel T. McSeveney, "Religious Conflict, Party Politics, and Public Policy in New Jersey," *New Jersey History* 110 (Spring–Summer 1992): 18–44.

The unraveling of Republicans' experiment with Reconstruction in the South, internal disagreements among northern Republicans about how to respond to that unraveling, and Democrats' attempts to exploit northerners' growing frustration with "the Southern question" without providing ammunition for northern Republicans' bloody-shirt campaigns constituted the most important context for the 1876 election. The literature on Reconstruction itself is far too vast to be listed here. Interested readers are directed to Foner's magisterial *Reconstruction: America's Unfinished Revolution* and to its monumental bibliography. Although drawing heavily on Foner for the story of southern blacks' experience during Reconstruction, I present a somewhat different account of Reconstruction in the chapters I wrote for David H. Donald, Jean H. Baker, and Michael F. Holt, *The Civil War and Reconstruction,* 3rd rev. ed. (New York: W. W. Norton, 2002). One source of our different interpretations is that I place far greater weight than does Foner on the interpretation of Michael Perman in his *Road to Redemption: Southern Politics, 1869–1879* (Chapel Hill: University of North Carolina Press, 1979), which I consider the finest analysis of southern politics during Reconstruction ever written.

For federal policy makers in the 1870s, the central issue was the extent of white violence against black voters and Republican governments in the South and what to do about it. Three studies document that Democratic terrorism: Allen W. Trelease, *White Terror: The Ku Klux Klan Conspiracy and Southern Reconstruction* (New York: Harper and Row, 1971); George C. Rable, *But There Was No Peace: The Role of Violence in the Politics of Reconstruction* (Athens: University of Georgia Press, 1984); and Nicholas Lemann, *Redemption: The Final Battle of the Civil War* (New York: Farrar, Straus, and Giroux, 2006). The last is an especially vivid account of white Democratic atrocities against blacks in Louisiana and Mississippi between 1873 and 1876.

Three different studies, in turn, provide an assessment of the response by the Grant administration and congressional Republicans to these events (superior to that offered in any existing biography of Grant): William Gillette, *Retreat from Reconstruction, 1869–1879* (Baton Rouge: Louisiana State University Press, 1979); Brooks D. Simpson, *The Reconstruction Presidents* (Lawrence: University Press of Kansas, 1998); and Charles W. Calhoun, *Conceiving a New Republic: The Republican Party and the Southern Question, 1869–1900* (Lawrence: University Press of Kansas, 2006). Each of these books possesses considerable merit, but because it addresses the southern policies of four presidents—Abraham Lincoln, Andrew Johnson, Ulysses S. Grant, and Rutherford B. Hayes—Simpson's deeply researched book deserves special mention. It demonstrates that Grant remained committed to the defense of southern blacks' right to vote far longer than most other northern Republicans, and it carefully explicates the hope of Hayes and other Ohio Republicans, such as James Garfield and Jacob Cox, of engendering a political realignment in the South by winning the support of former Whigs in that region.

My account of the 1875 election in Ohio is based heavily on a dissertation written at the University of Virginia under my supervision: Jack D. Morton, "Ohio's Gallant Fight: Northern State Politics during the Reconstruction Era, 1865–1878" (Ph.D. diss., University of Virginia, 2004).

One book was indispensable for my discussion of the creation and deliberations of the Federal Electoral Commission in 1877: Charles Fairman, *Five Justices and the Electoral Commission of 1877,* supplement to vol. 7 of the *Oliver Wendell Holmes Devise History of the Supreme Court of the United States* (New York: Collier Macmillan, 1988). Until I read this book, which almost qualifies as a primary source, I believed that I had a scoop concerning Republicans' warnings, as early as January 1875, of an impending crisis over counting the electoral votes. But the meticulous Fairman had already discovered it. Although his book details the creation of the electoral commission and the role of all the Supreme Court justices on it, his primary agenda, wholly successful in my opinion, is to defend the actions of the much-abused Joseph R. Bradley and to explode the partisan myths that emerged about his role.

Numerous political historians, including the above-mentioned Paul Kleppner and Dale Baum; Joel H. Silbey in *The American Political Nation, 1838–1893* (Stanford, Calif.: Stanford University Press, 1991); as well as numerous political scientists have noted that the primary political impact of the presidential election of 1876 was to restore a nationally competitive political balance between the Republican and Democratic parties for the first time since the 1850s.

INDEX